Microsoft®

WORD FOR WINDOWS® 95

Step by Step

Other titles in the Step by Step series:

For Microsoft Windows 95

(available in Fall 1995)

Integrating Microsoft Office 95 Applications Step by Step, for Windows 95

Microsoft Access for Windows 95 Step by Step

Microsoft Access/Visual Basic 95 Step by Step

Microsoft Excel/Visual Basic Step by Step

Microsoft PowerPoint for Windows 95 Step by Step

Microsoft Project for Windows 95 Step by Step

Microsoft Visual Basic 4 Step by Step

Microsoft Windows 95 Step by Step

Microsoft Excel for Windows 95 Step by Step

Microsoft Works for Windows 95 Step by Step

More Microsoft Windows 95 Step by Step

Upgrading to Microsoft Windows 95 Step by Step

For Microsoft Windows 3.1

(available now)

Microsoft Access 2 for Windows Step by Step

Microsoft Excel 5 for Windows Step by Step

Microsoft Excel 5 Visual Basic for Applications Step by Step, for Windows

Microsoft Visual FoxPro 3 for Windows Step by Step

Microsoft Mail for Windows Step by Step, versions 3.0b and later

Microsoft Office for Windows Step by Step, version 4

Microsoft PowerPoint 4 for Windows Step by Step

Microsoft Project 4 for Windows Step by Step

Microsoft Word 6 for Windows Step by Step

Microsoft Works 3 for Windows Step by Step

Microsoft®

WORD FOR WINDOWS® 95
Step by Step

Microsoft Press

PUBLISHED BY
Microsoft Press
A Division of Microsoft Corporation
One Microsoft Way
Redmond, Washington 98052-6399

Copyright © 1995 by Catapult, Inc.

Library of Congress Cataloging-in-Publication Data
Microsoft Word for Windows 95 Step by Step / Catapult, Inc.
         p.   cm.
     Includes index.
     ISBN 1-55615-828-9
       1. Microsoft Word for Windows.   2. Word processing.   I. Catapult, Inc.
   Z52.5.M523M49   1995
   652.5'536--dc20   95-24055
                                                              CIP

Printed and bound in the United States of America.

3 4 5 6 7 8 9   QMQM   9 8

Distributed in Canada by ITP Nelson, a division of Thomson Canada Limited.

A CIP catalogue record for this book is available from the British Library.

Microsoft Press books are available through booksellers and distributors worldwide. For further information about
international editions, contact your local Microsoft Corporation office, or contact Microsoft Press International
directly at fax (425) 936-7329. Visit our Web site at mspress.microsoft.com.

Macintosh is a registered trademark of Apple Computer, Inc. Microsoft, MS, MS-DOS, and Windows are registered
trademarks of Microsoft Corporation. Other product and company names mentioned herein may be the trademarks
of their respective owners.

Companies, names, and/or data used in screens and sample output are fictitious unless otherwise noted.

For Catapult, Inc.
Managing Editor: Donald Elman
Writers: Marie L. Swanson and Shari Dornquast
Project Editor: Ann T. Rosenthal
Production/Layout Editor: Jeanne K. Hunt
Technical Editor: Brett R. Davidson

For Microsoft Press
Acquisitions Editor: Casey D. Doyle
Project Editor: Wallis Bolz

Catapult, Inc. & Microsoft Press

Microsoft Word for Windows 95 Step by Step has been created by the professional trainers and writers at Catapult, Inc. to the exacting standards you've come to expect from Microsoft Press. Together, we are pleased to present this self-paced training guide, which you can use individually or as part of a class.

Catapult, Inc. is a software training company with years of experience in PC and Macintosh instruction. Catapult's exclusive Performance-Based Training system is available in Catapult training centers across North America and at customer sites. Based on the principles of adult learning, Performance-Based Training ensures that students leave the classroom with confidence and the ability to apply skills to real-world scenarios. *Microsoft Word for Windows 95 Step by Step* incorporates Catapult's training expertise to ensure that you'll receive the maximum return on your training time. You'll focus on the skills that increase productivity the most while working at your own pace and convenience.

Microsoft Press is the independent—and independent-minded—book publishing division of Microsoft Corporation. The leading publisher of information on Microsoft software, Microsoft Press is dedicated to providing the highest quality end-user training, reference, and technical books that make using Microsoft software easier, more enjoyable, and more productive.

Contents at a Glance

Table of Contents

Table of Contents

Table of Contents

Table of Contents

Inserting merge fields for form letters, see Lesson 16, page 293

Changing the design and size of text, see Lesson 1, page 20

Inserting today's date, see Lesson 1, page 22

Adding space between paragraphs, see Lesson 3, page 58

Changing line spacing within a paragraph, see Lesson 3, page 59

Creating bulleted lists, see Lesson 3, page 49

Indenting paragraphs, see Lesson 3, page 46

Adding borders to paragraphs, see Lesson 3, page 55

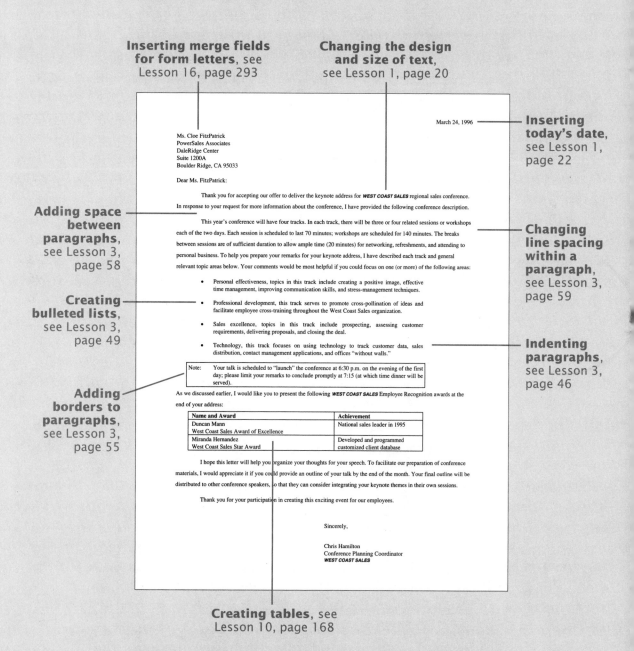

March 24, 1996

Ms. Cloe FitzPatrick
PowerSales Associates
DaleRidge Center
Suite 1200A
Boulder Ridge, CA 95033

Dear Ms. FitzPatrick:

Thank you for accepting our offer to deliver the keynote address for *WEST COAST SALES* regional sales conference. In response to your request for more information about the conference, I have provided the following conference description.

This year's conference will have four tracks. In each track, there will be three or four related sessions or workshops each of the two days. Each session is scheduled to last 70 minutes; workshops are scheduled for 140 minutes. The breaks between sessions are of sufficient duration to allow ample time (20 minutes) for networking, refreshments, and attending to personal business. To help you prepare your remarks for your keynote address, I have described each track and general relevant topic areas below. Your comments would be most helpful if you could focus on one (or more) of the following areas:

- Personal effectiveness, topics in this track include creating a positive image, effective time management, improving communication skills, and stress-management techniques.
- Professional development, this track serves to promote cross-pollination of ideas and facilitate employee cross-training throughout the West Coast Sales organization.
- Sales excellence, topics in this track include prospecting, assessing customer requirements, delivering proposals, and closing the deal.
- Technology, this track focuses on using technology to track customer data, sales distribution, contact management applications, and offices "without walls."

Note: Your talk is scheduled to "launch" the conference at 6:30 p.m. on the evening of the first day; please limit your remarks to conclude promptly at 7:15 (at which time dinner will be served).

As we discussed earlier, I would like you to present the following *WEST COAST SALES* Employee Recognition awards at the end of your address:

Name and Award	Achievement
Duncan Mann West Coast Sales Award of Excellence	National sales leader in 1995
Miranda Hernandez West Coast Sales Star Award	Developed and programmed customized client database

I hope this letter will help you organize your thoughts for your speech. To facilitate our preparation of conference materials, I would appreciate it if you could provide an outline of your talk by the end of the month. Your final outline will be distributed to other conference speakers, so that they can consider integrating your keynote themes in their own sessions.

Thank you for your participation in creating this exciting event for our employees.

Sincerely,

Chris Hamilton
Conference Planning Coordinator
WEST COAST SALES

Creating tables, see Lesson 10, page 168

*Quick*Look Guide

Choosing menu options, see Getting Ready, page xxix

Identifying spelling errors as you type, see Lesson 1, page 6

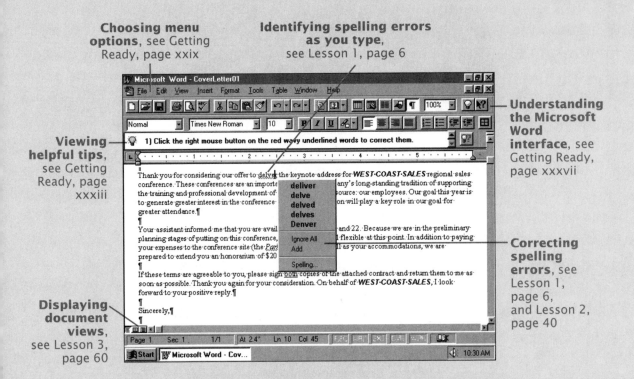

Understanding the Microsoft Word interface, see Getting Ready, page xxxvii

Viewing helpful tips, see Getting Ready, page xxxiii

Correcting spelling errors, see Lesson 1, page 6, and Lesson 2, page 40

Displaying document views, see Lesson 3, page 60

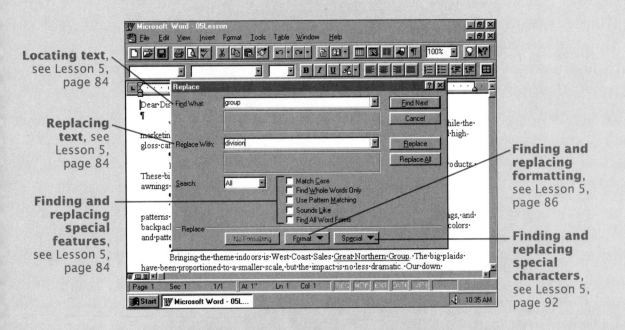

Locating text, see Lesson 5, page 84

Replacing text, see Lesson 5, page 84

Finding and replacing special features, see Lesson 5, page 84

Finding and replacing formatting, see Lesson 5, page 86

Finding and replacing special characters, see Lesson 5, page 92

Establishing document margins, see Lesson 7, page 108

Creating headers and footers, see Lesson 7, page 109

Entering information in a header, see Lesson 7, page 111

Establishing the look of a page, see Lesson 7, page 107

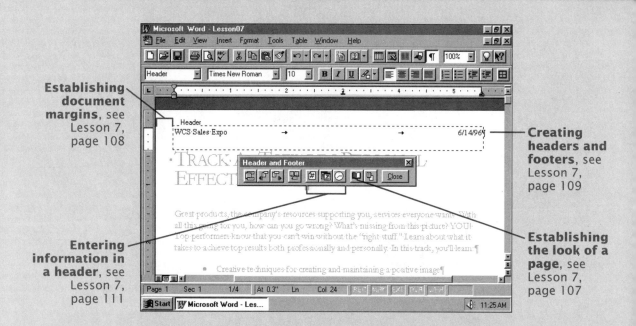

Promoting and demoting headings, see Lesson 13, page 241

Expanding and collapsing headings, see Lesson 13, page 245

Viewing body text, see Lesson 13, page 246

Moving blocks of text, see Lesson 13, page 247

Viewing specific headings, see Lesson 13, page 243

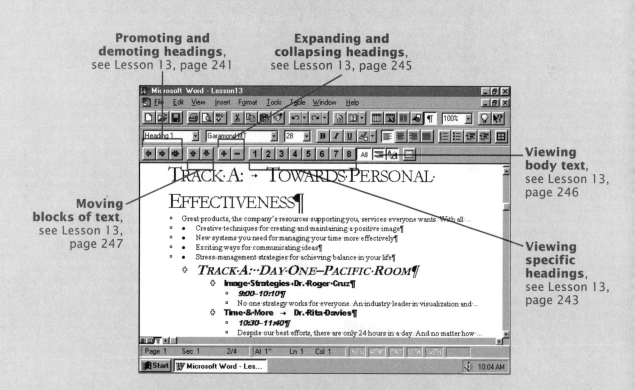

Formatting columns,
see Lesson 11, page 192

Inserting WordArt objects,
see Lesson 12,
page 211

Cropping graphics, see
Lesson 12,
page 201

Creating and modifying styles, see
Lesson 8,
page 124

Inserting and positioning text, see
Lesson 12,
page 216

Creating drop caps, see
Lesson 12,
page 210

Inserting graphics, see
Lesson 12,
page 200

Using AutoFormat,
see Lesson 8,
page 128

Creating callouts,
see Lesson 12,
page 208

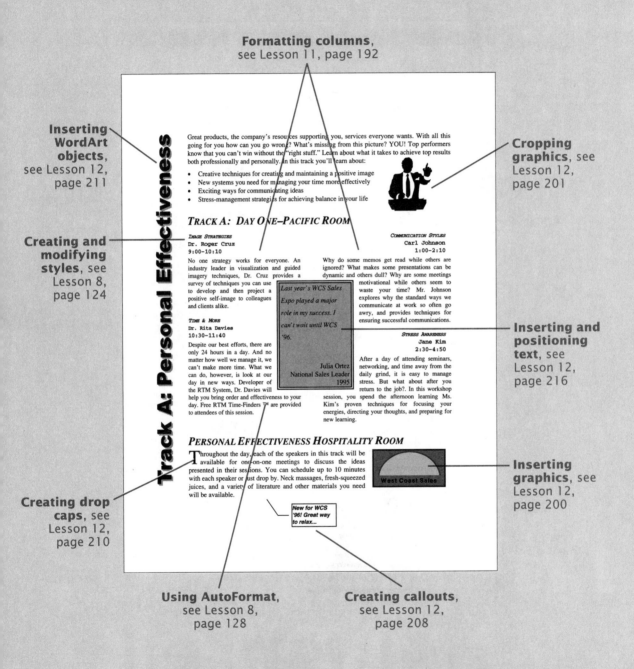

Track A: Personal Effectiveness

Great products, the company's resources supporting you, services everyone wants. With all this going for you how can you go wrong? What's missing from this picture? YOU! Top performers know that you can't win without the "right stuff." Learn about what it takes to achieve top results both professionally and personally. In this track you'll learn about:

- Creative techniques for creating and maintaining a positive image
- New systems you need for managing your time more effectively
- Exciting ways for communicating ideas
- Stress-management strategies for achieving balance in your life

TRACK A: DAY ONE–PACIFIC ROOM

IMAGE STRATEGIES
Dr. Roger Cruz
9:00–10:10

No one strategy works for everyone. An industry leader in visualization and guided imagery techniques, Dr. Cruz provides a survey of techniques you can use to develop and then project a positive self-image to colleagues and clients alike.

TIME & MORE
Dr. Rita Davies
10:30–11:40

Despite our best efforts, there are only 24 hours in a day. And no matter how well we manage it, we can't make more time. What we can do, however, is look at our day in new ways. Developer of the RTM System, Dr. Davies will help you bring order and effectiveness to your day. Free RTM Time-Finders ™ are provided to attendees of this session.

COMMUNICATION STYLES
Carl Johnson
1:00–2:10

Why do some memos get read while others are ignored? What makes some presentations can be dynamic and others dull? Why are some meetings motivational while others seem to waste your time? Mr. Johnson explores why the standard ways we communicate at work so often go awry, and provides techniques for ensuring successful communications.

Last year's WCS Sales Expo played a major role in my success. I can't wait until WCS '96.

Julia Ortez
National Sales Leader
1995

STRESS AWARENESS
Jane Kim
2:30–4:50

After a day of attending seminars, networking, and time away from the daily grind, it is easy to manage stress. But what about after you return to the job?. In this workshop session, you spend the afternoon learning Ms. Kim's proven techniques for focusing your energies, directing your thoughts, and preparing for new learning.

PERSONAL EFFECTIVENESS HOSPITALITY ROOM

Throughout the day, each of the speakers in this track will be available for one-on-one meetings to discuss the ideas presented in their sessions. You can schedule up to 10 minutes with each speaker or just drop by. Neck massages, fresh-squeezed juices, and a variety of literature and other materials you need will be available.

West Coast Sales

New for WCS '96! Great way to relax...

About This Book

In "About This Book" you will learn:

- How to find your best starting point in this book based on your level of experience.
- What the conventions in this book mean.
- Where to get additional information about Windows 95.

Microsoft Word for Windows 95 is a powerful word processing program that you can use for creating and editing documents, inserting and deleting text and graphics, and creating documents for special projects (such as creating forms and merging form letters). *Microsoft Word for Windows 95 Step by Step* shows you how to use Microsoft Word to simplify your work and increase your productivity. With this book, you can learn at your own pace and at your own convenience, or you can use it in a classroom setting.

 IMPORTANT This book is for use with Microsoft Word for the Windows 95 operating system. To determine what software you are running, you can either check the software documentation, the installation disk labels, or the exterior product packaging, or you can click the About Microsoft Word command on the Help menu in Word.

You get hands-on practice by using the practice files on the disk located in the back of this book. Each lesson explains when and how to use the appropriate practice files. Instructions for copying the practice files to your computer hard disk are in "Getting Ready," the next chapter in this book.

Finding the Best Starting Point for You

This book is designed for new users learning Microsoft Word for the first time, and for experienced users who want to learn and use the new features in Microsoft Word for Windows 95. Either way, *Microsoft Word for Windows 95 Step by Step* will help you get the most out of Microsoft Word.

This book is divided into four major parts, each containing several related lessons. Each lesson takes approximately 20 to 45 minutes, with an optional practice exercise at the end of each lesson. At the end of each part is a Review & Practice section that gives you the opportunity to practice the skills you learned in that part. Each Review & Practice section allows you to test your knowledge and prepare for your own work.

Use the following table to determine your best path through the book.

If you are	Follow these steps
New to a computer or graphical environment, such as Microsoft Windows 95	Read "Getting Ready," the next chapter in this book, and follow the instructions to install the practice files. Carefully read the section "If You Are New to Microsoft Windows 95." Next, work through Lessons 1 through 4 for a basic introduction to Microsoft Word. Work through Lessons 5 through 16 in any order.
Familiar with the Microsoft Windows 95 graphical computer environment, but new to using Microsoft Word	Follow the instructions for installing the practice files in "Getting Ready," the next chapter in this book. Next, work through Lessons 1 through 4 for a basic introduction to Microsoft Word. Work through Lessons 5 through 16 in any order.
Experienced with Microsoft Word	Follow the instructions for installing the practice files in "Getting Ready," the next chapter in this book. Next, read through "New Features in Word for Windows 95," the chapter following "Getting Ready," for an introduction to the new features in this version of Microsoft Word. Complete the lessons that best fit your needs.

Using This Book As a Classroom Aid

If you're an instructor, you can use *Microsoft Word for Windows 95 Step by Step* for teaching computer users. You might want to select certain lessons that meet your students' particular needs and incorporate your own demonstrations into the lessons.

If you plan to teach the entire contents of this book, you should probably set aside up to three days of classroom time to allow for discussion, questions, and any customized practice you might create.

Conventions Used in This Book

Before you start any of the lessons, it's important that you understand the terms and notational conventions used in this book.

Procedural Conventions

- Hands-on exercises that you are to follow are given in numbered lists of steps (1, 2, and so on). An arrowhead bullet (➤) indicates an exercise with only one step.
- Characters or commands that you type appear in **bold lowercase** type.

Print

- You can carry out many commands by clicking a button at the top of the program window. If a procedure instructs you to click a button, a picture of the button appears in the left margin, as the Print button does here.

Mouse Conventions

- If you have a multiple-button mouse, it is assumed that you have configured the left mouse button as the primary mouse button. Any procedure that requires you to press the secondary button will refer to it as the right mouse button.
- *Click* means to point to an object, and then press and release the mouse button. For example, "Click the Cut button on the Standard toolbar." *Use the right mouse button to click* means to point to an object, and then press and release the right mouse button.
- *Drag* means to point to an object, and then press and hold down the mouse button while you move the mouse. For example, "Drag the window edge downward to enlarge the window."
- *Double-click* means to rapidly press and release the mouse button twice. For example, "Double-click the Microsoft Word icon to start Microsoft Word."

Keyboard Conventions

- Names of keyboard keys that you are instructed to press are in small capital letters, for example, TAB and SHIFT.
- A plus sign (+) between two key names means that you must press those keys at the same time. For example, "Press ALT+TAB" means that you hold down the ALT key while you press TAB.
- Procedures generally emphasize use of the mouse, rather than the keyboard. However, you can choose menu commands with the keyboard by pressing the ALT key to activate the menu bar. You can sequentially press the keys that correspond to the underlined letter of the menu name and command name. For some commands, you can also press a key combination listed in the menu.

Notes

- Notes or Tips that appear either in the text or in the left margin provide additional information or alternative methods for a procedure.

- Notes labeled "Important" alert you to essential information that you should check before continuing with the lesson.

Other Features of This Book

- The "One Step Further" exercise at the end of each lesson introduces new options or techniques that build on the commands and skills you used in the lesson.

- Each lesson concludes with a Lesson Summary that lists the skills you have learned in the lesson and briefly reviews how to accomplish particular tasks.

- References to Microsoft Word online Help at the end of each lesson direct you to Help topics for additional information. The Help system provides a complete online reference to Microsoft Word. You'll learn more about Help in "Getting Ready," the next chapter in this book.

- The "Review & Practice" activity at the end of each part provides an opportunity to use the major skills presented in the lessons for that part. These activities present problems that reinforce what you have learned and demonstrate new ways you can use Microsoft Word.

- In the Appendix, "Matching the Exercises," you can review the options used in this book to get the results you see in the illustrations. Refer to this section of the book when your screen does not match the illustrations or when you get unexpected results as you work through the exercises.

Getting Ready

- Copy the practice files to your computer hard disk.
- Start Microsoft Windows 95 and use the mouse.
- Use basic Windows 95 features such as windows, menus, dialog boxes, and Help.
- Start Microsoft Word and get acquainted with some of its tools.

This chapter prepares you for your first steps into the Microsoft Word for Windows 95 environment. You will learn how to install the practice files that come with this book and how to start both Microsoft Windows 95 and Microsoft Word. You will also get an overview of some useful Windows 95 techniques, and you'll get an introduction to some terms and concepts that are important to understand as you learn Microsoft Word.

If you have not yet installed Windows 95 or Microsoft Word, you'll need to do that before you start the lessons. For instructions on installing Windows 95, see your Windows 95 documentation. For instructions on installing Microsoft Word for Windows 95, see your Microsoft Word documentation.

IMPORTANT Before you break the seal on the practice disk in the back of this book, be sure that you have the correct version of the software. This book is designed for use with Microsoft Word, an application that runs on the Windows 95 operating system. To determine what software you are running, you can either check the software documentation, the installation disk labels, or the exterior product packaging, or you can click the About Microsoft Word command on the Help menu in Word.

Installing the Step by Step Practice Files

The disk attached to the inside back cover of this book contains practice files that you'll use as you work through this book. You'll use the practice files in many of the lessons to perform the exercises. For example, the lesson that teaches you how to find documents stored on your computer instructs you to find and open one of the practice files. Because the practice files simulate tasks you'll encounter in a typical business setting, you can easily transfer what you learn from this book to your own work.

 NOTE If you would like an introduction to using the mouse before you set up your Step by Step practice files, refer to the section "If You Are New to Windows 95" later in this chapter. When you are finished practicing with the mouse, return to this section and copy the practice files to your hard disk.

Copy the practice files to your hard disk

You must have Microsoft Windows 95 installed on your computer in addition to Microsoft Word for Windows 95 to use the practice files. Follow these steps to copy the practice files to your computer hard disk so that you can use them with the lessons.

If you do not know your user name or password, contact your system administrator for further help.

1 If your computer isn't already on, turn it on now. Windows 95 starts automatically when you turn on your computer. If you see a dialog box asking for your user name and password, type them in the appropriate boxes, and then click OK. If you see the Welcome dialog box, click the Close button.

My Computer icon

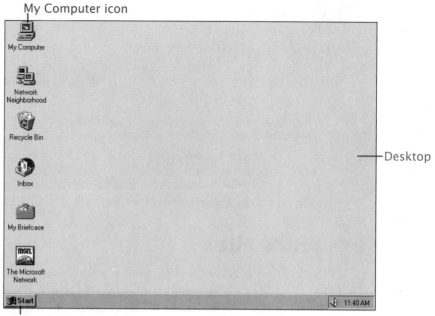

Desktop

Start button

2 Remove the disk from the package on the inside back cover of this book.

3 Put the disk in drive A or drive B of your computer.

4 On the taskbar at the bottom of your screen, click the Start button.

5 On the Start menu, click Run.

...and then click Run.

Click Start...

6 In the Run dialog box, type **a:setup** (or **b:setup** if the disk is in drive B), and then click the OK button. Do not type a space anywhere in the command.

7 Follow the directions on the screen.

The setup program window appears with recommended options preselected for you. For best results in using the practice files with this book, accept the recommendations made by the program.

8 After the files are copied, remove the disk from your computer, and replace it in the envelope on the inside back cover of the book.

The Step by Step setup program copies the practice files from the floppy disk onto the hard disk in a subfolder called Winword SBS Practice. The setup program makes use of the Windows 95 Favorites folder. Follow the steps presented in each lesson to open or save your practice files.

Using the Practice Files

The text in each lesson in this book explains when and how to use the practice file for that lesson. The installation doesn't create any icons—when it's time to use a practice file in a lesson, the book will list instructions for how to open the file.

 NOTE In this book, you won't be directed to use a practice file until Lesson 2.

Be sure to follow the directions for saving the files and giving them new names. Renaming the practice files allows you to use the renamed copy of a file to complete a lesson while leaving the original file intact. That way, if you want to start a lesson over or repeat a lesson later, you can reuse the original file.

Most lessons begin by opening a new practice file whose name corresponds to the lesson number. Be sure to close any open practice files, and then open the correct practice file when you are directed to do so in a lesson. Using a practice file from another lesson might not give you the correct results.

Lesson Background

For these lessons, suppose you are the president for West Coast Sales, Inc., a retail distributor of a variety of products for outdoor recreation and casual living. Throughout these lessons, you will use Microsoft Word to develop effective and exciting documents that communicate information about West Coast Sales products. You will also create documents needed for upcoming sales conference.

If You Are New to Microsoft Windows 95

Microsoft Windows 95 is an easy-to-use work environment that helps you handle the daily work that you perform with your computer. Microsoft Windows 95 also provides a common look and functionality among the many different programs you might use—both in the way they share data and in the way you use the programs. This makes it easy for you to learn and use different programs in Windows 95. In this section, you'll get an introduction to Windows 95. If you are already familiar with Windows 95, you can skip to the section, "Working with Microsoft Word."

Start Windows 95

Starting Windows 95 is as easy as turning on your computer.

If you do not know your user name or password, contact your system administrator for further help.

▶ If your computer isn't already on, turn it on now. If you see a dialog box asking for your user name and password, type them in the appropriate boxes and then click OK. If you see the Welcome dialog box, click the Close button or press ENTER.

Windows 95 starts automatically when you turn on your computer. Your screen looks similar to the following illustration.

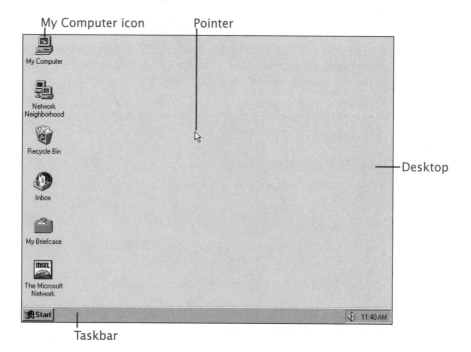

My Computer icon   Pointer

Desktop

Taskbar

Using the Mouse

Windows 95 is designed for use with a mouse. Although you can use the keyboard for most actions in Windows 95, many of these actions are easier to do with a mouse.

The mouse controls a pointer on the screen, as shown in the preceding illustration. You move the pointer by sliding the mouse over a flat surface in the direction you want the pointer to move. If you run out of room to move the mouse, lift it up and then put it down in a more comfortable location. The pointer moves only when the mouse is touching a flat surface.

Moving the mouse pointer across the screen does not affect the information that you see; the pointer simply indicates a location on the screen. When you press the mouse button, an action occurs at the location of the pointer.

You will use four basic mouse actions throughout the lessons in this book.

Pointing   Moving the mouse to place the pointer on an item is called *pointing*.

Clicking   Pointing to an item on your screen, and then quickly pressing and releasing the mouse button is called *clicking*. You select items on the screen by clicking. Occasionally there are operations you perform by pressing the right mouse button, but unless you are instructed otherwise, use the left mouse button to click.

Double-clicking   Pointing to an item, and then quickly pressing and releasing the mouse button twice is called *double-clicking*. This is a convenient shortcut for many tasks. Whenever you are unsure of the command to use for an operation, try double-clicking the item you want to affect. This often displays a dialog box in which you can make changes to the item you double-clicked.

Dragging   Pointing to an item, and then holding down the mouse button as you move the pointer is called *dragging*. You can use this action to select data and to move and copy text or objects.

Try the mouse

Take a moment to test-drive the mouse.

1   Slide the mouse pointer over the Windows 95 Desktop.

    The pointer is a left-pointing arrow.

2   Move the mouse pointer on top of the Start button at the bottom of the screen, and then press the left mouse button.

    The Start menu opens.

3 Move the mouse pointer outside the Start menu, and click the Desktop.

The Start menu closes.

My Computer

4 Point to the My Computer icon, and then use the left mouse button to double-click the icon.

The My Computer window opens, where you can view the disk drives and folders stored there.

5 Move the mouse pointer over the bottom edge of the My Computer window until the pointer changes to a double-headed arrow.

When you move the mouse pointer over different parts of the Windows 95 Desktop or different areas in a program window, the pointer can change shape to indicate what action is available at that point.

6 Hold down the left mouse button, and move (drag) the mouse pointer downward.

7 Release the mouse button.

The My Computer window is resized.

Using Windows-Based Programs

After you become familiar with the basic operation of Windows 95, you can apply these skills to learn and use Windows-based programs—programs that are designed for use with Windows 95.

All Windows-based programs have similar characteristics as to how they appear on the screen and how you use them. All the windows in Windows-based programs have common controls that you use to scroll, size, move, and close a window.

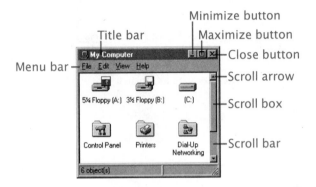

To	Do this	Button
Scroll through a window	Click a scroll bar or scroll arrow, or drag the scroll box.	
Enlarge a window to fill the screen	Click the Maximize button, or double-click the title bar.	▣
Restore a window to its previous size	Click the Restore button, or double-click the title bar. When a window is maximized, the Maximize button changes to the Restore button.	▣
Reduce a window to a button on the taskbar	Click the Minimize button. To display a minimized window, click its button on the taskbar.	▬
Move a window	Drag the title bar.	
Close a window	Click the Close button.	✕

You'll try out these Windows techniques and learn more about them in the following sections.

Using Menus

To choose a command on a menu, you click the menu name to open the menu, and then you click the command name on the menu. When a command name appears dimmed, it doesn't apply to your current situation, or it is unavailable. For example, the Paste command on the Edit menu appears dimmed if the Copy or Cut command has not been used first.

Some commands have a *shortcut key* combination shown to the right of the command name. Once you are familiar with the menus and commands, you might prefer to use these shortcut keys to save time if your hands are already at the keyboard.

To close a menu without choosing a command, you can click the menu name again or click anywhere outside of the menu. You can also press ESC to close a menu.

Open the Edit menu

1   In the My Computer window, click Edit in the menu bar.

    The Edit menu appears. Notice which commands are dimmed and which have shortcut key combinations listed.

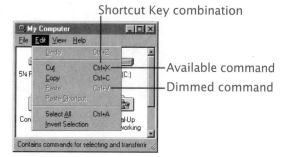

Shortcut Key combination

Available command

Dimmed command

2   Click the Edit menu name to close the menu.

    The menu closes.

Make menu selections

Commands on a menu are grouped by common functions. Commands that are in effect are indicated by a check mark or a bullet mark to the left of the command name. A check mark indicates that multiple items in this group of commands can be in effect at the same time. A bullet mark indicates that only one item in this group can be in effect at the same time.

1 Click View in the menu bar.

The View menu looks like the following illustration.

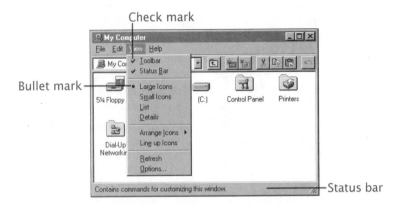

2 On the View menu, click Toolbar.

The View menu closes, and a toolbar appears below the menu bar.

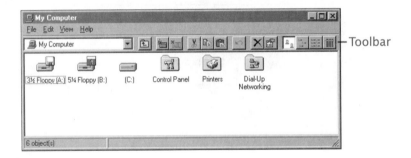

3 On the View menu, click List.

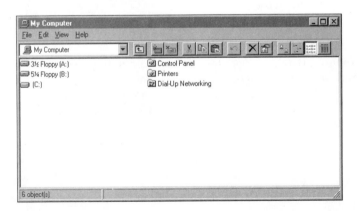

The items in the My Computer window are now displayed in a list, rather than by icons.

Large Icons

4 On the toolbar, click the Large Icons button.

If you do not see the button, drag a corner of the window to enlarge it until you see the button. Clicking a button on a toolbar is a quick way to select a command.

5 On the View menu, point to Arrange Icons.

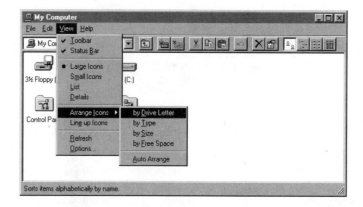

A cascading menu appears listing additional menu choices. When a right-pointing arrow appears after a command name, it indicates that additional commands are available.

6 Click the menu name or anywhere outside the menu to close the menu.

7 On the menu bar, click View, and then click Toolbar again.

The View menu closes and the toolbar is now hidden.

Close

8 Click the Close button in the upper-right corner of the My Computer window to close the window.

Using Dialog Boxes

When you choose a command name that is followed by an ellipsis (...), Windows-based programs display a dialog box in which you can provide more information about how the command should be carried out. Dialog boxes consist of a number of standard features as shown in the following illustration.

Text box   Tab

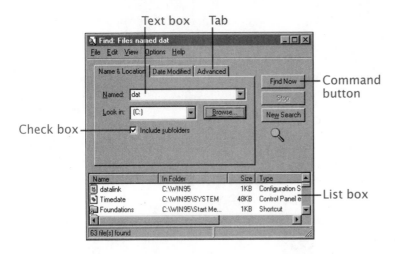

Check box

Command button

List box

To move around in a dialog box, you click the item you want. You can also hold down ALT as you press the underlined letter. Or you can press TAB to move between items.

After you enter information or make selections in a dialog box, you either choose the OK button in the dialog box or press the ENTER key on the keyboard to carry out the command. Click the Cancel button or press ESC to close a dialog box and cancel the command.

Display the Taskbar dialog box

Some dialog boxes provide several categories of options displayed on separate tabs. You click the top of an obscured tab to bring it forward and display additional options.

1   On the taskbar, click the Start button. On the Start menu, point to Settings, and then click Taskbar.

2   In the Taskbar Properties dialog box, click the Start Menu Programs tab.

Click here.

On this tab, you can customize the list of programs that appears on your Start menu.

3   Click the Taskbar Options tab, and then click Show Small Icons In Start Menu.

Clicking a check box that is selected (the box displays a check mark) turns the option off.

4   Click the check box a couple of times, and observe how the display in the dialog box changes.

Clicking any check box or option button will turn the option off or on.

5   Click the Cancel button in the dialog box.

This closes the dialog box without changing any settings.

Getting Help with Windows 95

When you need information about a procedure or how to use a particular feature on your computer, the online Help system is one of the most efficient ways to learn. The online Help system for Windows 95 is available from the Start menu, and you choose the type of help you want from the Help dialog box.

For instructions on broad categories, you can look at the Help contents. Or you can search the Help index for information on specific topics. The Help information is short and concise, so you can get the exact information you need quickly. There are also shortcut buttons in many Help topics that you can use to directly switch to the task you want to perform.

Viewing Help Contents

The Help Contents tab is organized like a book's table of contents. As you choose top-level topics, or "chapters," you see a list of more detailed topics from which to choose. Many of these chapters have special "Tips and Tricks" subsections that can help you work more efficiently.

If you are new to Windows 95, you might be interested in the Help topic under "Introducing Windows" named "Ten minutes to using Windows."

Find Help on general categories

In this exercise, you'll look up information in the online Help system.

1   Click Start. On the Start menu, click Help.

The Help dialog box appears.

2   If necessary, click the Contents tab to make it active.

3 Double-click "Introducing Windows."

The book icon opens to display a set of subtopics.

4 Double-click "Using Windows Accessories."

5 Double-click "For General Use."

6 Double-click "Calculator: for making calculations."

A Help topic window appears.

Maximize

7 Click the Maximize button on the Help window.

The Help topic window fills the entire screen.

Minimize

8 Click the Minimize button to reduce the Help window to a button on the taskbar.

Whenever you minimize a window, its button appears on the taskbar.

Finding Help on Specific Topics

There are two methods for finding specific Help topics: the Index tab and the Find tab. The Index tab is organized like a book's index. Keywords for topics are organized alphabetically. You can either scroll through the list of keywords or type the keyword you want to find. One or more topic choices are then presented.

With the Find tab, you can also enter a keyword. The main difference is that you get a list of all Help topics in which that keyword appears, not just the topics that begin with that word.

Find Help on specific topics using the Help index

In this exercise, you'll use the Help index to learn how to change the background pattern of your Desktop.

1 Click the Windows Help button on the taskbar.

The Help dialog box appears as you left it.

Restore

2 Click the Restore button so that you can see both the Help window and the Desktop.

3 Click the Help Topics button at the top of the Help dialog box, and then click the Index tab.

The Help index appears.

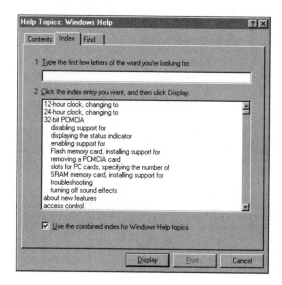

4 In the text box, type **display**

A list of display-related topics appears.

5 Double-click the topic named "background pictures or patterns, changing."

The Topics Found window appears.

6 Double-click the topic named "Changing the background of your Desktop."

7 Read the Help topic.

Jump

Close

8 Click the jump button in Step 1 of the Help topic.

The Properties For Display dialog box appears. If you want, you can immediately perform the task you were looking up in Help.

9 Click the Close button on the Display Properties dialog box.

10 Click the Close button on the Windows Help window.

> **NOTE** You can print any Help topic. Click the Options button in the upper-left corner of any Help topic window, click Print Topic, and then click OK. To continue searching for additional topics, you can click the Help Topics button in any open Help topic window.

Find Help on specific topics using the Find tab

In this exercise, you'll use the Find tab to learn how to change your printer's settings.

1 Click Start. On the Start menu, click Help.

The Help dialog box appears.

2 Click the Find tab to make it active.

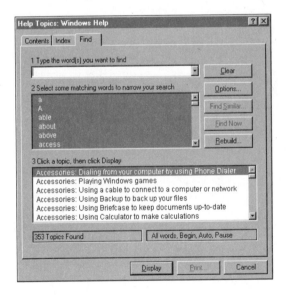

3   If you see a wizard, select the best option for your system, and then click Next. Click Finish to complete and close the wizard.

The wizard creates a search index for your Help files. This might take a few minutes. The next time you use Find, you won't have to wait for Windows 95 to create a topic list.

4   In the text box under step 1, type **print**

All topics that have to do with printing appear in the list box at the bottom of the tab.

5   In the list box under step 3, click the topic "Changing printer settings," and then click Display.

The Help topic appears.

6   Read the Help topic, using the scroll bar as necessary.

7   Click the Close button on the Windows Help window.

NOTE   You can also get help about the controls in a dialog box by clicking the question mark button in the upper-right corner of the dialog box. When you click this button and then click any dialog box control, a Help window pops up that explains what the control is and how to use it.

Working with Microsoft Word

Now that you are familiar with the Windows 95 operating environment, you can start Microsoft Word. The easiest way to start Microsoft Word is from the Programs menu, but you can also use My Computer.

Start Microsoft Word from the Programs menu

NOTE   If you do not see Microsoft Word listed on the Programs menu when you do step 1 below, skip to the exercise, "Start Microsoft Word from My Computer" to start Microsoft Word.

1   Click Start. On the Start menu, point to Programs, and then click Microsoft Word.

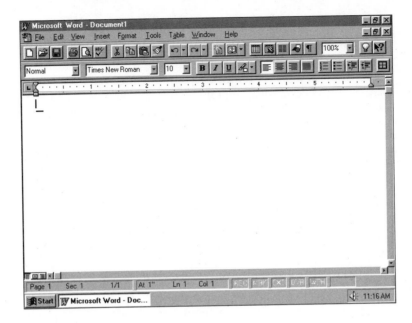

2 If you see the Welcome dialog box, click OK.

3 If you see the Tip Of The Day dialog box, read the tip, and then click OK.

The dialog box closes, and you see a blank window.

Maximize

4 If the window is not already maximized, as shown in the above illustration, click the Maximize button.

Start Microsoft Word from My Computer

If Microsoft Word is not listed on the Windows 95 Programs menu, you can start the program from My Computer.

1 Double-click the My Computer icon.

2 In the My Computer window, double-click the Drive C icon to display the files and folders stored there.

3 Find and double-click the Winword folder to open it.

You might have to scroll downward in the list to find the folder.

4 Double-click the Microsoft Word program file called Winword.exe to start the program.

Understanding Word Processing

You use word processing software when you want to create a new document—such as a letter, memo, or report—or when you want to modify a document that you or someone else has already created. You can use Microsoft Word to type in text, edit existing text, and format text to add emphasis, clarify ideas, and arrange text attractively on the page. You can also use Microsoft Word to insert graphics, tables, and charts, as well as to check your document for spelling and grammatical mistakes.

If Microsoft Word was limited to just these features, you would have a tool that already is significantly more powerful than a typewriter. But beyond these capabilities, Microsoft Word has many more features that make creating and modifying documents much easier. Below is a quick summary of the ones you will use most often, but be sure to review the New Features section for a list of the lessons in which features that are new in this version of Microsoft Word are covered.

- As your typing reaches the end of a line, Microsoft Word automatically moves to the next line. This is called *wordwrap*. With wordwrap, you do not need to press ENTER at the end of a line (unless you want to start a new paragraph or create a blank line in the document).

- If you misspell certain words, the AutoCorrect feature will correct your spelling as you type. The Automatic Spelling feature identifies additional misspelled words with a wavy, red underline so that you can quickly locate and correct errors.

- If you use hyphens in lists, fractions, ordinal numbers (such as 3RD), and trademark or other symbols in your documents, the AutoFormat feature automatically inserts the correct symbol as you type.

- If you need to arrange text in a grid of rows and columns, you can always use tabs to create a table; but using Word's table feature is much easier. With tables you can quickly format your text attractively, and if your table contains numbers, you can quickly represent your table as a chart.

- The Preview feature allows you to display the document as it will appear when you print, giving you an opportunity to get the "big picture" of all the pages at once, so you can make adjustments to the document before you print it.

You can also take advantage of many timesaving features, including:

- AutoText for storing and inserting frequently used text and graphics
- Styles for storing and applying formatting combinations consistently
- Mail Merge for creating form letters, envelopes, and labels
- Macros for storing and executing sequences of commands you use frequently
- Document wizards for creating a variety of attractively formatted documents

Exploring the Microsoft Word program window

When you start Microsoft Word, a new (and empty) document appears in a *document window*. The document window is the Microsoft Word equivalent of a sheet of paper in a typewriter—it is where you type your text. The buttons and ruler you see at the top of the window offer easy ways to work on your documents. By using the mouse to click a button, select an option from a list, or adjust margins and indents on the ruler, you can change the way your document looks, check spelling, or perform any number of other common word processing tasks.

The two rows of buttons and the ruler near the top of the Microsoft Word window are actually three separate items. You can display or hide them independently of each other if you need more viewing room on your screen. They are designed to speed your work by helping you perform the tasks you use most often. You will find it most convenient to display all three.

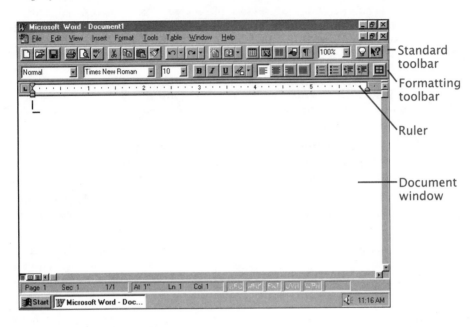

Using Toolbars

The first row of buttons below the Microsoft Word menu bar is the *Standard toolbar*. This toolbar contains buttons for performing basic operations for working with the program, such as opening, closing, and printing a document. The following illustration identifies the buttons on the Standard toolbar.

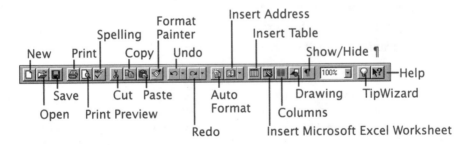

There are several toolbars in Microsoft Word, which you can display or hide depending on your needs. Each toolbar is composed of buttons that perform related tasks. For example, you'll use the Formatting toolbar (located below the Standard toolbar) to enhance the appearance of your document, including the style and size of your type. It is generally much faster to click a button on a toolbar than to select a command from a menu.

When you click certain buttons on a toolbar, such as the Print button, Microsoft Word carries out the corresponding command using the command's default options. If you want to specify different options for carrying out a command, use the command from the menu. Other buttons turn features on and off, such the Show/Hide button, which displays or hides special nonprinting characters. Still other buttons, such as the Open button, perform in the same way as the corresponding command. The instructions in this book emphasize using the toolbar for almost all Microsoft Word operations.

Take a quick tour of the Standard toolbar

Take a moment to get acquainted with the buttons on the Standard toolbar. If you accidentally click a button, you can press the ESC key or click the Undo button on the Standard toolbar.

If you do not see the button name, choose Toolbars from the View menu. Click the Show Tool Tips check box.

> Move the pointer over a button and wait.

After a moment, the name of the button appears.

ToolTip

Using Wizards

Wizards are intelligent assistants that guide you through the steps of performing specific tasks, such as creating resumes, letters, or meeting agendas. When you run a wizard, it asks you for the information and text that will be incorporated into your document. There are also TipWizards that monitor how you use Microsoft Word and offer suggestions to help you work more effectively. The TipWizard appears below the Formatting toolbar; clicking the Show Me button next to the wizard will display a related help topic, while scroll bars allow you to review previous tips. Various wizards will be used or described throughout this book.

The Answer Wizard, available from the Microsoft Word Help menu, can assist you in finding a topic of your choice. In this wizard, you type a topic or question, and then the wizard presents you with a list of related topics from which you can choose. After you choose a topic, the wizard displays additional information for completing the task or provides a demonstration of the steps.

Use the Answer Wizard

As you type text in the document window, you might notice a number of changes that occur as you type. Some of these changes are the result of Microsoft Word's AutoCorrect feature. In the next exercise, you will use the Answer Wizard to learn about the kinds of changes made by the AutoCorrect feature.

1 On the Help menu, click Answer Wizard.

The Answer Wizard window appears.

2 In the first box, type **AutoCorrect**, and then click the Search button.

In this box, you can type any word, phrase, or question about which you want more information. A list of topics related to using Microsoft Word's automatic correction features appears.

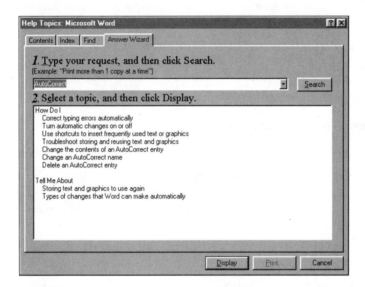

3 In the Tell Me About area, click Types Of Changes That Word Can Make Automatically, and then click the Display button.

An overview of these changes appears in the Help window. Read the information, and then continue on to the next step.

4 Click the button next to What Happens When I Use AutoCorrect.

The help topic related to using Word's AutoCorrect feature appears. You can click the Back button to return to the previous help topic, or you can return to the document window.

5 Click the Close button on the Help Topics window to close it.

Quitting Microsoft Word and Windows 95

Now that you are introduced to Windows 95 and Microsoft Word, you can proceed to Lesson 1. If you would like to quit Microsoft Word or Windows 95 for now, follow these steps.

Quit Microsoft Word

Close

1 Hold down the ALT key and press F4.

2 If you see a message box asking whether you want to save changes, choose the No button.

Quit Windows 95

1 Close all open windows by clicking the Close button in the upper-right corner of each window.

2 Click Start, and then click Shut Down.

3 When you see the message dialog box, click the Yes button.

 ∠ **WARNING** To avoid loss of data or damage to Windows 95, always quit Windows 95 by using the Shut Down command on the Start menu before you turn your computer off.

New Features in Word for Windows 95

The following table lists the major new features in Microsoft Word for Windows 95 that are covered in this book. The table shows the lesson in which you can learn about each feature. For more information about new features, see the list of topics you can look up in the Answer Wizard (located at the end of each lesson).

To learn how to	See
Get answers to your questions about Microsoft Word with the Answer Wizard.	Getting Ready
Vividly highlight text in color using the Highlighter button.	Lesson 1
Find and correct spelling errors at a glance with Automatic Spell Checking. Wavy, red underlines make it easy.	Lesson 1
Use AutoFormat features to correctly format hyphens, fractions, trademarks, and ordinal numbers.	Lesson 8
Preview your document before opening it. The new Open dialog box provides additional ways to get more information about your documents at a glance.	Lesson 4
Use a new search-and-replace feature that locates and replaces all forms (such as tense, and singular versus plural).	Lesson 6
Create new documents based on new document templates. Preview template formatting in the New dialog box.	Lesson 9
Use the Address Book to store and insert names and addresses in your documents and form letters.	Lesson 16

Basic Skills

Part **1**

Creating a
Simple Document

In this lesson you will learn how to:

Estimated time
30 min.

- Type text in a new document window.
- Correct spelling errors using Automatic Spell Checking.
- Select text to edit or format.
- Delete, replace, and move text.
- Change the appearance of text and its position on the page.
- Name and save your document for future use.

In Microsoft Word, it's easy to create documents and make them look the way you want. In this lesson, you will type a short letter and then use many of the formatting and editing options that are available with a click of the mouse button. At the end of the lesson, your document should look similar to the following illustration.

Buttons for emphasizing words and phrases

Buttons for formatting paragraphs

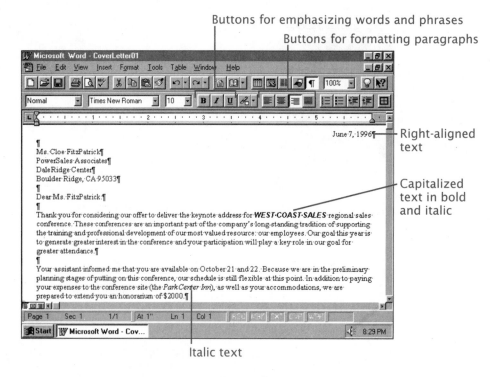

Right-aligned text

Capitalized text in bold and italic

Italic text

Working in the Document Window

If you haven't yet started Microsoft Word, see "Getting Ready," earlier in this book.

When you start Microsoft Word, you see an empty document, called the document window. When the document window is maximized, "Document1" appears in the title bar of the program window. When the document window is not maximized, the document name appears in the title bar of its own document window. Microsoft Word uses a standard 8.5-by-11-inch paper with 1.25-inch left and right margins and 1-inch top and bottom margins.

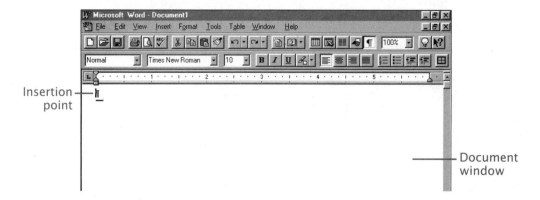

Insertion point

Document window

Typing Text

Later in this book, you will learn about templates and wizards, which are like online forms you can complete to help you create attractive documents (including letters) quickly.

As part of your responsibilities in coordinating the West Coast Sales Regional Conference, you must obtain the services of a keynote speaker. One of your tasks is to write a letter to a motivational speaker who has expressed interest in delivering the address.

You can begin typing in the empty document window, just as you would on a clean sheet of paper. The blinking insertion point, which is already positioned for you at the top of the window, shows where the text you type will appear. As you type, the insertion point moves to the right, leaving behind a stream of text. If you make a typing mistake, you can press the BACKSPACE key to delete the mistake and then type the correct text. For the next exercise, you'll start with the salutation. Later you will insert the date and inside address.

Type text in a letter

1 Type **Dear Ms. FitzPatrick:** and press ENTER.

Pressing ENTER places the insertion point at the start of a new blank line. If a red, wavy underline appears below a word you type, it means that the automatic spell checking feature is enabled and the word is identified as misspelled. You will learn more about this feature later in this lesson.

2 Press ENTER to create another blank line.

Type a paragraph of text

When you type paragraphs that are longer than one line, you do not need to press ENTER at the end of each line. Instead, you can just keep typing. When the insertion point approaches the right margin, it automatically moves to the next line as you continue typing. This is known as wordwrap. You press ENTER to begin a new paragraph or to create a blank line.

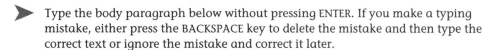 Type the body paragraph below without pressing ENTER. If you make a typing mistake, either press the BACKSPACE key to delete the mistake and then type the correct text or ignore the mistake and correct it later.

Thank you for considering our recent offer to deliver the keynote address for our company's regional sales conference. These conferences are an important part of the company's long-standing tradition of supporting the training and professional development of our most valued resource: our employees. Our goal this year is to generate interest in the conference and your participation will play a role in our goal for greater attendance.

Working with Automatic Corrections

If you make certain kinds of spelling or typographical errors, you might notice that Microsoft Word automatically makes the necessary corrections as you type. For example, some common spelling mistakes (such as typing 'adn' instead of 'and') are corrected as soon as you type the first space after the word. Similarly, if you type two capitalized letters in a row, the program automatically changes the second character to lowercase as you continue typing (with the exception of state abbreviations, such as 'MA'). These corrections are examples of Microsoft Word's *AutoCorrect* feature.

If you misspell a word that is not corrected right away, the program underlines the word with a red, wavy underline. Repeated words (such as 'the the') are identified this same way. This feature is called *Automatic Spell Checking*. After you finish typing, you can use the right mouse button to click the word to display a shortcut menu of correction options. You can:

- Choose the correct spelling from the suggested words at the top of the list.

- Choose Ignore All to remove the underlining and ignore every occurrence of the misspelled word.

- Choose Add to add the word to the dictionary (in the future, Microsoft Word will no longer identify the word as misspelled).

- Choose the Spelling command to display the Spelling dialog box in which you can specify additional spelling options.

- If no suggested spelling appears on the shortcut menu, click the misspelled word and edit the text to correct the spelling.

You will learn more about using the Spelling command in Lesson 2.

Correct typing errors

If you did make spelling errors as you typed text in the previous exercise, you might have observed the message below the Formatting toolbar. This message was generated by the TipWizard. This wizard monitors the commands you use as you work in Microsoft Word and displays suggestions for working more effectively. When you first make a spelling mistake, the TipWizard displays a message that explains how to correct errors, which you will learn how to do in the next exercise.

1   Use the right mouse button to click the word "FitzPatrick."

The Spelling shortcut menu appears, as shown in the following illustration.

Word identified as misspelled

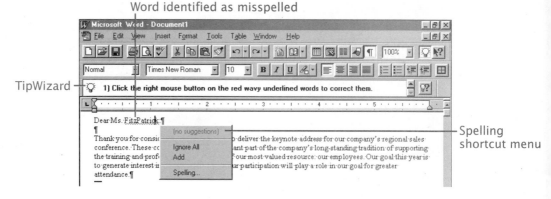

2   Click Ignore All to ignore all occurrences of this word in the document.

3   Use the right mouse button to click any other words underlined with a red, wavy line. On the shortcut menu, click the correct spelling of the word or click Ignore All. If you repeated a word, click Delete Repeated Word.

For now, do not click Add or Spelling. You will learn how to use these options in Lesson 2.

4   On the Standard toolbar, click the TipWizard button to hide the TipWizard for now.

TipWizard

NOTE   The Automatic Spell Checking feature is enabled by default. If you wish to turn it off or hide the red, wavy underlines (which you can turn back on later), on the Tools menu, click Options. Then click the Spelling tab. Clear the Automatic Spell Checking check box to disable the Automatic SpellChecking feature. (Until you enable the feature again, this setting remains in effect every time you use Microsoft Word.) You can also leave Automatic SpellChecking turned on, but hide the red, wavy underlines by clearing the Hide Spelling Errors in Current Document check box.

Display paragraph marks and special symbols

When you typed the salutation for the letter, Microsoft Word inserted a paragraph mark (¶) each time you pressed ENTER. If you cannot see the paragraph marks, you can display them by clicking the Show/Hide ¶ button.

Show/Hide ¶

▶   On the Standard toolbar, click the Show/Hide ¶ button if paragraph marks are not already displayed.

In Microsoft Word, a paragraph can be any amount of text that ends with a paragraph mark, from a word or two (as in your name) to several lines. Even a blank line is a paragraph; it's called an *empty paragraph*. Microsoft Word also displays small dots that represent the spaces between words; these spaces are created when you press the SPACEBAR. Paragraph marks and dots are nonprinting symbols. They will not appear in printed documents. Your document should look similar to the following illustration.

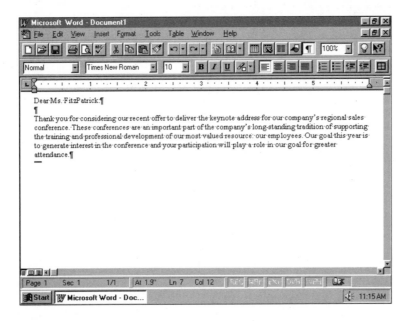

You can display or hide paragraph marks and space marks by clicking the Show/Hide ¶ button. With the marks displayed, you can see how many empty paragraphs fall between lines of text and the number of spaces between words.

Type additional paragraphs of text

▶ Type the following body paragraphs of text. Be sure to press ENTER to insert blank paragraph marks where indicated.

¶

Because we are in the preliminary planning stages of putting on this conference, our schedule is still flexible at this point. Your assistant informed me that you are available on October 21 and 22. In addition to paying your expenses to the conference site (the ParkCenter Inn), as well as your accommodations, we are prepared to extend you an honorarium of $1000.

¶

If these terms are agreeable to you, please sign both copies of the attached contract and return them as soon as possible to me. ¶

¶

Thank you again for your consideration. On behalf of West Coast Sales, I look forward to your positive reply. ¶

¶

Sincerely, ¶

¶

¶

Chris Hamilton ¶

Conference Planning Coordinator ¶

West Coast Sales

Inserting and Deleting Text

Editing text simply means making changes by inserting new text, removing (*deleting*) existing text, or replacing text by removing old text and inserting new text in its place. There are a variety of techniques you can use to modify text. To indicate the text you want to delete or replace, you must first *select* it. Once you've selected the text, you can click a button to do something to the text. Selected text is highlighted (that is, shown in white letters against a dark background), depending on your Display settings.

Selected text

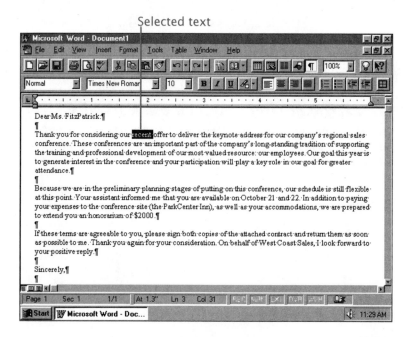

Insert text in a sentence

You can easily insert new text anywhere in a document.

1   Press CTRL+HOME to place the insertion point at the beginning of the document.

2   Position the pointer just before the word "role," as shown in the following illustration, and then click. If you are working with paragraph and space marks displayed, click immediately to the right of the space mark.

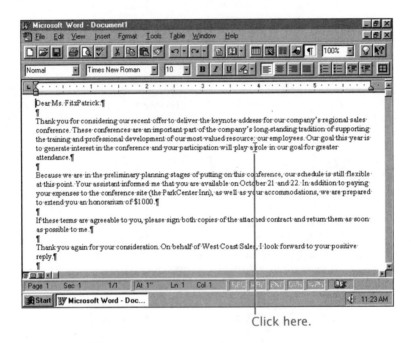

Click here.

3   Type **key** and then press the SPACEBAR to insert a space between the two words.

Delete extra spacing between paragraphs

If your typing types over the existing text, press the INSERT key or double-click OVR on the status bar to turn off overtype mode.

You can del text one character at a time using either BACKSPACE or DEL. Use BACKSPACE to remove characters to the left of the insertion point. Use DEL to remove characters to the right of the insertion point.

1   Place the insertion point before the first word ("Thank") of the last body paragraph—the last paragraph in the main body of the document.

2   Press BACKSPACE twice.

3   Press the SPACEBAR to insert a space between the two sentences.

Edit text in a sentence

Pressing DEL removes characters to the right of the insertion point. After removing text, you can insert new text in its place.

1 Place the insertion point before the number "1" in $1000.

2 Press DEL and then type **2**

Select and delete a word

You can always press BACKSPACE or DEL to remove characters one at a time if you make a mistake as you type. Of course, it would be cumbersome to backspace through an entire document. Instead you can delete text, whether the text is one word or many paragraphs, by first selecting the text you want to remove.

1 In the first body paragraph, place the pointer on the word "recent."

2 Double-click to select the word and the space that follows it.

This maintains the correct spacing after you delete a word.

3 Press DEL to remove the word from the text.

The text in the document moves over to fill the space left by the deleted word.

Select text and replace it

Double-clicking a word selects it, but you can select any amount of text by dragging across it with the mouse. Once you've selected text, the next text you type—regardless of its length—replaces the selection.

1 In the first body paragraph, drag to select the text "our company's"

2 Type **West Coast Sales**

3 Check the spacing before and after the new text you typed. If you need to add a space, position the insertion point and press the SPACEBAR.

Reversing Your Changes

A useful feature in Microsoft Word is the Undo button, which reverses your changes. For example, clicking the Undo button in the next exercise will remove the new text and restore the original text to your document. Whenever something happens that is confusing or is not what you intended, click the Undo button.

NOTE You can undo most (but not all) Microsoft Word commands; operations that cannot be undone include saving, printing, opening, and creating documents.

Undo

> On the Standard toolbar, click the Undo button to reverse your last change.

If this action did not remove the new text and restore the original text to the paragraph, you might have pressed another key before you clicked the Undo button. Clicking Undo once reverses only the last change. You can click the button again until the original text is restored.

Undo more changes

You can also click the arrow next to the Undo button to see a list of actions you can reverse. For example, if you want to return the document to the way it looked before you made the last three changes, you would scroll to the last of the three changes listed in the Undo list and select it. This action would undo all three changes. In the next exercise, you'll see how this works.

> On the Standard toolbar, click the arrow next to the Undo button, and then select the third change in the list to undo your last three actions: deleting the word "recent," typing the "2," and deleting the "1" in $1000.

All of the changes you made between then and now are reversed. The changes in the Undo list appear so that your most recent change is at the top of the list, with each previous change appearing below it. Because several changes in sequence often depend on preceding changes, you cannot select an individual action without undoing all the actions that appear above it in the list.

Change your mind again

The Redo button on the Standard toolbar allows you to reverse an undo action. You can reverse the results of the last change by clicking the Redo button.

Redo

> On the Standard toolbar, click the Redo button to redo your last undo action.

The "1" is again deleted from $1000.

Redo all changes

> On the Standard toolbar, click the arrow next to the Redo button, and then select all of the changes in the list to redo all actions.

Your document should look like the following illustration.

Deleted text   Replacement text

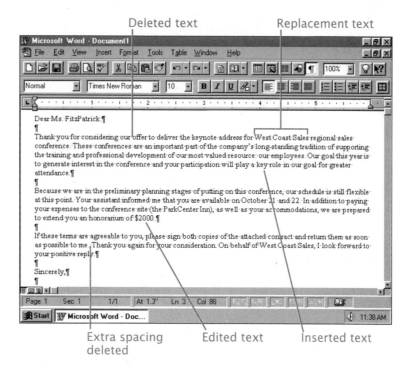

Extra spacing   Edited text   Inserted text
deleted

Moving and Copying Text with Drag-and-Drop Editing

You can re-use and rearrange text in your documents with the *drag-and-drop* feature in Microsoft Word. By dragging selected text to where you want, you can quickly copy or move text to a new location.

Select text and move it

In this exercise, you'll move the second sentence of the second body paragraph to the beginning of the paragraph by selecting and dragging the sentence.

1 Select the sentence, "Your assistant informed me that you are available on October 21 and 22." Be sure that you select the period and the space that follows the sentence.

TIP You might find it easier to select a large amount of text if you click where you want the selection to begin and then, while holding down the SHIFT key, click where you want the selection to end. Microsoft Word selects everything between the first place you clicked and the second place you clicked. This technique is useful when you want to select a large amount of text that does not appear on the screen at one time.

Text Move pointer

2 Position the mouse pointer over the selection until the pointer turns into a left-pointing arrow.

3 Hold down the left mouse button. A small, dotted box and a dotted insertion point appear. Drag until the dotted insertion point is at the beginning of the paragraph, as shown in the following illustration. Then release the mouse button.

Move selected text here.

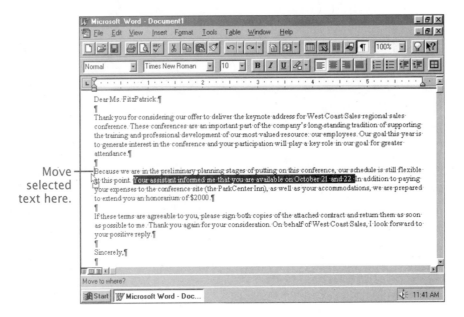

4 Click anywhere outside the selected text to remove the highlighting.

Your moved text should look like the following illustration.

Moved text ——————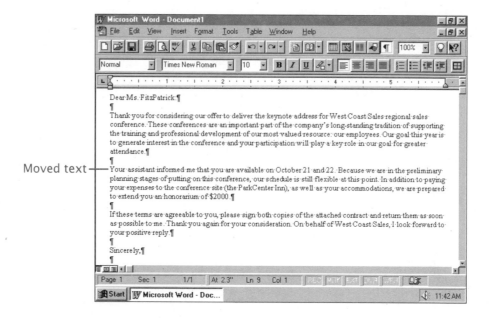

Copy text using the mouse

Copying text with the mouse is similar to moving text with the mouse. For example, you can quickly copy the word "greater" and insert it at another location in the sentence.

1 Double-click to select the word "greater" in the last sentence of the first body paragraph.

2 Hold down the CTRL key on the keyboard, point to the selected text, and then hold down the mouse button.

3 Drag the dotted insertion point to the place immediately before the word "interest" in the same sentence. Release the mouse button and then the CTRL key.

A copy of the selected text is inserted; the original remains where it was, unchanged.

4 Click anywhere outside the selected text to deselect the text.

5 If you need to insert a space between the new text and the old text, place the insertion point where a space is needed, and then press the SPACEBAR.

Your screen should look like the following illustration.

Copied text

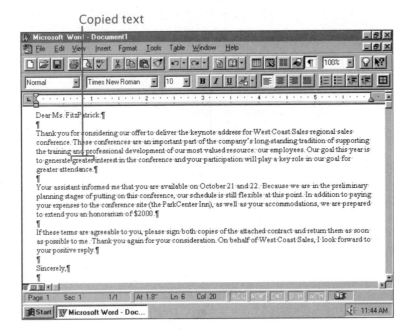

Using Smart Cut and Paste

As you noticed when you double-click to select a word, the space after the word is automatically selected. When you move your selection to a new location in the middle of a sentence, you don't need to type a space to separate it from the other words. However, there are times (at the end of a sentence, for example) when you do not want this space in the new location. With Microsoft Word, you have the option to automatically eliminate the space before a period when you move a selection to the end of a sentence. With the smart-cut-and-paste feature turned on, you don't have to remember to add or delete extra spaces between words or at the end of sentences.

Activate the smart-cut-and-paste feature

You can activate context-sensitive drag-and-drop editing with the smart-cut-and-paste feature. In this exercise you'll activate this feature using the Options command on the Tools menu.

1   On the Tools menu, click Options.

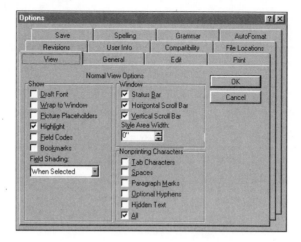

2 In the Options dialog box, click the Edit tab to make it active.

Activate this feature —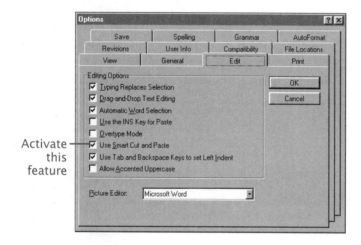

3 Click the Use Smart Cut And Paste check box if it is not checked.

If this check box has a check in it, it means that the smart-cut-and-paste feature is already active. If you clear the check box, you deactivate it; so leave it checked.

4 Click OK to return to your document.

Select text and move it

With the smart-cut-and-paste feature activated, you don't have to remember to add or delete extra spaces between words or at the end of sentences.

1   Select the words "as soon as possible" in the last body paragraph.

2   Position the mouse pointer over the selection until the pointer turns into a left-pointing arrow.

3   Hold down the left mouse button. A small, dotted box and a dotted insertion point appear. Drag until the dotted insertion point is at the end of the sentence. Then release the mouse button.

    No space appears between the last word and the period. To complete the remaining lessons in this book, you need to activate the smart-cut-and-paste option.

Changing the Look of Your Text

When you change the appearance of text—by centering it or making it bold or italic, for example—you are *formatting* it. The concept of "select, then do" is important in formatting. You first select the text you want to format, and then you apply one or more formats to it.

Bold, italic, and underlining are formats you can apply or remove quickly by clicking buttons on the Formatting toolbar. For example, you can select text and then click the Bold button to apply bold formatting. If you select the text and then click the Bold button again, you remove the formatting. Other character formats are available in the Font dialog box.

 NOTE   Your printer might not be able to print both underlining and bold, or other combinations of formatting, if these formats are applied to the same word. Check your printer documentation for any limitations.

Display the Formatting toolbar

To format your text quickly, you need to display the Formatting toolbar. Follow these steps if the Formatting toolbar is not already displayed.

Formatting toolbar

1   On the View menu, click Toolbars.

2   In the Toolbars dialog box, click the Formatting check box if it is not already checked.

3 Click the OK button to display the formatting toolbar.

Select a line of text

At the left of every paragraph, there's an invisible selection bar. By clicking in the selection bar, you can select an entire line. You can also drag the mouse pointer down the selection bar to select several lines at once. In this exercise, you will select the company name in the signature block.

1 Press CTRL+END to move to the end of the document.

2 Position the mouse pointer to the left of the company name "West Coast Sales."

When the mouse pointer is in the selection bar, the pointer changes to a right-pointing arrow.

3 Click to select the line.

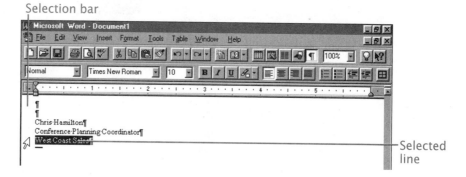

Selection bar

Selected line

Change the look of the text

▶ With this line selected, click the Bold and Italic buttons on the Formatting toolbar.

The Bold, Italic, and Underline buttons apply formatting the first time you click the button, and then remove the formatting when you click the button again. Click anywhere to deselect the text. The formatted text should look like the following illustration.

Bold

Italic

Underline

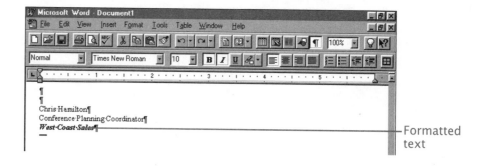

Formatted text

Change the design and size of text

Microsoft Word displays your text in the *font* and *font size* in which it will print. The font is the design of the text characters (letters and numbers); the font size is their size. You can change the font and font size for selected text by making selections from the Font and Font Size lists on the Formatting toolbar.

1 Click in the selection bar of the company name to select the line.

2 To display the list of fonts, click the down arrow next to the Font box.

The font names in your list may be different from those in this illustration.

Fonts you can use for formatting text

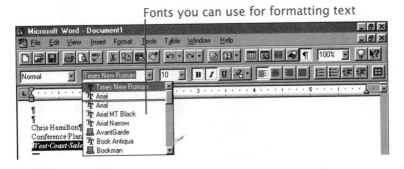

If you see symbols or lines instead of text, you selected a font that displays your text as symbols or lines. To see the text again, select another font.

3 Click Arial from the list of font names.

You might have to click the up arrow in the list scroll bar to find it. The selected text changes to the Arial font.

4 To display a list of font sizes for the font you've selected, click the down arrow next to the Font Size box.

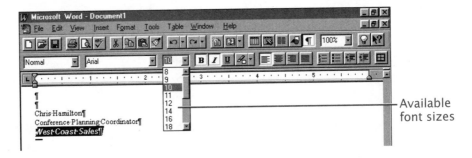

Available font sizes

5 Click 9 from the list of font sizes.

NOTE A point is a standard measurement used in the publishing industry. There are 72 points in an inch, 36 points in one-half inch, and 18 points in one-quarter inch.

Copy formatting to text

The Standard and Formatting toolbars provide the basic tools you need to format and edit documents. After using various formatting combinations in your document, you can save time by reapplying formats with the Format Painter button. Double-clicking the Format Painter button allows you to copy formatting to several locations, while single-clicking the Format Painter button copies formatting only once.

Format Painter

Format Painter pointer

1 Select the line "West Coast Sales" in the signature block if it is not already selected.

2 On the Standard toolbar, double-click the Format Painter button to copy formatting information.

The mouse pointer now appears with a paint brush next to it.

3 Press CTRL+HOME to move to the beginning of the document.

4 Drag the pointer across the text "West Coast Sales" in the first body paragraph.

The formatting from the signature block text is applied to this text as well.

5 Drag the pointer across the text "West Coast Sales" in the last body paragraph to apply the formatting from the signature block line to this text.

6 Click the Format Painter button to turn off the copy formatting feature.

Apply additional formatting to text

Underline

Italic

1 In the last body paragraph, place the insertion point in the word "both."

To change the formatting of a single word, you do not need to select the word first.

2 On the Formatting toolbar, click the Underline button.

3 In the second body paragraph, drag to select the text "ParkCenter Inn."

4 On the Formatting toolbar, click the Italic button.

Click anywhere to deselect the text. Your document should look like the following illustration.

Italicized text

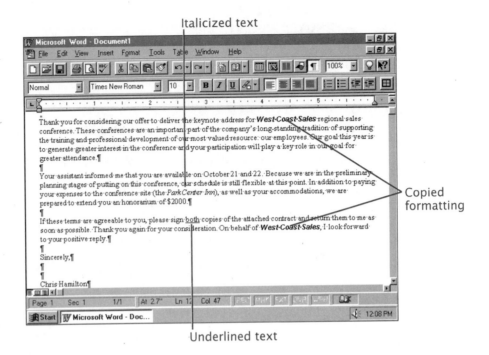

Copied formatting

Underlined text

Insert and right-align today's date

1 Press CTRL+HOME to place the insertion point at the top of the document.

2 On the Insert menu, click Date and Time.

The Date and Time dialog box appears.

3 In the Available Formats box, click the fourth date format from the top, and then click OK.

The current date is inserted at the insertion point. This date is based on your computer's date and time setting.

4 Press ENTER.

5 Place the insertion point anywhere in the date line.

To change the alignment of a single paragraph, you do not need to select the paragraph first.

6 On the Formatting toolbar, click the Align Right button.

Align Right

The date is now aligned at the right margin of the page. Your document should look like the following illustration.

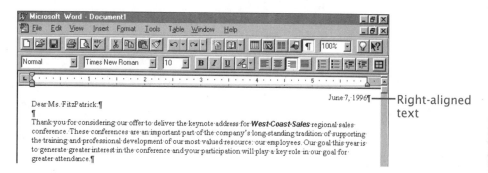

Right-aligned text

Insert the inside address

Microsoft Word stores formatting information in the paragraph mark at the end of each paragraph. Pressing ENTER in front of a paragraph mark copies the paragraph mark to the next line and carries the paragraph formatting into the new paragraph.

TIP If you do not want a new paragraph to have the formatting of the one preceding it, press CTRL+Q before you begin typing the new paragraph. This removes, or *clears,* the formatting. To return character formatting to its default font and size (and remove bold, italics, underlining or other effects), press CTRL+SPACEBAR.

1 Press END to place the insertion point at the end of the date line.

2 Press ENTER.

The new line has the same right-aligned formatting as the paragraph above it.

3 On the Formatting toolbar, click the Align Left button.

Align Left

The new line is now aligned at the left margin of the page.

4 Press ENTER to create a blank line.

5 Type **Ms. Cloe FitzPatrick** and press ENTER.

6 Type **PowerSales Associates** and press ENTER.

7 Type **DaleRidge Center** and press ENTER.

8 Type **Boulder Ridge, CA 95033** and press ENTER.

Saving Documents

The work you've done is currently stored in the computer's memory. To save the work for future use, you must give the document a name and store it on a disk. After you save it, the document is available each time you want to use it. You specify how you want to save your file in the Save As dialog box.

Save the document

When you save a document, you must give it a name and specify where you want to store it. For the documents you create in this book, save them in the same folder as the Step by Step practice files so that you can quickly locate the documents you created.

Save

1 On the Standard toolbar, click the Save button.

Microsoft Word displays the Save As dialog box. This dialog box appears the first time you save a document. In this dialog box, you enter the name you wish to give your document. You can also specify in which folder you wish to save your document.

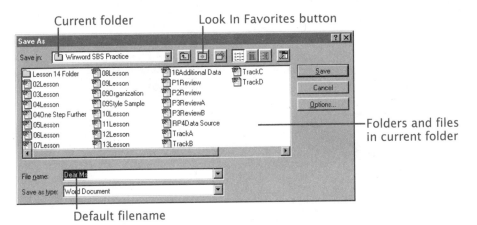

Current folder   Look In Favorites button

Default filename

Folders and files in current folder

2 If the Winword SBS Practice folder is not currently displayed in the Save In box, click the Look In Favorites button, and then double-click on the Winword SBS Practice Folder icon.

3 Click in the File Name box, and type **Cover Letter 01**

You can enter a filename that is up to 255 characters long. You can also use spaces and other characters as part of the name. You can enter a name in lowercase or uppercase; however, text in mixed case (capitalizing the first letter, followed by lowercase letters) is usually easier to read than text in all capital letters.

4 Click the Save button, or press ENTER, to close the dialog box and save the document as you've specified.

Your letter is saved with the name Cover Letter 01 in the Winword SBS Practice folder on your Desktop.

It is best to name and save a document soon after you start working on it. After that, it's a good idea to save a document every 15 minutes or so as you work. The Save button on the Standard toolbar makes this quick and easy to do. By saving your work every 15 minutes, you minimize the amount of work lost if power to your computer is interrupted.

One Step Further: Changing Text Case

Microsoft Word makes it easy to change the capitalization of characters in selected text. The Change Case command gives you the option to select from five standard capitalization schemes. In this exercise, you'll capitalize all of the characters of each word. Then, you'll use the F4 key to repeat the command and copy the uppercase formatting to additional text.

Change the case of text

1 Press CTRL+END and then select the company name line at the bottom of the letter.

2 On the Format menu, click Change Case.

The Change Case dialog box appears.

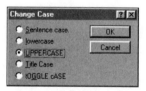

3 Click the UPPERCASE option button if it is not selected.

4 Click the OK button to return to your document.

The selected text appears in uppercase.

5 Press CTRL+HOME and, in the first body paragraph, select the text "West Coast Sales."

6 Press F4 to repeat the Change Case command.

7 In the last body paragraph, select the text "West Coast Sales" and press F4.

If You Want to Continue to the Next Lesson

1   On the File menu, click Close.

2   If a message appears asking whether you want to save changes, click the Yes button.

   Choosing this command closes the active document; it does not exit the Microsoft Word application.

If You Want to Quit Microsoft Word for Now

1   On the File menu, click Exit.

   This command closes both the document and the Microsoft Word application.

2   If a message appears asking whether you want to save changes, click the Yes button.

   Microsoft Word will prompt you to save your changes if you attempt to close the document or the application before you save your most recent changes.

Lesson Summary

To	Do this	Button
Create a new paragraph or a blank line	Press ENTER.	
Display or hide paragraph marks	On the Formatting toolbar, click the Show/Hide ¶ button.	¶
Insert text into existing text	Position the insertion point where you want the new text, and then type.	
Delete characters	Press BACKSPACE to remove characters to the left of the insertion point. Press DELETE to remove characters to the right of the insertion point.	
Select a word	Double-click the word you want to select.	
Select any amount of text	Drag over the text you want to select, or click where you want the selection to begin, hold down SHIFT, and then click where you want the selection to end.	
Select entire lines	Point to the left of the line in the selection bar, and then click. To select more than one line, select a line, and then drag up or down in the selection bar.	

To	Do this	Button
Delete text	Select the text, and then press DELETE or BACKSPACE.	
Replace text	Select the text, and then type new text.	
Undo an action	Click the Undo button immediately after an action.	
Undo multiple actions	Click the Undo arrow, and select the first in the sequence of actions you want undone.	
Reverse an undo action	Click the Redo button immediately after an undo action.	
Reverse multiple undo actions	Click the Redo arrow, and select the first in the sequence of undo actions you want reversed.	
Move or copy text	Select the text, and then drag the selection to a new location. To copy text, hold down CTRL while dragging the text.	
Activate the smart-cut-and-paste feature	From the Tools menu, choose Options. Click the Edit tab, and then select the Smart Cut And Paste option.	
Apply bold, italic, or underline formatting	Select the text, and then click the appropriate buttons on the Formatting toolbar.	
Copy formatting	Select the formatted text. On the Standard toolbar, click the Format Painter button. Drag the pointer across the unformatted text.	
Change a font or font size	Select the text, click the down arrow next to the Font or Font Size list box, and then click a font or font size.	
Change text alignment	Select the text, and click one of the alignment buttons on the Formatting toolbar.	
Save a new document	On the Standard toolbar, click the Save button. Display the appropriate folder in the Save In box, and then type a name in the File Name box.	

To	Do this
Change the case of text	Select the text to change. On the Format menu, click Change Case. Select the desired case option.
Repeat a command	Press F4.
End a Microsoft Word session	On the File menu, click Exit.

For online information about	Use the Answer Wizard to search for
Creating and formatting a simple document	**New document**, and then display Create a new document
Opening documents	**Open document**, and then display Open a document
Saving documents	**Save document**, and then display Save a document
Typing and editing text	**Typing**, and then display Trouble-shooting typing problems
Inserting text	**Inserting**, and then display Type over editing text

To learn more about the Answer Wizard, see "Getting Ready," earlier in this book.

Preview of the Next Lesson

In the next lesson, you'll learn how to revise and rearrange text in an existing document. You'll also learn how to move around quickly in a document and move text by using the buttons on the Standard toolbar. At the end of the lesson, you'll use the Microsoft Word spelling checker to correct spelling errors in a completed document.

Moving Around in a Document

In this lesson you will learn how to:

Estimated time
30 min.

- Open an existing document and save it with a new name.
- Scroll through a document.
- Display a document in page layout view.
- Move text to a new location in a document.
- Copy text to a new location in a document.
- Check and correct spelling.

By copying and moving text, you can easily take advantage of work you've already done. For example, you can copy text, move it to a different location, and edit it. In this lesson, you'll copy and move text within a document using buttons on the Standard toolbar. You'll also learn how to correct typing and spelling mistakes using the Microsoft Word spelling checker.

Opening a Document

As you learned in Lesson 1, a new, empty document window is displayed when you start Microsoft Word. You can also open an existing document and work on it in the same way you work on a new document.

Open a practice file

If you have not yet started Microsoft Word or set up the Word SBS practice files, refer to "Getting Ready," earlier in this book.

In this exercise, you'll open the practice file called 02Lesson and then save the file with a different name, Lesson02. This process creates a duplicate of the file that you can work on and modify during the lesson. The original file, 02Lesson, will remain unchanged in case you want to start the lesson again.

1   On the Standard toolbar, click the Open button.

The Open dialog box appears. In this dialog box, you select the folder and document you wish to open. The text box labeled Look In shows the folder that is currently selected.

Open

Depending on how your system is configured, your dialog box might look different from this illustration.

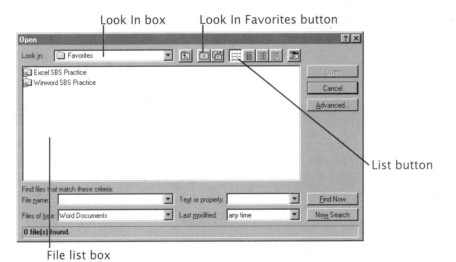

Look In box   Look In Favorites button

List button

File list box

List

If you do not see folders listed, click the Commands and Settings button in the Open dialog box, and select Search Sub-folders to remove the check mark.

2   On the toolbar of the Open dialog box, click the List button if it is not selected.

The names of all folders and files that are contained within the selected folder are listed in the file list box.

3   Be sure that the Favorites folder appears in the Look In box, as shown in the previous illustration.

If a folder name other than Favorites or Winword SBS Practice appears in the Look In box, click the Look In Favorites button on the toolbar.

4   In the file list box, double-click the folder named Winword SBS Practice.

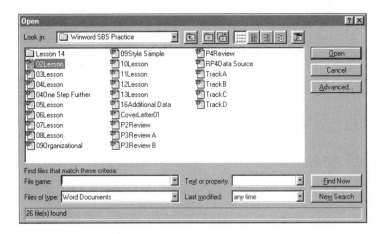

5   In the file list box, double-click the file named 02Lesson.

The dialog box closes, and the file 02Lesson appears in the document window.

Save the practice file with a new name

When you save a file, you give it a name and specify where you want to store it. For each file you use in this book, you'll usually save it in the Step by Step practice files folder with a new name so that the original practice file will remain unchanged.

1   On the File menu, click Save As.

The Save As dialog box appears.

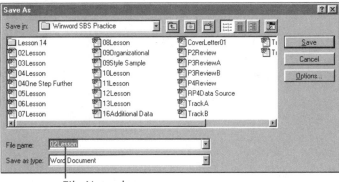

File Name box

2   Be sure that Winword SBS Practice appears in the Save In box.

If the Winword SBS Practice folder does not appear, follow the suggestions under step 3 of the previous exercise to select the folder.

3   Drag to select all text in the File Name box if the text is not selected, and then type **Lesson02**

4 Click the Save button in the dialog box, or press ENTER, to close the dialog box and save the file.

Your file is saved with the name Lesson02 in the Winword SBS Practice folder.

With Automatic Spell Checking enabled, the misspelled words in this document appear underlined with red, wavy lines. To help you focus first on moving around in the document (rather than on the misspelled words), you can hide the red, wavy underlines for now.

Hide spelling errors

1 On the Tools menu, click Options and then click the Spelling tab.

2 Click the Hide Spelling Errors in Current Document check box so that there is a check mark in the check box.

This option hides the red, wavy underlines in the document.

3 Click the Close button to close the dialog box and return to the practice document.

The misspelled words are no longer underlined with red, wavy underlines.

Display paragraph marks

Show/Hide ¶

➤ If you cannot see the paragraph marks on your screen, click the Show/Hide ¶ button on the Standard toolbar.

Moving Around in a Document

When you are working in a multiple page document, it is essential that you know how to quickly display the parts of the document you wish to edit. In Microsoft Word, there are two ways you can move around in a document: by scrolling or by moving to a specific page.

Scrolling Through a Document

The sample document you're working on contains more text than you can see on the screen at one time. To see the rest of the text, you need to *scroll* through the document. Scrolling means moving into view the text that's currently above or below the window. You use the *scroll arrows* to move very short distances (one line at a time) and the *scroll box*, located on the *vertical scroll bar*, to move one window at time or to move to a relative position in the document (near the beginning, near the midpoint, and so on).

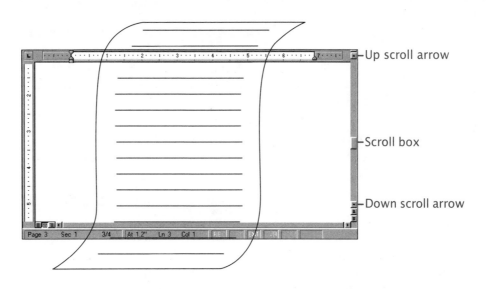

—Up scroll arrow

—Scroll box

—Down scroll arrow

*Double-headed
arrow*

> **NOTE** Double-clicking or dragging the *split box* (at the top of the vertical scroll bar), divides the document window into two parts, in which you can scroll independently. To remove the horizontal line, point to the bar in the middle of the scroll bar (the split box) between the two scroll arrows. When the mouse pointer changes to a double-headed arrow, double-click or drag the split box back up to the top of the scroll bar.

You can use any of the following three methods for scrolling, depending on how quickly you want to move through the document. You can scroll line by line, window by window, or you can jump immediately to the beginning, middle, or end of the document.

Scroll line by line

Each time you click a scroll arrow, the screen changes to show you one more line.

1   Click the down scroll arrow until you see the lines of text that are currently below the window. Click the down scroll arrow a few more times.

2   Click the up scroll arrow a few times to see the text that is currently above the window.

33

3   Point to the down scroll arrow, and hold down the mouse button.

Text will "roll" by rapidly, line by line. To stop scrolling, release the mouse button. As you scroll through the document, you might notice a dotted line that extends across the page; this line represents a new page in the document. Microsoft Word adjusts the page break (called *pagination*) as you add and delete text.

Scroll window by window

To view text that lies above or below the text currently displayed in the document window, you can click in the area above or below the scroll box.

You can also press the PAGE UP and PAGE DOWN keys to move through a document one window at a time.

1   To view the text above what you are currently viewing, click in the scroll bar above the scroll box.

Until you click in a new page, the status bar (at the bottom of your screen) displays the page number of the text in the document displayed at the top of the window.

2   To view the text below what you are currently viewing, click in the scroll bar below the scroll box.

3   Scroll to the beginning of the document by clicking in the scroll bar above the scroll box.

Jump to a different part of the document

Dragging the scroll box on the scroll bar is a quick way to jump to the beginning, middle, or end of a document, or anywhere in between. For example, if you want to work on text at the end of the document, you can drag the scroll box all the way down to the bottom of the scroll bar.

1   To view the end of the document, drag the scroll box to the bottom of the scroll bar.

2   To view the text in the middle of the document, drag the scroll box to the middle of the scroll bar.

As you drag, the page number of the location in the document where the scroll box is positioned appears to the left of the scroll bar.

3   Drag the scroll box to the top of the scroll bar. (You cannot drag it off the scroll bar.)

The beginning of the document appears.

Moving to a Specific Page

If you know the number of the page you wish to see, you can double-click the page number on the left side of the status bar to display the Go To dialog box. In this dialog box, you can type the number of the page and click the Go To button. After you close the dialog box, the insertion point appears on the page you entered. You can use this technique when you are familiar with the contents of the document you are editing and know exactly where you want to work.

Move to page three

You can also press F5 to display the Go To dialog box.

1   Double-click the page number on the status bar.

The Go To dialog box appears. It looks like the following illustration.

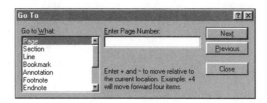

2   In the Go To dialog box, be sure that Page is selected in the Go To What box, and then type **3** in the Enter Page Number box.

3   Click the Go To button.

The dialog box remains open, so you can read the text on the page and verify that this is the page you want to view before you close the dialog box.

4   Click the Close button to close the dialog box and return to your document.

The insertion point moves to the top of page three in your document (the status bar indicates the number of the currently displayed page).

Displaying a Document in Page Layout View

In the document window, there are several display options (called *views*) for viewing your document. In each view, you can focus on different parts of the editing process. For example, you will probably most often use the default, normal view. In this default view, you can see basic text and paragraph formatting, making it the best view for focusing on text and revising your document. On the other hand, page layout view is the best view to use when you want to see the arrangement of text and graphics on the page while you edit text. You can switch between views quickly with the View buttons located to the left of the horizontal scroll bar.

Switch to Page Layout view

Page Layout View

1   Click the Page Layout View button.

The document appears in page layout view.

2   Scroll downward until the middle of the third page appears in the document window.

You can now see that parts of the document are formatted in multiple columns. You also see where graphics appear in relation to text on the page. Your document should look similar to the following illustration.

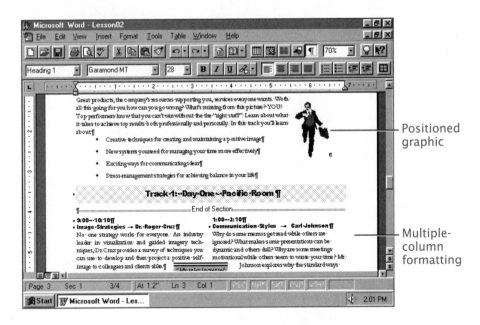

Positioned graphic

Multiple-column formatting

Remain in page layout view as you move and copy text in the next part of this lesson.

Moving and Copying Text Using the Standard Toolbar

In Lesson 1, you learned a quick way to move and copy text using the mouse. In both cases, you could see the final destination for the text on the screen. If you need to move or copy text to a location not visible at the moment, you can also use buttons on the Standard toolbar to store the text until you display the new location.

The following illustration shows how you can use the Copy and Paste buttons on the Standard toolbar to insert text in a new location. When you copy text, Microsoft Word stores the copy on the *Clipboard*—a temporary storage area. The text remains on the Clipboard, so you can insert the same text multiple times. The contents of the Clipboard remain the same until you cut or copy other text, or until you shut down your computer.

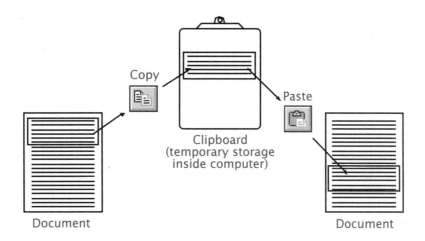

Copy

Paste

Clipboard
(temporary storage
inside computer)

Document

Document

Copy a heading

Remember, the area to the left of the text is called the selection bar.

By copying and editing existing text, you save time and reduce errors. If you copy the heading "Track 1: Day One" and insert the text in a new location, you need to change only one word to create a new heading, "Track 1: Day Two." Its formatting is identical to the original heading.

1   Select the text "Track 1: Day One – Pacific Room." Be sure to include the paragraph mark.

2   On the Standard toolbar, click the Copy button.

You'll see no change in the document, but a copy of the selected text is placed on the Clipboard.

Copy

3   Scroll to the top of page four, and select the first blank paragraph mark.

4   On the Standard toolbar, click the Paste button.

Microsoft Word inserts a copy of the heading.

Paste

Edit the new heading

➤   Double-click "One" in the new heading, and then type **Two**

The word "two" should replace the word "one." If text is inserted next to the selection, be sure that the Typing Replaces Selection check box is selected on the Edit tab of the Options dialog box. For more information, see "Edit Options" in the Appendix, "Matching the Exercises."

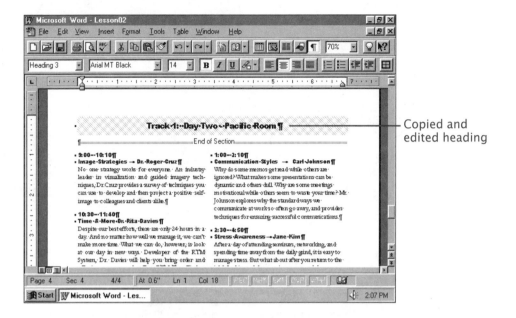

Copied and edited heading

Moving Text Over a Long Distance

Moving text over a long distance within a document is similar to copying text over a long distance, as you just did. The Standard toolbar provides buttons to make this easy. The difference is that instead of copying the text, you *cut* the text from its original place in the document and store it on the Clipboard. Then you scroll to where you want to insert the text and paste it back into the document.

Move text from the end of the document to the middle

The text in the last three paragraphs after the schedule for Day Two might be overlooked by people attending on the first day. In this exercise, you'll move the last three paragraphs so that they appear at the end of the first day's schedule, on page three.

1 Click the down scroll arrow until you can see all of the text under the heading "Personal Effectiveness Hospitality Room."

2 Select the two heading paragraphs and the paragraph under it.

3 On the Standard toolbar, click the Cut button.

The text from the document is removed and stored on the Clipboard.

Cut

4 Click the Previous Page scroll button at the bottom of the vertical scroll bar to move quickly to the previous page.

Previous Page

5 Scroll downward, if necessary, and select the paragraph mark above the line labeled "End of Section."

6 On the Standard toolbar, click the Paste button to insert the text from the Clipboard.

Paste

7 Press BACKSPACE to delete the extra paragraph mark and move text up to the previous page.

Pages three and four of your document should look similar to the following illustration.

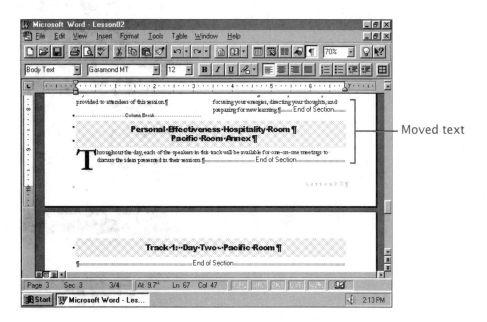

Moved text

Save the document

Save

➤ On the Standard toolbar, click the Save button.

The current version replaces the previous version. You will not see any change to the document. The status bar, however, displays a brief message indicating your document is being saved.

Checking the Spelling in an Entire Document

Before you complete any document, you'll want to check for typographical and spelling errors. Earlier, you learned how Microsoft Word identifies spelling errors as you type and create a new document. You can also use the Spelling button or Spelling command to *proof* the document after you have finished editing it.

When you check the spelling in a document, the check begins at the insertion point and proceeds downward from there. Microsoft Word compares each word in the document to a standard, built-in dictionary. The spelling checker might find words such as your name, your company name, and a technical term that are spelled correctly but that are not in the standard dictionary. You can add such words to a custom dictionary as you check the spelling.

Microsoft Word not only displays the misspelled word in the dialog box, but also highlights the word in the document. You can read the surrounding text to determine the correct spelling. If a word is spelled incorrectly, you have two choices for correcting it: you can retype it, or you can select the correct spelling from a list.

Check the spelling

You can also press CTRL+HOME to move the insertion point to the start of the document.

Spelling

1   Scroll to the beginning of the document and position the insertion point in front of the first line.

2   On the Standard toolbar, click the Spelling button.

The Spelling dialog box appears when the spelling checker finds an unrecognized word that is not in its dictionary. In this case, Microsoft Word identifies "personaly" as a possibly misspelled word.

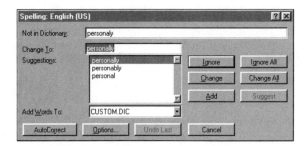

The suggested spelling "personally" appears in the Change To box.

3   Click the Change button.

Microsoft Word corrects the spelling and selects the next misspelled word.

If WCS is not selected as a misspelled word in step 4, click Options on the Tools menu, and then select the Spelling tab. Clear the check mark next to Words In UPPERCASE , and then click OK.

4   "WCS" is a company abbreviation that is used often. To have Microsoft Word recognize this instance of the name and all future instances in this and future documents, click the Add button.

5   Continue checking and correcting the spelling in the document.

For this word	Do this
woth	Click "with" in the list of suggested spellings, and then click the Change button.
the	The label in the dialog box has changed to "Repeated Word." The sentence contains two instances in a row of the word "the." Click the Delete button.

For this word	Do this
youneed	Click the entry in the Not In Dictionary box, and then correct the text in the Change To box by inserting a space after the "u." Because you make this mistake frequently, click the AutoCorrect button. The next time you type "youneed" and a space, Microsoft Word will automatically correct the spelling for you.

6 Click the Ignore All button for all remaining spelling errors found (these are all proper nouns that are not found in the dictionary).

7 Click the OK button when the spelling check is complete.

Save the document

➤ On the Standard toolbar, click the Save button.

Save

Microsoft Word saves the current version of this document in place of the previous version.

One Step Further: Spell Checking Selected Text

You might realize that you must make changes to your document after you have already checked its spelling. So that you don't have to check the spelling of the entire document again, you can restrict the spelling check to only the text you select.

Check spelling of selected text

In this exercise, you'll enter the text, and then check the spelling of the new text only.

1 Scroll to display the end of the third page.

2 Place the insertion point at the end of the last sentence of the last paragraph on the page, and press the SPACEBAR.

3 Type the following text. Misspell the words as indicated so that you can see AutoCorrect make corrections for you.

You can schdule up to 10 minutes with each each speaker or just drop by. Neck massages, frash-squeezed juices, and a vriety of literature and other materials youneed will be available.

Spelling

4 Limit the spelling check to the new text you added by selecting the last two sentences you typed.

5 On the Standard toolbar, click the Spelling button.

6 Microsoft Word checks the spelling of the selected text only. Respond to each correction that appears in the Spelling dialog box.

For this word	Do this
schdule	Click "schedule" in the list of suggested spellings, and then click the Change button.
each	Click the Delete button to remove the repeated word.
frash	Click "fresh" in the list of suggested spellings, and then click the Change button.
vriety	Click "variety" in the list of suggested spellings, and then click the Change button.

7 Click the No button when you see the message asking whether you want to continue checking the remainder of the document.

If You Want to Continue to the Next Lesson

1 On the File menu, click Close.

2 If a message appears asking whether you want to save changes, click the Yes button.

Choosing this command closes the active document; it does not exit the Microsoft Word program.

If You Want to Quit Microsoft Word for Now

1 On the File menu, click Exit.

2 If a message appears asking whether you want to save changes, click the Yes button.

Lesson Summary

To	Do this	Button
Open an existing document	On the Standard toolbar, click the Open button, and then select the document name from the File Name list. If you don't see the document name, check to make sure that the correct drive and folder are selected.	
Scroll through a document	Click the scroll arrows on the scroll bar, drag the scroll box, or click above or below the scroll box.	
Move or copy text to a location not currently visible	Select the text, and click the Cut or Copy button on the Standard toolbar. Scroll to the new location, and click to place the insertion point. Click the Paste button to insert the selection.	
Display a document in different views	Click the appropriate view button located to the left of the horizontal scroll bar.	
Check and correct the spelling in a document	On the Standard toolbar, click the Spelling button, and then change or ignore words as Microsoft Word selects them.	

For online information about	Use the Answer Wizard to search for
Opening and saving documents	**opening documents**, and then display Open a document **saving documents**, and then display Save a document
Moving and copying text	**moving and copying text**, and then display Move or copy text or graphics
Scrolling through a document	**scrolling**, and then display Use the mouse to scroll through a document
Checking the spelling of a document	**spelling**, and then display Correct spelling

Preview of the Next Lesson

In the next lesson, you'll learn to affect the appearance of entire paragraphs using paragraph formatting techniques. You'll add bullets or numbers to lists. You'll also learn how to indent paragraphs and how to set page margins.

Formatting Paragraphs

In this lesson you will learn how to:

Estimated time
35 min.

- Set left, right, first-line, and hanging indents.
- Create numbered and bulleted lists.
- Add a border around a paragraph.
- Sort a list.
- Change the line spacing in a paragraph and between paragraphs.
- Change the size of page margins.
- View an entire page on the screen.

Just as you can change the appearance of text using the toolbars, you can change the appearance of paragraphs. In this lesson, you'll learn about using the Formatting toolbar to indent text, adjust the margins, create tables, create a border around a paragraph, and add bullets and numbers to lists. Using commands from the menu, you'll further customize the appearance of paragraphs by changing line spacing and sorting lists. When you complete this lesson, your document should look like the following illustration.

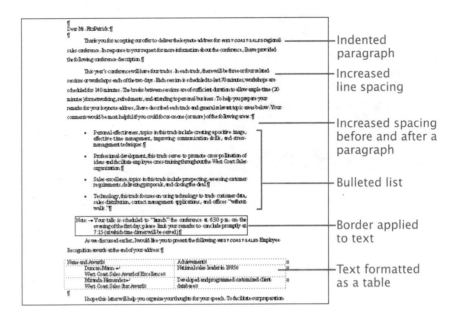

Indented paragraph

Increased line spacing

Increased spacing before and after a paragraph

Bulleted list

Border applied to text

Text formatted as a table

Start the lesson

Follow the steps below to open the practice file called 03Lesson, and then save it with the new name Lesson03.

Open

To select the folder containing your practice files, refer to "Open a practice file" near the start of Lesson 2.

1   On the Standard toolbar, click the Open button.

2   Make sure that the Winword SBS Practice folder appears in the Look In box.

3   In the file list box, double-click the file named 03Lesson to open it.

4   On the File menu, click Save As.

The Save As dialog box opens. Make sure the Winword SBS Practice folder appears in the Save In box.

5   Select and delete any text in the File Name box, and then type **Lesson03**

6   Click the Save button, or press ENTER.

If you share your computer with others who use Microsoft Word, the screen display might have changed since your last lesson. If your screen does not look similar to the illustrations as you work through this lesson, see the Appendix, "Matching the Exercises."

Setting Indents and Creating Lists

You can quickly indent the left edge of a line or paragraph by using the TAB key or by clicking a button on the Formatting toolbar. You can also use the Formatting toolbar buttons to automatically add bullets or numbers to lists.

Using the Tab Key to Indent Text

One of the simplest ways to indent a single line of text is with the TAB key. You can insert a tab in front of the first character you want to indent. If you are entering new text, you can press TAB before typing your text. If the text continues on one or more additional lines, however, the TAB only indents the first line of a paragraph.

Use a tab to indent a line

1 Move the insertion point in front of the word "Thank" in the first body paragraph.

2 Press TAB.

Your paragraph should look like the following illustration.

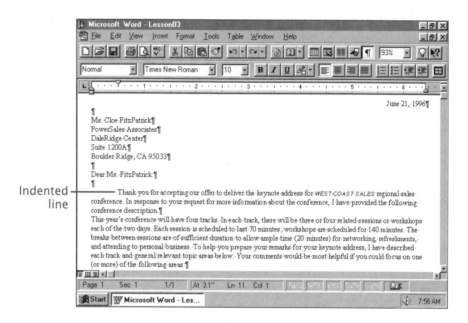

Indented
line

If you cannot see the Formatting toolbar, use the right mouse button to click a gray area on the Standard toolbar, and then select Formatting from the menu.

Using the Formatting Toolbar to Set Indents

With buttons on the Formatting toolbar, you can quickly indent one or more paragraphs. Each time you click the Increase Indent button, Microsoft Word indents all lines of the selected paragraph (or the paragraph containing the insertion point) one-half inch. Microsoft Word has preset, or *default,* tab stops every one-half inch, so you are actually indenting to the next tab stop. The Formatting toolbar also has a Decrease Indent button if you've indented a paragraph too far.

Decrease Indent

Increase Indent

Use the indent buttons

1   Be sure that the insertion point is still in the first body paragraph.

2   On the Formatting toolbar, click the Increase Indent button.

Increase Indent

Your indented paragraph should look like the following illustration.

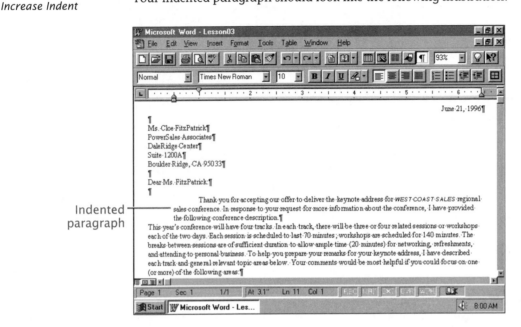

Indented paragraph

3   Click the Increase Indent button two more times.

Each time you click the button, the paragraph indents one-half inch and the text breaks to accommodate the shorter lines of text.

4   On the Formatting toolbar, click the Decrease Indent button to move the paragraph to the left. Continue clicking until the paragraph reaches the left margin—it will not move beyond the margin.

Decrease Indent

Indent several paragraphs

1   Select four paragraphs of the sample document, starting with the paragraph that begins with "Personal effectiveness" and ending with the paragraph that begins with "Note."

2   On the Formatting toolbar, click the Increase Indent button to indent the selected paragraphs one-half inch.

3   Click anywhere to deselect the text. Your document should look like the following illustration.

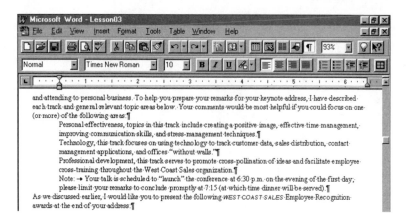

Creating Bulleted and Numbered Lists

Bulleted and numbered lists are common elements in many documents. Bullets clearly separate list items from one another, emphasizing each point; numbers show sequence. The AutoFormat As You Type feature inserts a bullet (and a tab) whenever you type a hyphen and a space (or tab) at the beginning of a line. To format existing text with bullets, you can click the Bullets button on the Formatting toolbar. You can also use the Numbering button to create a numbered list when you are typing new text or when you want to format existing text.

Create a numbered list

In this exercise, you will convert three paragraphs of the document into a numbered list.

1   Select the first three indented paragraphs, starting with the paragraph that begins with "Personal effectiveness" and ending with the paragraph that begins with "Professional development."

2   On the Formatting toolbar, click the Numbering button.

3   Click anywhere to deselect the text.

Numbering

A number appears in front of each selected paragraph, and the indents adjust to separate the text from the numbers. When the paragraph is longer than one line, the second line of text aligns with the one above, as shown in the following illustration.

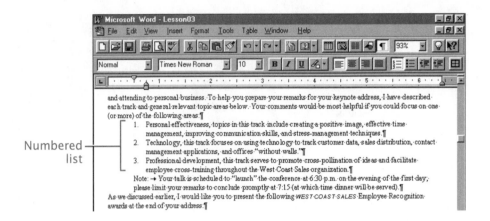

Numbered list

Insert another numbered paragraph

In this exercise, you will insert a new numbered paragraph within the existing numbered list.

1 With the insertion point in the last line of the first numbered paragraph, press END.

2 Press ENTER.

A new numbered line is inserted. Notice that the remaining paragraphs are renumbered to reflect the addition of a new item in the list.

3 Type the following text: **Sales excellence, topics in this track include prospecting, assessing customer requirements, delivering proposals, and closing the deal.**

Change the list to bullets

Because these items do not require sequential order, you can list them with bullets rather than with numbers.

1 Select the numbered paragraphs.

2 On the Formatting toolbar, click the Bullets button.

The numbers are replaced with bullets. Click anywhere to deselect the text.

Bullets

*If you do not
see bullets,
but you see
{symbol ...}
instead, you
are viewing
the codes that
produce the
bullets. To see
the bullets,
select Options
from the Tools
menu. On the
View tab, clear
the Field Codes
check box.*

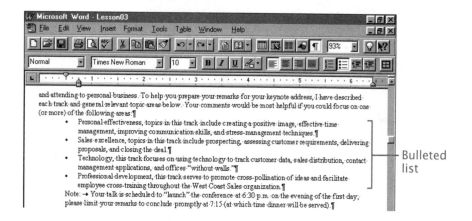

Bulleted
list

  TIP Although using the Formatting toolbar buttons is the quickest way to create a numbered or bulleted list, many more options are available with the Bullets And Numbering command on the Format menu.

Setting Custom Indents

Clicking the Formatting toolbar buttons is the fastest way to adjust a left indent in one-half-inch increments. Sometimes, however, you might want to use different settings in your document. You can use the ruler at the top of your screen to set custom indents. The ruler is preset to show inches, and each inch is divided into eighths.

The triangular markers on the ruler control the indents of the current paragraph (the one you've selected or the one that contains the insertion point). The left side of the ruler has three icons. The top triangle controls the first line of the paragraph; the bottom triangle controls the remaining lines of the paragraph. The small square under the bottom triangle, called the *paragraph indent marker,* controls the entire left edge of the paragraph. The triangle on the right side of the ruler controls the right edge of the paragraph.

First-line indent marker

Left indent marker

Right indent marker

Paragraph indent marker

Display the ruler

To complete this lesson, you will need to display the ruler. Do this step if your ruler is not already displayed.

➤ From the View menu, click Ruler.

Set a custom left indent

In this exercise, you will drag the paragraph indent marker to adjust the entire left edge of the signature block.

1 Select the four paragraphs of the signature block at the end of the document.

2 Drag the paragraph indent marker to the 4-inch mark on the ruler, and then release the mouse button.

If only one marker moves, it means the mouse pointer dragged a triangle instead of the square. On the Standard toolbar, click the Undo button. Then point to the square and try again.

Both the top and bottom triangles move with the square. A dotted line appears to help you see where the new indent will be. When you release the mouse button, the text moves to align with the paragraph indent marker. Click anywhere to deselect the text.

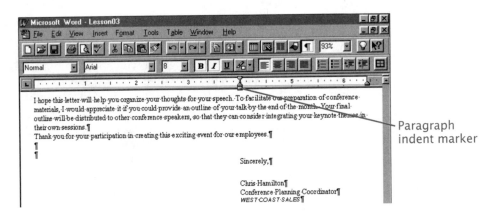

Paragraph indent marker

Set a right indent

1 Select the four bulleted items and the "Note" paragraph.

2 Drag the *right indent marker* (the triangle at the right end of the ruler) to the 5.5-inch mark.

You might need to scroll to the right to see the right indent marker; scroll back to the left edge when you are done. Click anywhere to deselect the text.

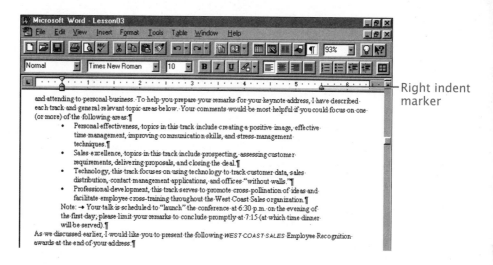

Right indent marker

Set a hanging indent

The top triangle on the left of the ruler is called the *first-line indent marker*. This marker controls only the first line of a paragraph.

Only the top, or first-line indent, marker should move. If both markers move, it means you dragged the square instead of the top triangle. On the Standard toolbar, click the Undo button. Then point to the top triangle and try again.

➤ With the insertion point positioned in the "Note" paragraph, drag the first-line indent marker to the left to the one-quarter-inch mark on the ruler.

The first line extends to the left of the paragraph, with the rest of the paragraph "hanging" below it. This creates what is called a *hanging indent*.

First-line indent marker

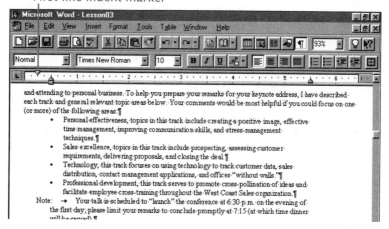

Customize the hanging indent

1 Be sure that the insertion point is still in the "Note" paragraph.

2 Drag the left indent marker (the bottom triangle) to the three-quarter-inch mark on the ruler.

The first line does not move, but the "hanging" text is now aligned with the items in the bulleted list. The paragraph should look like the following.

Left indent marker

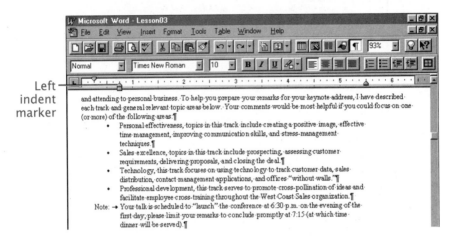

Indent the first line

1 Click in the paragraph that begins with "This year's conference."

2 Drag the first-line indent marker (the top triangle) to the one-half-inch mark.

The paragraph should look similar to the following illustration.

Indented first line

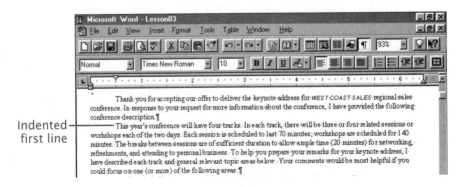

TIP If you know the exact measurements that you need for indents and you prefer to enter the measurements in a dialog box instead of dragging markers on the ruler, use the Paragraph command on the Format menu.

Add borders to a paragraph

To create a line around text, you can use the Border toolbar. You can display the Border toolbar by clicking the Borders button on the Formatting toolbar. When you no longer want to display the Borders toolbar, click the Borders button again.

Borders toolbar

Borders

To change the type of line in a border, select the line style you want from the Line Style list before you select where you want the border to appear.

1 On the Formatting toolbar, click the Borders button.

The Borders toolbar appears below the Formatting toolbar.

2 With the insertion point in the "Note" paragraph, click the Outside Border button on the Formatting toolbar.

The "Note" paragraph is surrounded by a thin black border as shown in the following illustration.

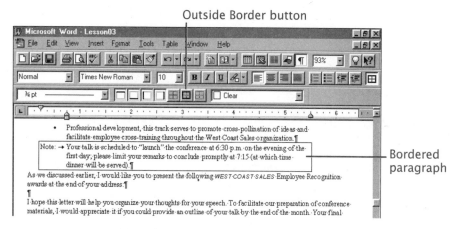

3 On the Formatting toolbar, click the Borders button.

When the Borders toolbar is displayed, clicking the Borders button hides this toolbar.

Sorting a List

Sorting a list in alphabetical order helps organize information in your document. You can sort a list by selecting all the items in the list you want sorted and choosing the Sort Text command on the Table menu. The following steps show you how easy it is to sort a list.

Sort a list

1   Select the four bulleted items describing conference topics.

2   On the Table menu, click Sort Text.

The dialog box appears and displays different sorting options from which you can choose. Because you want to sort the list in ascending order (from A to Z) you don't need to make any changes in this dialog box.

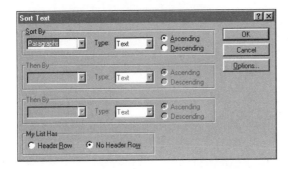

3   Click the OK button.

Your list is sorted alphabetically by the first character in each paragraph.

Changing Paragraph Formatting

In addition to formatting with the ruler and toolbars, you can change the appearance of paragraphs with the Paragraph command on the Format menu. In the Paragraph dialog box, you can change the line spacing of a paragraph and the space between paragraphs, as well as indentation and alignment. Options you set with this command affect entire paragraphs.

If you know the exact measurement you want for indents, the Paragraph dialog box provides an opportunity for greater precision in comparison to what is available on the Formatting toolbar and ruler. For instance, you can specify exact measurements and preview the effect on a sample paragraph displayed in the dialog box.

Indent the first line

1   Select the last two body paragraphs, beginning with "I hope" through "Thank you."

2   On the Format menu, click Paragraph.

Microsoft Word displays the Paragraph dialog box.

3   Click the Indents and Spacing tab if it is not activated.

In the Preview box, you see a preview of the options as you set them. This dialog box shows you the formatting of the current paragraph.

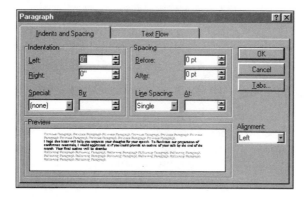

4   In the Indentation area, click the down arrow next to the Special box, and then click First Line.

The first line of the paragraph will be indented to the first default tab stop. The Preview box changes to reflect the new setting.

5   Click the OK button.

Change the right indent and alignment

1   Select the four bulleted items and the "Note" paragraph.

2   On the Format menu, click Paragraph.

3   In the Indentation area, click the up arrow next to the Right box so that "1" " appears.

4   From the Alignment drop-down list, click Justified.

This option aligns text evenly between the left and right margins.

5   Click the OK button to return to the document, and then click to deselect the text.

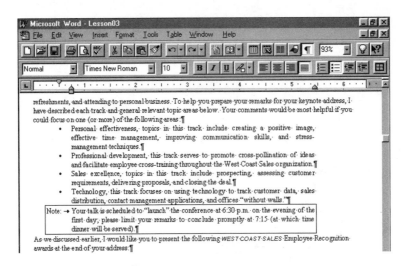

Add vertical spacing between paragraphs

Instead of pressing ENTER to add blank lines before and after a heading or text paragraph, you can make the vertical spacing part of the paragraph's formatting. Later, if you need to move the paragraph to another location in the document, the correct spacing travels with it. This method also gives you more flexibility and precision, because you can increase spacing by a fraction of a line—for example, by 1.5 or 1.75 lines.

1 Place the insertion point in the first body paragraph.

2 On the Format menu, click Paragraph.

3 In the Spacing area, click the up arrow in the After box once so that "6 pt" appears.

Remember to check the sample in the Preview box to see the results.

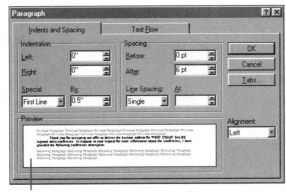

Preview of selected paragraph settings

4 Click the OK button to return to the document.

5 With the insertion point in the body paragraph that begins "I hope," click Repeat Paragraph Formatting on the Edit menu to repeat your last editing command.

Add spacing before and after paragraphs

1 Select the four bulleted items and the "Note" paragraph.

2 On the Format menu, click Paragraph.

3 In the Spacing area, click the up arrow in the Before box once so that "6 pt" appears.

4 Press TAB and, in the After box, type **3**

These settings will insert 6 points of space before and 3 points of space after each selected paragraph.

5 Click the OK button to return to the document.

Change the line spacing within a paragraph

Microsoft Word is preset to create single-spaced lines. If you prefer a different line spacing, you can change the setting.

1 Place the insertion point anywhere in the first body paragraph, and then on the Format menu, click Paragraph.

2 Click the down arrow next to the Line Spacing box to display the spacing options.

3 Select 1.5 Lines.

4 Click the OK button to apply the formatting and close the dialog box.

Your paragraph should look like the following illustration.

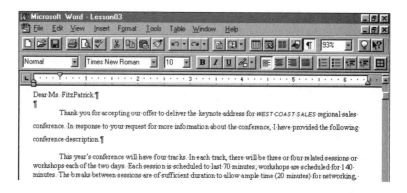

59

5 Repeat steps 1 through 4 for all body paragraphs, except the bulleted items and "Note" paragraph.

TIP If you want to change the line spacing for an entire document, use the Select All command on the Edit menu to select the entire document, and then choose the Paragraph command and set the spacing.

Setting Margins with the Ruler

You've seen how you can use the ruler to set indents. In page layout view, the ruler can also display margin markers, which you can drag to change the page margins. In this view, you can see the effect that changing the margins has on the layout of the entire page. You can also quickly switch between normal and page layout views by clicking the buttons to the left of the horizontal scroll bar.

Change to page layout view

In page layout view, you can see the edge of the page to better examine the changes to your margins. This view shows how your page will appear when you print your document.

Page Layout View

▶ Click the Page Layout View button to the left of the horizontal scroll bar.

Display the margin boundaries on the ruler

When you display indents on the ruler, the numbers indicate inches from the left margin. On the other hand, margins are measured in inches from the left edge of the page. Just as you can adjust indents from the ruler, you can adjust the margins on the ruler. After adjusting your margins, you can change the magnification to see your changes.

1 Press CTRL+HOME to place the insertion point at the top of the document.

2 Scroll the document all the way to the top and to the left.

3 Position the pointer near the left margin on the horizontal ruler until the pointer changes to a two-sided arrow, as shown in the following illustration.

Margin pointer

4 To adjust the left margin, drag to the right to the 1.25-inch mark on the gray scale, as indicated in the illustration callout below.

TIP You can hold down the ALT key while you drag to see the measurements for the margins as you adjust them in the ruler.

1.25-inch left margin

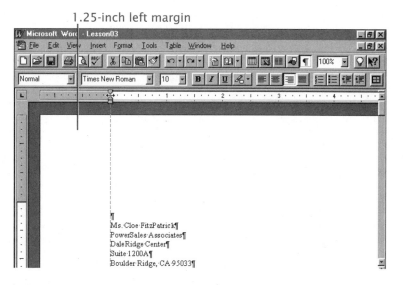

5 Position the pointer near the top of the white part of the vertical ruler.

6 To adjust the top margin, drag upward to the 1-inch mark on the gray scale.

You'll be dragging the ruler until the gray portion is 1 inch in length.

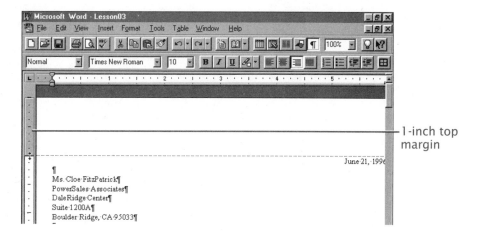

1-inch top margin

NOTE If you know the exact measurements that you want for your document's margins, you can choose the Page Setup command on the File menu and enter them in the dialog box. You can also divide the document into sections and set different margins for each section.

Change the magnification

As in normal view, you can adjust the magnification in page layout view to get an overall view of the page.

▶ In the Zoom Control drop-down list, click Whole Page.

Your document should look like the following illustration.

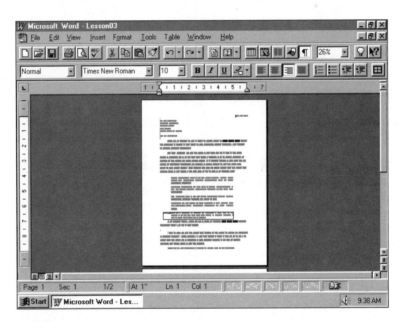

Switch back to normal view

Normal View

▶ Click the Normal View button to the left of the horizontal scroll bar to return to normal view.

Save the changes

Save

▶ On the Standard toolbar, click the Save button. Microsoft Word saves this version of the document in place of the previous version.

One Step Further: Creating a Table with the Standard Toolbar

When you want to create paragraphs that should appear side by side, you can use the Insert Table button on the Standard toolbar. With this button, you can create a grid of any size. For example, if you want to create a table containing two columns and four rows, click the Insert Table button and drag to create a table that contains the number of rows and columns you want. In each cell of the grid, you can enter text of any length. Microsoft Word handles all the formatting, ensuring correct alignment and line spacing.

Create a table

Insert Table

1 Place the insertion point in front of the blank paragraph mark located below the "As we discussed" paragraph.

2 From the Standard toolbar, click the Insert Table button, and drag to highlight a group of cells that is three rows long and two columns wide.

When you release the mouse button, your screen should look like the following illustration.

If the gridlines in the table are not visible, click Gridlines on the Table menu.

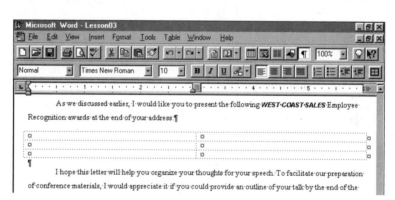

Enter text in the table

1 With the insertion point in the first cell of the left column, type **Name and Award** and press TAB.

The insertion point moves to the first cell in the right column.

2 Type **Achievement** and press TAB.

The insertion point moves to the second cell in the left column.

3 Type **Duncan Mann West Coast Sales Award of Excellence**

The text in the cell wraps to the following line.

63

4   Place the insertion point before the word "West" in the current cell.

5   Press SHIFT+ENTER.

The award name is placed on a separate line, but without creating a new paragraph. Any paragraph formatting you apply to one line will affect the other.

Increase Indent

6   On the Formatting toolbar, click the Increase Indent button.

The text moves one-half inch to the right in the cell.

7   Press TAB, and type **National sales leader in 1995**

8   Press TAB, and type **Miranda Hernandez**

9   Press SHIFT+ENTER, and type **West Coast Sales Star Award**

10   On the Formatting toolbar, click the Increase Indent button.

11   Press TAB, and type **Developed and programmed customized client database**

This introduction to tables is intended to help you see how easy it is to make tables in Microsoft Word. In Lesson 10 of this book, you will learn more about working in tables.

If You Want to Continue to the Next Lesson

1   On the File menu, click Close.

2   If a message appears asking whether you want to save changes, click the Yes button.

Choosing this command closes the active document; it does not exit the Microsoft Word program.

If You Want to Quit Microsoft Word for Now

1   On the File menu, click Exit.

2   If a message appears asking whether you want to save changes, click the Yes button.

Lesson Summary

To	Do this	Button
Set indents	Click the Increase Indent or Decrease Indent button.	
Create bulleted lists	Select the paragraphs to format, and click the Bullets button.	
Create numbered lists	Select the paragraphs to format, and click the Numbering button.	
Set custom indents	Drag the triangular indent markers on the ruler to set the first-line, left, and right indents.	
Add a border to a paragraph	Click the Borders button to display the Borders toolbar. Select a line style from the Line Style box. Click the appropriate border button.	
Sort text in a list	On the Table menu, click Sort Text.	
Adjust spacing between paragraphs	On the Format menu, click Paragraph. Select the spacing you want in the Spacing area.	
Adjust line spacing within a paragraph	On the Format menu, click Paragraph. Select the line spacing you want in the Line Spacing drop-down list.	
Set margins	In page layout view, drag the left and right margins on the ruler to the measurement you want.	
View an entire page	On the View menu, click Page Layout. *or* Click the Page Layout View button.	
Return to normal view	Click the Normal View button.	

For online information about	Use the Answer Wizard to search for
Setting indents	**indents**, and then display Types of paragraph indentation
Creating bulleted or numbered lists	**lists**, and then display Numbered and bulleted lists
Setting margins	**margins**, and then display Changing margins

Preview of the Next Lesson

In the next lesson, you'll prepare to print a document. You'll first view your document in Print Preview to examine it before you print it. Then you will select a printer and print the document.

Printing Your Document

Estimated time
25 min.

In this lesson you will learn how to:

- Examine one or more pages of a document in the Print Preview window.
- Edit text in the Print Preview window.
- Insert page breaks.
- Print your document using the Standard toolbar and menu commands.

After creating documents and getting them to look the way you want, you can print the results of your labors. In this lesson, you'll use buttons on the Standard toolbar to examine the layout of a document. After editing text and manually inserting hard page breaks, you'll print your document if you have a printer available. If not, you can still preview your document and see how it will look when you are able to print it.

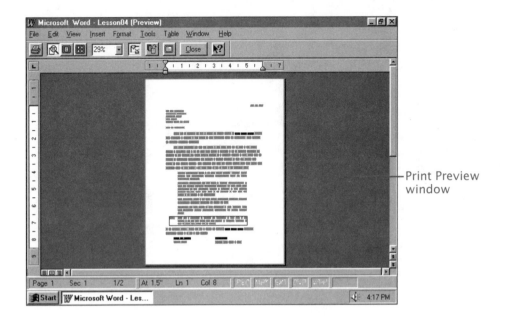

Print Preview window

Start the lesson

Follow the steps below to open the practice file called 04Lesson, and then save it with the new name Lesson04.

Open

To select the folder containing your practice files, refer to "Open a practice file" near the start of Lesson 2.

1 On the Standard toolbar, click the Open button.

In the Look In box, be sure that the Winword SBS Practice folder appears.

2 In the file list box, double-click the file named 04Lesson to open it.

3 On the File menu, click Save As.

The Save As dialog box opens. Be sure that the Winword SBS Practice folder appears in the Save In box.

4 In the File Name box, type **Lesson04**

5 Click the Save button, or press ENTER.

If you share your computer with others who use Microsoft Word, the screen display might have changed since your last lesson. If your screen does not look similar to the illustrations as you work through this lesson, see the Appendix, "Matching the Exercises."

Previewing Your Document

To get a better idea of how your document will look when you print it, you can use the Print Preview window. In this window, you can see the overall appearance of one page or all the pages. You can see where text falls on a page before it continues on to the next page. After you examine your document, you can make more adjustments to get everything just right. Previewing the document can save you time, because it reduces the number of times you print the document before it looks exactly the way you want. Previewing saves paper, too.

Preview the document

Print Preview

➤ On the Standard toolbar, click the Print Preview button.

Your document in the Print Preview window should look like the following illustration.

If your screen does not match this illustration, choose View, Ruler to display the ruler in Print Preview. Click the One Page button if you see more than one page of the document.

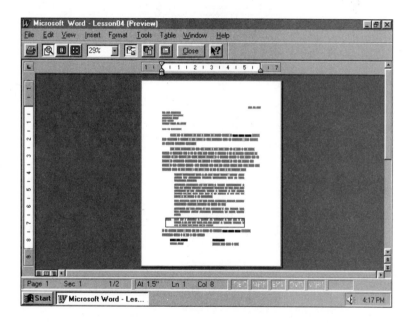

Microsoft Word displays the current page of your document in the Print Preview window. A toolbar contains the buttons you can use in this window. The menu bar still contains the usual Microsoft Word menu items.

View other pages

Multiple Pages

➤ On the Print Preview toolbar, click the Multiple Pages button, and then drag across two boxes.

Now you can see all pages of your document side by side.

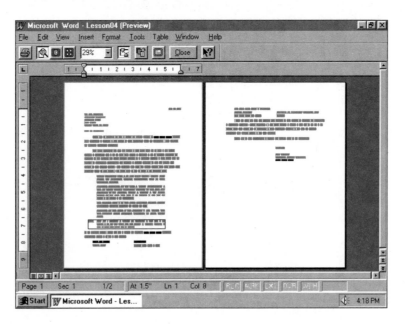

Editing Text

When you need to make changes to your document, such as inserting, deleting or formatting text, you do not need to return to the document window. Basic edits can be accomplished right in the Print Preview window. However, because nonprinting characters are not displayed in print preview, complicated editing or formatting tasks in this view are not recommended.

Edit text in Print Preview

1   With the magnifier pointer, click near the first body paragraph on page one to get a closeup view of the page.

Your screen should look similar to the following illustration.

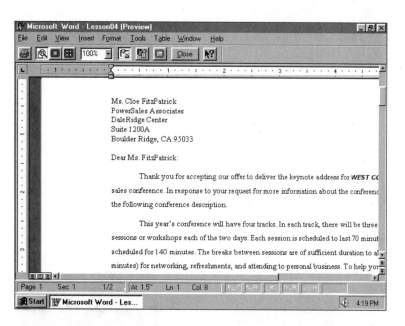

Magnifier

2 On the Print Preview toolbar, click the Magnifier button to change the magnifier pointer to the editing pointer.

3 Place the insertion point immediately in front of the sentence that begins with "In response to your request."

4 Type the following text:

As I mentioned when we spoke on the phone the other day, your participation will play a key role in our goal for greater attendance.

5 Press the SPACEBAR.

Inserting Page Breaks

As text fills a page, Microsoft Word inserts a page break called a *soft page break*. You cannot delete these soft page breaks. If you wish to improve the balance of text on pages, you can insert or delete manual page breaks (also called *hard page breaks*), either in the document window or in the Print Preview window. Microsoft Word automatically repaginates the document after you insert or delete a break. This means that the text flows from page to page throughout the document without requiring you to reposition the text on each page.

Insert a page break

In this exercise, you will insert a page break so that the table does not split across two pages.

Zoom Control

1   On the Print Preview toolbar, click the down arrow next to the Zoom Control box, and then click Page Width.

2   Scroll to the bottom of the page, and then place the insertion point immediately in front of the sentence that begins with "As we discussed earlier."

3   Press CTRL+ENTER.

Microsoft Word inserts a page break just above the insertion point and places the text after the insertion point on the next page.

4   On the Print Preview toolbar, click the Multiple Pages button, and drag across two boxes.

Your Print Preview window should look like the following illustration.

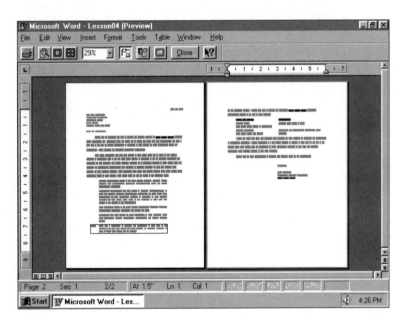

5   On the Print Preview toolbar, click the Close button.

6 Scroll downward, if necessary, to view the bottom of page one.

In normal and page layout views, the page break is represented by a dotted line labeled Page Break. Neither the line nor the label appear when you print the document.

New page break

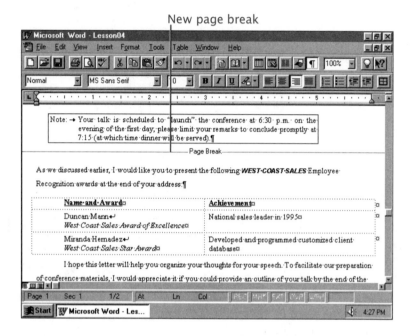

Save the changes

Save

➤ On the Standard toolbar, click the Save button.

Printing Your Document

Now that you are satisfied with the appearance of your document, you are ready to print it. You can either click the Print button on the Standard toolbar to print the entire document using default settings or use the Print command to select different printing options.

If you don't have a printer connected to your computer, you can skip to the end of this lesson.

Before You Begin Printing

If you are the only person who uses this computer and you have not printed a document using a Windows-based program, you might have to install or select a printer. For complete instructions about installing and setting up a printer, see your Windows documentation. If you share this computer with others, it's likely that a printer is installed and ready to use.

Print a document from the Standard toolbar

The Print button prints all pages of the currently active document on the default printer connected to your computer.

1   Be sure that the printer is on.

Print

2   On the Standard toolbar, click the Print button.

The status bar displays an icon showing the pages being spooled to the printer.

Print a document from the menu

You can also print a document directly from the Print Preview window by using the Print button on the Print Preview toolbar or by clicking Print on the File menu.

Occasionally, you might want to print just a page or two from a long document, instead of printing all the pages. With the Print command, you have the option to print only the page that currently contains the insertion point.

1   Be sure that the printer is turned on.

2   Double-click anywhere in the page number display on the status bar, and then type 1 in the Go To dialog box.

3   Click Go To to move to page 1 of your document, and then click Close.

4   On the File menu, click Print.

The Print dialog box appears.

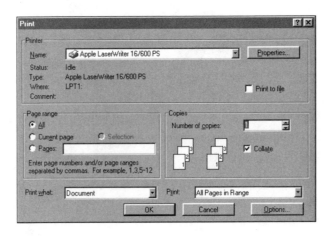

5   In the Page Range area, click the Current Page option button.

6   Click OK to begin printing.

One Step Further: Shrinking a Document to Fit

Occasionally, you may have a multiple-page document that contains only a small amount of text on the last page. In Print Preview, you can use the Shrink To Fit feature to reduce the number of pages by one. Microsoft Word accomplishes this by reducing the font size within the document.

Reduce the number of pages by one

Open

1   On the Standard toolbar, click the Open button.

2   In the Winword SBS Practice folder, open the file named 04One Step Further.

3   Save the file with the name **One Step Further04** and press ENTER.

Print Preview

4   On the Standard toolbar, click the Print Preview button.

5   Click the Multiple Pages button, and drag to display all pages if necessary.

Multiple Pages

6   On the Print Preview toolbar, click the Shrink To Fit button.

The document now fits on one page.

7   Click the Close button to return to normal view.

Scroll through the document to view the changes.

Shrink To Fit

If You Want to Continue to the Next Lesson

1   To close each document, on the File menu, click Close.

2   If a message appears asking whether you want to save changes, click the Yes button.

Choosing this command closes the active document; it does not exit the Microsoft Word program.

3   Repeat steps 1 and 2 to close the other document.

If You Want to Quit Microsoft Word for Now

1   On the File menu, click Exit.

2   If a message appears asking whether you want to save changes, click the Yes button.

Lesson Summary

To	Do this	Button
Display a document in Print Preview	On the Standard toolbar, click the Print Preview button.	⬛
View multiple pages of the document at one time	On the Print Preview toolbar, click the Multiple Pages button. Drag across the number of pages you want to see.	⬛
Display a document closeup in print preview	With the magnifier pointer, click the area of the document you want to view close up.	
Edit text in print preview	On the Print Preview toolbar, click the Magnifier button to change to the editing pointer.	⬛
Insert a page break	Place the insertion point where you want the page break. Press CTRL+ENTER.	
Print all pages of a document to the default printer	On the Standard toolbar, click the Print button. *or* On the Print Preview toolbar, click the Print button.	⬛
Print a document using dialog box options	On the File menu, click Print. Select the options you want from the Print dialog box.	

For online information about	Use the Answer Wizard to search for
Previewing text	**previewing text**, and then display Preview a document before printing
Printing documents	**printing**, and then display Print more than one copy at a time

Preview of the Next Lessons

The lessons in the next part of the book will show you how to get the most out of Microsoft Word. You'll learn how to increase your productivity by using styles to quickly format text and paragraphs. In the next lesson, you'll use such editing productivity tools as search and replace, AutoText, and AutoCorrect. In later lessons, you'll use proofing tools to check your spelling and grammar, and use the online Thesaurus. Finally, you'll learn how templates and wizards save you time when you create documents that use similar formatting.

Review & Practice

Estimated time
20 min.

You will review and practice how to:

- Open and modify a document.
- Save a document.
- Check the spelling in a document.
- Format characters and paragraphs.

In this Review & Practice section, you have an opportunity to fine-tune the basic editing and word processing skills you learned in Part 1 of this book. Use what you have learned about selecting, moving, and copying text to rearrange and reformat the text in the practice document.

Scenario

In this Review & Practice section, you will complete a cover letter that was started by an associate. This letter is going to accompany an annual report package for West Coast Sales. While your colleagues in the marketing department are working on the annual report itself, the task of making this cover letter more attractive has fallen on you. Most of the text of the letter has already been written, so you can focus on formatting text and paragraphs to give the letter more impact.

Step 1:   *Open and Modify a Document*

1   Open the document called P1Review, and save it as ReviewP1.

2   Place the insertion point at the beginning of the fifth line, and press ENTER.

3   At the insertion point, type the following paragraph. Be sure to make the typing mistakes as written so that you can practice using the spelling feature.

> **Enclosed is your copy of West Coast Sales Annual Report. The Annual Report contains all the detials about major progress and achievements at at West Coast Sales. The accompanying Executive Summary provides a breif overview of the past year's highlights.**

4   Delete the text "your copy of" in the first sentence, and replace it with **"the."**

5   In the first paragraph, move the third sentence in front of the second sentence.

6   Copy the text "West Coast Sales," and paste it in front of "Annual Report" throughout the letter.

7   Add this sentence to the end of the last paragraph, before the closing:

> **Thank you for your continued support and interest in West Coast Sales.**

For more information on	See
Opening a document	Lesson 2
Typing text	Lesson 1
Deleting text	Lesson 1
Copying text	Lesson 2

Step 2:   *Save a Document*

➤   Save your letter with the name Review P1.

For more information on	See
Saving a document with a new name	Lesson 2

Step 3:   *Check a Document's Spelling*

1   Return to the top of the document, and click the Spelling button on the Standard toolbar.

2   Add all proper names to the dictionary, and add AutoCorrect entries for words you misspell frequently.

3   After you have finished checking the spelling of the document, save your document.

For more information on	See
Checking spelling	Lesson 2

Step 4: *Format Characters and Paragraphs in a Document*

Use the following illustration as a guide for the kind of formatting you can apply to characters and paragraphs. When you have completed formatting, your document should look like the following.

<u>**Chris Hamilton**</u>
West Coast Sales
555 Plaza Avenue
Franklin, CO 54320

Enclosed is the **West Coast Sales** *Annual Report*. The accompanying Executive Summary provides a brief overview of the past year's highlights. The **West Coast Sales** *Annual Report* contains all the details about major progress and achievements at **West Coast Sales**. Year-end financial results are also included. But here is a quick overview:

- We moved our corporate headquarters to the renovated Elliott building in Franklin.

- After a year-long search and interviewing many highly qualified candidates, we hired a new director of Quality and Customer Satisfaction, Lisa Martinez, formerly of Sweet Lil's Bonbons.

- This year we increased profitability by 17% over last year, a fact that pleases shareholders and employees alike.

If you would like to continue to receive regular updates about our company, you need to complete the enclosed subscription card and return it to new our corporate offices in Franklin.

West Coast Sales
555 Plaza Avenue
Franklin, CO 54320

Be sure to indicate whether you want to receive the **West Coast Sales** *Annual Report*, the Executive Summary, or both. If you do not complete the card, you will no longer receive the **West Coast Sales** *Annual Report*. Thank you for your continued support and interest in West Coast Sales.

Sincerely,

Chris Hamilton
President/CEO
West Coast Sales

➤ When you have completed formatting your document, preview the document. If you have a printer connected to your computer, you can print your document and then save it.

For more information on	See
Formatting characters	Lesson 1
Formatting paragraphs	Lesson 3
Previewing and printing a document	Lesson 4

If You Want to Continue to the Next Lesson

1 On the File menu, click Close.
2 If a message appears asking whether you want to save changes, click the Yes button.

If You Want to Quit Microsoft Word for Now

1 On the File menu, click Exit.
2 If a message appears asking whether you want to save changes, click the Yes button.

Part
2

Everyday
Tasks Made Easy

Increasing Editing Productivity

Estimated time
30 min.

In this lesson you will learn how to:

■ Locate and replace text.

■ Locate and replace formatting.

■ Use AutoCorrect to insert boilerplate text as you type.

■ Use AutoText to insert boilerplate text into your document.

Sometimes after you complete a document, you discover a better word or phrase you would like to use instead of the original text. With Microsoft Word's Find and Replace features, you can search for and selectively (or globally) replace specific occurrences of both text and formatting. If you observe that you frequently use the same phrases in your document, you'll appreciate how to work more productively by using Find and Replace, AutoCorrect, and AutoText features. In this lesson, you'll learn how to reduce the amount of repetitive typing or actions you make in a document so that you can produce documents more quickly and with fewer errors.

Start the lesson

Follow the steps below to open the practice file called 05Lesson, and then save it with the new name Lesson05.

1 On the Standard toolbar, click the Open button.

2 In the Look In box, make sure that the Winword SBS Practice folder appears.

3 In the file list box, double-click the file named 05Lesson to open it.

Open

83

To select the folder containing your practice files, refer to "Open a practice file" near the start of Lesson 2.

4 On the File menu, click Save As.

The Save As dialog box opens. Make sure that the Winword SBS Practice folder appears in the Save In box.

5 Select and delete any text in the File Name box, and then type **Lesson05**

6 Click the Save button, or press ENTER.

If you share your computer with others who use Microsoft Word, the screen display might have changed since your last lesson. If your screen does not look similar to the illustrations as you work through this lesson, see the Appendix, "Matching the Exercises."

If Automatic Spell Checking is enabled, the misspelled words in this document appear underlined with red, wavy lines. You can hide the red, wavy lines by clicking Options on the Tools menu and then clicking the Spelling tab. Click the Hide Spelling Errors In Current Document check box.

Finding and Replacing Text

In your role to motivate the West Coast Sales sales force, you have decided to prepare a list of products for several new lines. Your assistant has drafted a simple document that you would now like to finish. You can use the Find and Replace commands on the Edit menu to quickly find—and, if necessary, replace—all occurrences of a certain word or phrase. For example, you might want to find every instance of an outdated product name in a brochure and substitute its new name. You can change all instances at once, or you can accept or reject each change individually. Either method ensures that the change is made consistently throughout the document.

Identify text to find and replace

The sample document you opened refers to "groups" at West Coast Sales, but these should really be called "divisions." In this exercise, you'll use the Replace command to locate the word "group" and replace it with "division."

To find and replace all forms of a word, such as singular and plural, or present and past tense, check the Find All Word Forms check box in the Replace dialog box.

1 On the Edit menu, click Replace.

2 In the Find What box, type **group**

If you share your computer with others who have used the Find command or the Replace command in the current work session, the text they last searched for might appear in the Find What box. You can select the text and type over it.

3 Make sure that the No Formatting button is dimmed so that Microsoft Word does not search for any formatting. If it isn't dimmed, click No Formatting.

4 In the Replace With box, type **division**

If text is already in the Replace With box, select the text and type over it.

5 Again, make sure that the No Formatting button is dimmed so that Microsoft Word does not format the replacement text. If it isn't dimmed, click No Formatting.

6 In the Search drop-down list, click the down arrow and select All, if it is not already selected.

Your completed dialog box should look like the following illustration.

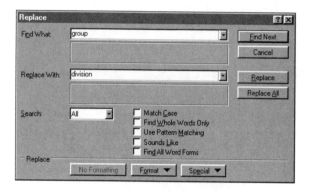

Find and replace the text

1 To begin the search, click the Find Next button.

The word "group" is highlighted. You might need to drag the Replace dialog box to a new location to see the selected word in the document window.

2 Click the Replace button.

The word "division" replaces the word "group," and the next occurrence of "group" is highlighted.

3 Click the Replace button.

The word "Division" replaces the word "Group," and the next occurrence of "group" is highlighted.

4 Because "group" is the word you want in this case and you do not want to replace it, click the Find Next button.

The next occurrence of "group" is highlighted.

5 Click the Replace button for each of the remaining occurrences.

6 In the message box that appears when the end of the document is reached, click the OK button to continue.

Replacing All Occurrences of Text

When you do not want to confirm each change, you can use the Replace All option in the Replace dialog box. This option makes changes without asking you to confirm each one. In the next exercises, you change all occurrences of "we are" to "West Coast Sales is."

Identify text to replace

The text you last searched for is selected in the Find What box. You can type over it.

1 In the Find What box, type **we are**
2 In the Replace With box, select the existing text, and type **West Coast Sales is**

Your completed dialog box looks like the following illustration.

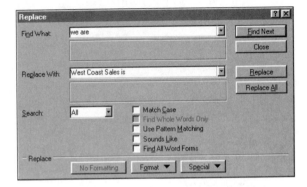

Find and replace all occurrences

1 To replace all occurrences, click the Replace All button.

A dialog box indicates how many changes were made.

2 Click the OK button to return to the Replace dialog box.
3 Click the Close button to return to the document and view the changes.

Scroll through the document. "West Coast Sales is" is substituted throughout the document.

Finding and Replacing Formatting

You can locate text that has a specific format, such as bold or underlined, and change the formatting as well as the text. You can also search for and change only the formatting without changing the text. For example, suppose you had at first underlined division names but now you want to make them italic and bold instead. With the Replace command, you can quickly find any underlined text and change the underline to italic and bold. In the price list document you are creating, you have decided to replace underlined division names with another kind of formatting.

Specify which formatting to find and replace

In this exercise, you'll scroll through the document to view the formatting. Then you'll return to the beginning and use the Replace command to change underlined text to italic and bold. Because the formatting you will use is available on the Formatting toolbar, you can make your formatting selections by clicking the Formatting toolbar while the Replace dialog box is still open.

1 Scroll through the document to view current formatting.

2 Press CTRL+HOME to place the insertion point at the top of the document.

3 On the Edit menu, click Replace.

 NOTE If the formatting you want to search for or replace is not available on the Formatting toolbar (such as Small Caps), you can click the Format button at the bottom of the dialog box, and select Font from the list. Then, in the Find Font dialog box, which looks like the Font dialog box in which you format characters, select the formatting you wish to locate or replace.

4 Delete the text in the Find What box.

Underline

5 On the Formatting toolbar (outside of the dialog box), click the Underline button.

6 Select the text in the Replace With box, and then press the BACKSPACE key.

7 On the Formatting toolbar (outside of the dialog box), click the Bold and Italic buttons.

Bold

8 On the Formatting toolbar, click the Underline button twice.

Your completed dialog box looks like the following illustration.

Italic

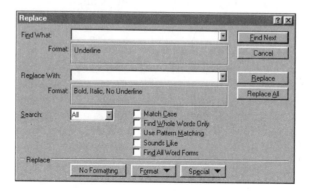

Find and replace formatting

Now that you've specified the formatting to find and replace, you are ready to start the search.

1   In the Replace dialog box, click the Replace All button.

A dialog box indicates how many changes were made.

2   Click the OK button to return to the Replace dialog box.

3   Click the Close button to return to the document and view the changes.

Scroll through the document. The text that was underlined is now italic and bold.

Inserting Text with AutoCorrect and AutoText

As you learned in Lesson 1, you can use the AutoCorrect feature in the Spelling dialog box to identify words that you often misspell. The next time you misspell that word and type a space (or some form of punctuation), it is automatically corrected as you type. In addition, you can use AutoCorrect to insert words and phrases you use frequently, even if they are not misspelled. An *AutoCorrect entry* automatically inserts the text as you type.

Similarly, you can use the AutoText feature to insert frequently used text only when you press the F3 key after typing the *AutoText entry*. Use the AutoText feature when you want greater control over when repeated text is inserted. AutoText entries are particularly useful when entering numbers or text that requires complicated formatting.

Creating an AutoCorrect Entry

Suppose you are creating a list of products in which each line begins with the same name. Instead of typing the repeated part of the product name each time, you can type the AutoCorrect entry followed by the rest of the name. Microsoft Word inserts the word or phrase as you type.

Create an AutoCorrect entry

Product names appear in a table in the Price List section of this document. Each product name should begin with the text "Big Plaid," but because you often misspell "plaid" as "pld," you can create an AutoCorrect entry to insert the correct spelling automatically when you type "pld" followed by a space. While you're at it, modify the AutoCorrect entry so that it will also insert the word "Big." When you type "pld" and a space, the text "Big Plaid" will be inserted automatically. You will save time because you have to type less text.

1   Scroll to the price list near the end of the document.

2   In the first row under the Description heading of the price list, select the text "Big Plaid."

3   On the Tools menu, click AutoCorrect.

The AutoCorrect dialog box appears.

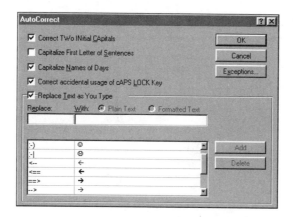

4   With the insertion point in the Replace box, type **pld**

5   Click the Add button.

The new entry is added to the list of AutoCorrect entries in the dialog box.

6   Click the OK button to return to the document.

Use AutoCorrect to insert text

Try your new AutoCorrect entry to insert the text "Big Plaid" in front of each product in the list. You can press TAB to move from cell to cell in the table. Press SHIFT+TAB to move to a previous cell. In Lesson 10, you will learn more about working in tables.

1   In the price list part of the document, place the insertion point in the second column and fourth row of the table.

2   Type **pld** and a space, and **Awning**

The text "Big Plaid" appears as soon as you type "pld" and a space.

3   Place the insertion point in front of the word "Mountain" in the next group of products in the price list.

If you don't want to type "pld" again, click Repeat Typing on the Edit menu.

4   Type **pld** and a space.

The text "Big Plaid" appears in front of the word "Mountain."

5   Repeat step 4 for each remaining product in the list.

When you have completed inserting text, your document should look like the following illustration.

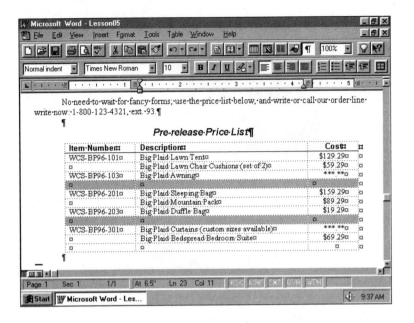

Creating an AutoText Entry

Suppose your list of products also includes item numbers that begin with the same characters. Instead of typing these item numbers for each product, you can type the AutoText entry followed by the F3 key, and Microsoft Word inserts the rest.

Create an AutoText entry

The item number for each product should be listed under the Item Number heading in the price list. Each item number begins with the text "WCS-BP96-." In this exercise, you will create an AutoText entry to insert this text when you type "wcs" followed by the F3 key.

1   In the second row of the price list table, select the text "WCS-BP96-".

    Be sure to include the second hyphen.

2   On the Edit menu, click AutoText.

    The AutoText dialog box appears.

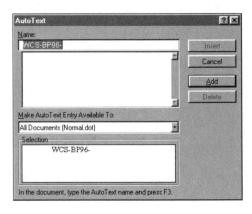

3 In the Name box, replace the existing text by typing **wcs**

4 Click the Add button to return to the document.

Use AutoText to insert text

In this exercise, you will apply your new AutoText entry to insert the text "WCS-BP96-" to begin item numbers in the list. After you insert this text, you can type in the rest of the missing numbers.

1 Place the insertion point in the third row of the first column in the table.

2 Type **wcs**

3 Press F3.

The text "WCS-BP96-" appears.

4 After the inserted text, type **102**

5 Repeat steps 3 and 4 for each product missing an item number in the price list. For example, for the second item in the next group of products, insert the AutoText entry followed by "202." For the second item in the third group of products, use the AutoText entry followed by "302."

Use AutoText and AutoCorrect to insert text

In this exercise, you can see the difference between AutoCorrect and AutoText for inserting repeated text in a document by adding a new product to the price list. Remember, AutoCorrect entries are inserted as soon as you type a space, while AutoText entries are inserted only after you press F3.

1 Place the insertion point in the first cell of the last row in the table.

2 Type **wcs**

3 Press F3.

4 Type **303** and press TAB.

5 Type **pld Down Bedroom Suite** and press TAB.

6 Type **$89.29**

Your completed price list should look like the following illustration.

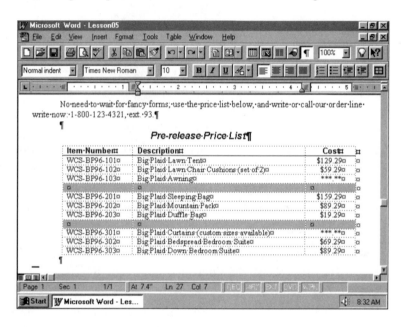

Save your work

Save

▶ On the Standard toolbar, click the Save button.

One Step Further: Finding and Replacing Special Characters

You can use the Find and Replace feature to help you replace special characters, such as paragraph marks, tab characters, and manual page breaks, in your document. If you want to remove extra spacing between paragraphs in your document, you can use the Special button to locate two paragraph marks in a row and replace them with one paragraph mark.

Identify the special character to find and replace

1 On the Edit menu, click Replace.

2 With the insertion point in the Find What box, click the Special button, and select Paragraph Mark.

Microsoft Word inserts a code that represents a paragraph mark.

3 Click the Special button, and select Paragraph Mark again.

4 Click the No Formatting button to clear any formatting specified from a previous search.

5 With the insertion point in the Replace With box, click the Special button, and select Paragraph Mark.

6 Click the No Formatting button to clear any formatting specified from a previous search.

7 Click the arrow next to the Search drop-down list, and select Up.

This option searches backward through the document. Use this option when the insertion point is located at the end of the document.

Find and replace the text

1 Click the Find Next button.

Microsoft Word highlights the two paragraph marks above the price list. You want to keep this spacing intact.

2 Click the Find Next button.

You want to delete the extra spacing between these two paragraphs.

3 Click the Replace button.

4 Click the Replace button for the next three highlighted occurrences.

Microsoft Word highlights the spacing between the salutation and first paragraph. You want to keep this spacing intact.

5 Click the Find Next button.

6 When you see the message box, click the Yes button to continue.

7 Click OK in the next message box, and then click the Close button to return to the document.

If You Want to Continue to the Next Lesson

1 On the File menu, click Close.

2 If a message appears asking whether you want to save changes, click the Yes button.

If You Want to Quit Microsoft Word for Now

1 On the File menu, click Exit.

2 If a message appears asking whether you want to save changes, click the Yes button.

3 If you see the message asking whether you want to save changes to Normal, click the No button if you share your computer with others or are connected to a network. Your AutoText and AutoCorrect entries will not be saved.

Click the Yes button if you are the only one who uses your computer and if you want to save the AutoText and AutoCorrect entries you created in this lesson.

 NOTE When you create AutoText and AutoCorrect entries, they are stored in a template document called Normal. This document contains information about how you work with Microsoft Word. The options you enable (or disable) and your AutoText and AutoCorrect entries are saved in this template as well. This means that the entries you create in this document will be available in all your documents.

Lesson Summary

To	Do this
Find and replace text	On the Edit menu, click Replace. In the Replace dialog box, type the text you want to find. Clear or select any formatting. Type the replacement text to use, and clear or select any formatting. Use the Find Next button to move to each occurrence. Click the Replace button to replace an occurrence and move to the next. Click Replace All to replace all occurrences at once.
Find and replace formatting	On the Edit menu, click Replace. Use the buttons and options available in the Replace dialog box to specify the kind of formatting to find and the replacement formatting. Use the Find Next button to move to each occurrence. Click the Replace button to replace an occurrence and move to the next. Click Replace All to replace all occurrences at once.

To	Do this
Create an AutoCorrect entry	Select the text for the entry. On the Tools menu, click AutoCorrect. With the insertion point in the Replace box, type the name of the entry. Click the Add button. Click the OK button to return to the document.
Insert an AutoCorrect entry	Type the name of the entry and a space.
Create an AutoText entry	Select the text for the entry. On the Edit menu, click AutoText. With the insertion point in the Replace box, type the name of the entry. Click the Add button to return to the document.
Insert an AutoText entry	Type the name of the entry and press F3.

For online information about	Use the Answer Wizard to search for
Finding and replacing text	**find and replace text**, and then display Find text and formatting *or* Replace text and formatting
Finding and replacing formatting	**find and replace formatting**, and then display Finding and replacing information
Inserting repeated text	**repeated text**, and then display Storing text and graphics to use again

Preview of the Next Lesson

In the next lesson, you'll learn to use and customize proofing tools that help improve the quality of your writing. You'll use the thesaurus to locate alternative words and write more precisely. You'll also customize the spelling checker dictionary to include special terms you use often. Finally, you'll use Microsoft Word to check your grammar and style in a document.

Proofing a Document

Estimated time
30 min.

In this lesson you will learn how to:

- Find synonyms and related words using the thesaurus.
- Check grammar and spelling.

After you've written and formatted a document, you'll probably want to *proof,* or check, the document one last time to make sure that no errors exist and that everything is in order. You've already seen how simple it is to check for spelling errors using the Spelling button on the toolbar. In this lesson, you'll learn how to use other proofing tools, such as the thesaurus to add interest and precision to your writing by asking Microsoft Word to suggest synonyms for selected words. You'll also work with the grammar checker to locate common grammatical or stylistic errors.

Start the lesson

Follow the steps below to open the practice file called 06Lesson, and then save it with the new name Lesson06.

Open

1   On the Standard toolbar, click the Open button.

2   In the Look In box, be sure that the Winword SBS Practice folder appears.

3   In the file list box, double-click the file named 06Lesson to open it.

4   On the File menu, click Save As.

The Save As dialog box opens. Be sure that the Winword SBS Practice folder appears in the Save In box.

To select the folder containing your practice files, refer to "Open a practice file" near the start of Lesson 2.

5 Select and delete any text in the File Name box, and then type **Lesson06**

6 Click the Save button, or press ENTER.

If you share your computer with others who use Microsoft Word, the screen display might have changed since your last lesson. If your screen does not look similar to the illustrations as you work through this lesson, see the Appendix, "Matching the Exercises."

 IMPORTANT The Setup program you use to install Microsoft Word on your computer gives you the option to install or not install the Microsoft Word proofing tools, which include the Thesaurus, Grammar, and Spelling commands. You need to have installed these components for them to appear on the Tools menu. You can run the Microsoft Word Setup program again and specify that you want to install the proofing commands only.

Using the Thesaurus

Using the thesaurus helps you add precision and variety to your writing. Like a printed thesaurus, the Microsoft Word thesaurus provides synonyms (words with a similar meaning) and sometimes antonyms (words with an opposite meaning) for a particular word. It also provides lists of related words and different forms of the selected word. For example, the word "work" can be used as a noun or as a verb; the thesaurus lists synonyms for both forms. When you select a word and then choose the Thesaurus command, the Thesaurus dialog box appears, where you can quickly search through a wide range of synonyms and related words until you find exactly the word you want.

Look up a word in the thesaurus

Suppose you want to find an alternative to the word "efficiently" and insert it in the document. In this exercise, you will use the Find command to find the word "efficiently." Then you'll use the Thesaurus command to select a synonym.

1 On the Edit menu, click Find.

2 Type **efficiently**

3 If the No Formatting button is not dimmed, click the button.

4 Click the Find Next button.

The word "efficiently" is found and highlighted.

5 Click the Cancel button to close the Find dialog box.

6 On the Tools menu, click Thesaurus.

The Thesaurus dialog box appears.

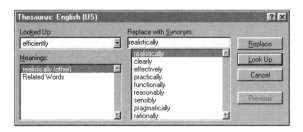

7   In the Replace With Synonym box, click "effectively" in the list, and then click the Replace button.

"Effectively" replaces "efficiently," and the dialog box closes.

Replace another word

In this exercise, you find an alternative to the word "strategies."

1   In the first paragraph under "Track B," select the word "strategies," as shown in the following illustration.

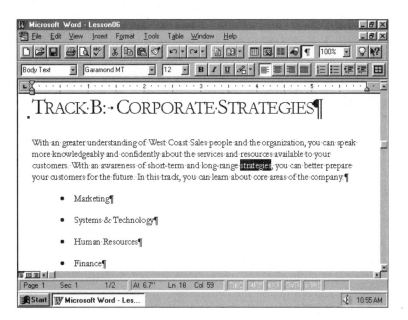

2   On the Tools menu, click Thesaurus.

Microsoft Word does not display alternatives for "strategies." Instead, it displays the singular form of the word "strategy." This indicates that you can look up alternatives for the singular form.

3 Click the Look Up button to see alternatives for the singular form of this word.

Microsoft Word lists the synonyms. The word "approach" would be a good alternative, but you'll need to add "es" to the end of it.

4 Select "approach" to have Microsoft Word copy it to the Replace With Synonym box.

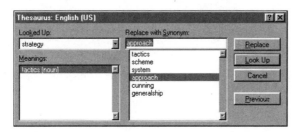

5 In the Replace With Synonym box, click at the end of "approach" and type **es**

6 Click the Replace button.

Microsoft Word replaces "strategies" with "approaches."

Using the Grammar Command

The Grammar command identifies sentences in your document that have possible grammatical errors or a nonstandard writing style. For many types of errors, the Grammar command suggests ways to correct the sentence. You can choose the correction you want to make so that Microsoft Word changes the sentence in your document. You can also make changes directly in your document and then continue checking.

Checking Grammar and Spelling

While checking your document for grammatical errors, spelling is also checked. If a questionable word is found, the Spelling dialog box appears over the Grammar dialog box so that you can correct the misspelling. Microsoft Word then continues checking the grammar.

The Grammar command provides a quick and convenient way to find many common grammatical errors. However, remember that no grammar checker can replace reading a document carefully.

Check the grammar and spelling together

Microsoft Word normally checks all of your document, beginning at the insertion point. Although you can position the insertion point anywhere in the document, in this exercise, you will position it at the top.

Dragging the scroll box is a fast way to scroll. However, this doesn't change the position of the insertion point.

1   Press CTRL+HOME to move the insertion point to the beginning of the document.

2   On the Tools menu, click Grammar.

This starts both the grammar checker and the spelling checker. The first highlighted error is a grammatical item.

NOTE   If the Grammar command is not available, it means that this feature was not installed when you set up Microsoft Word on your computer. To complete this lesson, you will need to run the Microsoft Word Setup program again and use the custom installation option to install the Grammar feature.

Get an explanation for a grammar rule

Microsoft Word provides explanations for the suggestions that it makes. The following procedure shows how to read about a grammar rule before you decide to make a change in your document.

1   With the suggested grammar replacement still displayed in the Grammar dialog box, click the Explain button.

Microsoft Word displays a window with an explanation of the grammar rule regarding contractions.

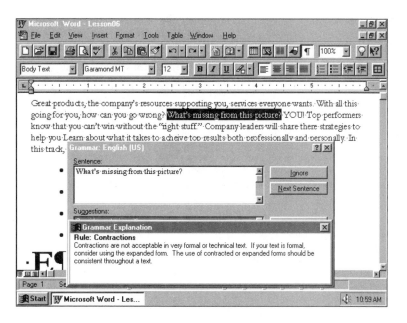

2   When you finish reading about the grammar rule, click the Close box in the upper-right corner of the explanation window.

Because this is not a formal document, you want to ignore this rule. Microsoft Word will not identify any other occurrences of this kind of grammatical error in the document.

3   Click the Ignore Rule button.

The spelling checker highlights the word "acheive." Microsoft Word displays the error and the suggested correction in the Spelling dialog box.

4   Click the Change button.

The word "acheive" changes to "achieve."

 NOTE   Each time the grammar checker finds a sentence with a possible error, you can click the Ignore button or the Next Sentence button if you don't want to change anything. If you click Ignore, Microsoft Word ignores this occurrence of the "error" and continues checking the sentence. If you click Next Sentence, Microsoft Word skips to the next sentence. You can also specify which grammatical and stylistic rules Microsoft Word applies when checking your documents by selecting the Grammar tab in the Options dialog box.

Continue checking grammar and spelling

The next error is a grammatical error: the use of "there" rather than "their." Microsoft Word suggests considering "their" instead of "there." This is an appropriate rule in this instance. In this sentence, you should accept the suggested change.

You can disable the spelling checker while doing a grammar check. On the Tools menu, click Options. On the Grammar tab, clear the Check Spelling check box. For this lesson, however, do not disable the spelling checker.

1 Click the Change button to insert the correct word.

The next error is a spelling error: the word "BonusBucks." Because you use this word often in your communications, you want to add it to the custom dictionary.

2 Click the Add button.

The next time you check a document that contains "BonusBucks," Microsoft Word will not identify the word as misspelled. The next error is a grammatical error. Microsoft Word suggests considering "a" instead of "an." This is an appropriate rule in this instance.

3 Click the Change button.

4 For each error found, do the following:

When Microsoft Word suggests	Do this
The word "LapWell" is misspelled	Click the Add button to add this word to the dictionary.
This sentence does not seem to contain a main clause	In the Sentence box, click after the word "you" and type "are" and a space. Then click the Change button.
The word "companys" is misspelled	Select the word "company's" in the Suggestions box and click the Change button.
Consider rephrasing to avoid ending this sentence with a preposition	Click the Ignore Rule button.
Consider using "are" instead of "is" *or* Using "tool" instead of "tools"	There are two possible ways to correct this sentence. In this case, be sure to select the first suggestion and click the Change button.

Viewing Readability Statistics

In the Readability Statistics dialog box that appears when the grammar check is finished, Microsoft Word displays information about the text that it checked. The readability statistics help you evaluate how easily the average adult reader can understand your writing. Most readability indexes assign a reading grade level. A grade level of 7, for example, indicates writing that can be understood by an average English-speaking reader who has completed seven years of education in the United States. By writing with shorter, simpler sentences and using smaller words, you can lower the grade level and improve the readability of your document.

View readability statistics

1 Note the grade level numbers in the dialog box before you continue.

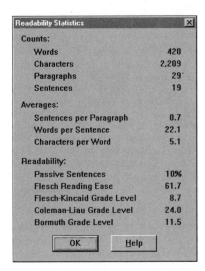

Readability Statistics	☒
Counts:	
Words	420
Characters	2,209
Paragraphs	29
Sentences	19
Averages:	
Sentences per Paragraph	0.7
Words per Sentence	22.1
Characters per Word	5.1
Readability:	
Passive Sentences	10%
Flesch Reading Ease	61.7
Flesch-Kincaid Grade Level	8.7
Coleman-Liau Grade Level	24.0
Bormuth Grade Level	11.5

| OK | Help |

2 Click the OK button to return to your document.

NOTE   If the Readability Statistics dialog box did not appear, it means the option has been disabled. To display the statistics the next time you run the grammar checker, click Options on the Tools menu. Click the Grammar tab. Select the check box next to Show Readability Statistics, and then click OK.

One Step Further: Using Word Count

You can easily determine how many words are included in a document using the Word Count command on the Tools menu. This is particularly useful when you need to limit text to a certain number of words. The Word Count dialog box also displays the number of pages, characters, paragraphs, and lines included in the document.

View Word Count statistics

1 On the Tools menu, click Word Count.

2 View the statistics displayed in the Word Count dialog box.

3 Click the Close button to close the dialog box.

If You Want to Continue to the Next Lesson

1 On the File menu, click Close.

2 If a message appears asking whether you want to save changes, click the Yes button.

Choosing this command closes the active document; it does not exit the Microsoft Word program.

If You Want to Quit Microsoft Word for Now

1 On the File menu, click Exit.

2 If a message appears asking whether you want to save changes, click the Yes button.

Lesson Summary

To	Do this
Use the Microsoft Word thesaurus	Select a word or phrase in the document, and then click Thesaurus on the Tools menu to see synonyms, related words, and, sometimes, antonyms.
Check grammar and spelling	On the Tools menu, click Grammar. As possible grammar or spelling errors are highlighted, make the suggested changes or ignore them.
Clarify a grammar rule	In the Grammar dialog box, click the Explain button.

For online information about	Use the Answer Wizard to search for
Checking spelling and grammar, or using the thesaurus	**proofing**, and then display Editing and proofing tools

Preview of the Next Lesson

In the next lesson, you'll learn to number pages automatically. You'll also learn how to add text, such as a company name or a chapter name, as well as a page number in the top or bottom margin of every page in the document.

Establishing the Look of a Page

Estimated time
40 min.

In this lesson you will learn how to:

- Establish margins for the entire document.
- Insert page numbers in a document.
- Create a header or footer that prints on every page.
- Create a unique header or footer for each part of the document.
- Create different headers on odd-numbered and even-numbered pages.

When you create multiple-page documents with Microsoft Word, it is easy to give all the pages of your document a consistent and polished appearance. In this lesson, you will first learn how to set the margins. Then you will learn how to print additional information on every page in headers and footers. Finally, in addition to creating different footers for different parts of the document, you will also create different headers and footers for odd-numbered and even-numbered pages.

Start the lesson

Follow the steps below to open the practice file called 07Lesson, and then save it with the new name Lesson07.

Open

1   On the Standard toolbar, click the Open button.
2   In the Look In box, be sure that the Winword SBS Practice folder appears.
3   In the file list box, double-click the file named 07Lesson to open it.

To select the folder containing your practice files, refer to "Open a practice file" near the start of Lesson 2.

4 On the File menu, click Save As.

The Save As dialog box opens. Be sure that the Winword SBS Practice folder appears in the Save In box.

5 Select and delete any text in the File Name box, and then type **Lesson07**

6 Click the Save button, or press ENTER.

Display paragraph marks

Show/Hide ¶

➤ If you cannot see the paragraph marks on your screen, click the Show/Hide ¶ button on the Standard toolbar.

If you share your computer with others who use Microsoft Word, the screen display might have changed since your last lesson. If your screen does not look similar to the illustrations as you work through this lesson, see the Appendix, "Matching the Exercises."

Setting Up Document Pages

With the Page Setup command on the File menu, you can define the margins, paper size, the paper source, and orientation for the document. You also have the option to change these settings for the current section, from the insertion point forward, for selected text, or for the entire document.

Establish document margins

1 On the File menu, click Page Setup.

The Page Setup dialog box appears.

If your dialog box does not look like this illustration, click the Margins tab to bring the Margins tab forward.

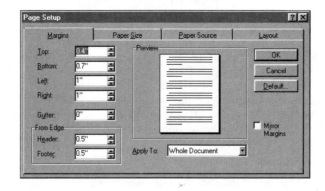

2   In the Top box, click or hold down the up arrow until .7" appears in the box.

This setting increases the distance between the Header text and the top edge of the document text. You can see the results of your changes in the Preview box.

3   In the Bottom box, decrease the bottom margin to .5".

4   In the Left box, increase the left margin to 1.5".

5   In the Right box, increase the right margin to 1.5".

6   In the From Edge area, click or hold down the down arrow next to the Header box until .3" appears in the box.

This setting decreases the distance between the Header text and the top edge of the page.

7   In the From Edge area, click or hold down the down arrow next to the Footer box until .3" appears in the box.

This setting decreases the distance between the Footer text and the bottom edge of the page.

8   Click the OK button to return to the document.

Creating Headers and Footers

In Microsoft Word, you can specify the information you want to appear on every page in the headers and footers. Text appearing at the top of every page is called the *header*; text appearing at the bottom of every page is called the *footer*. These parts of the document can contain whatever text you want, but you usually see information such as the date, the page number, or the document name in a header or footer.

There are two ways to insert page numbers in a header or footer. With the Page Numbers command, you can insert a page number, specify the starting page number, or select a format for the numbers, such as uppercase and lowercase Roman numerals. With the Header And Footer command, you can insert a date, time, text, fields that contain document information, as well as a page number.

Viewing Headers and Footers

In normal view, you cannot see headers or footers; in page layout view, the text in the header and footer areas appears in light gray. To create or edit headers and footers, you need to display the header or footer area with the Header And Footer command on the View menu (or if you are in page layout view, you can double-click the header or footer). When you display the header and footer areas, you will use the Header And Footer toolbar to help you add and modify headers and footers quickly.

When you view headers and footers, the header and footer areas are enclosed in a dotted line, and the body text is dimmed on the page. As a result, you cannot edit the body text while you are viewing and editing the headers or footers. You can use buttons on the Header And Footer toolbar to switch between the header area and the footer area, and insert the date, time, and page number. There is also a button that hides the dimmed text if you find it distracting. If you want to adjust document margins, change additional header and footer options, or modify some other part of the page setup, you can click the Page Setup button for quick access to the Page Setup dialog box.

View header and footer information

➤ On the View menu, click Header And Footer.

Your document looks like the following illustration.

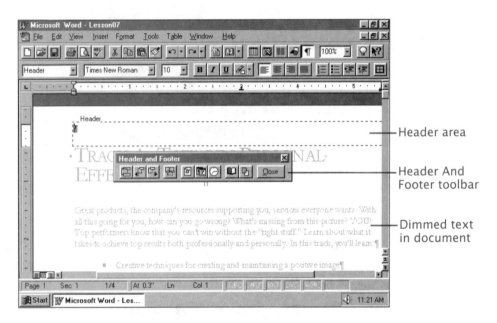

TIP If the Header And Footer toolbar obscures part of the document window you need to use, drag the title bar of the toolbar to position the toolbar anywhere in the document window. You can also double-click a gray area in the Header And Footer toolbar to place the toolbar above the ruler so that it does not obscure your view of the page.

Enter information in the header

In this exercise, you will insert text and a date in the header.

1 With the insertion point in the header area, type **WCS Sales Expo**

If you have completed the earlier lessons on the AutoCorrect feature, "WCS" might expand to "West Coast Sales."

2 Press TAB twice to align the text you will insert in the next step with the right margin.

3 On the Header And Footer toolbar, click the Date button.

The header looks like the following illustration.

Date

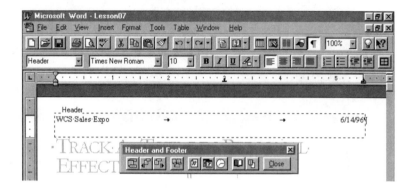

Enter text in a footer

Entering information in the footer is identical to entering information in the header. After moving the insertion point to the footer area, you can type and format text that you want to appear along with the page number you will insert.

Switch Between Header And Footer

1 On the Header And Footer toolbar, click the Switch Between Header And Footer button.

2 Type **Page** and press the SPACEBAR.

3 On the Header And Footer toolbar, click the Page Numbers button.

The page number appears next to the text "Page."

Page Numbers

4 On the Formatting toolbar, click the Align Right button.

5 On the Header And Footer toolbar, click the Close button to return to page layout view.

Align Right

Preview the document

Print Preview

Multiple Pages

1   On the Standard toolbar, click the Print Preview button.

2   Click the Multiple Pages button, and then drag two boxes to display two pages of the document.

3   Scroll to the third page.

Your document looks like the following illustration.

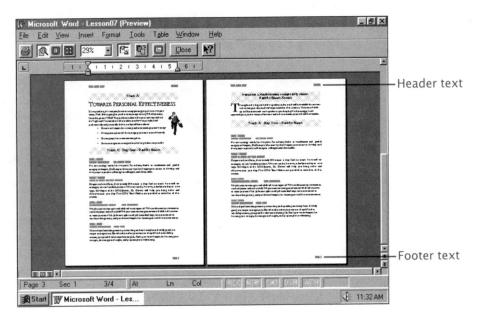

4   Click the Close button to return to page layout view.

Numbering Different Parts of a Document

In longer documents, it is common to see different parts of the document numbered differently. For example, the first section might be numbered as "Page 1-1, Page 1-2," and so on. The second section would restart its numbering at 1 and might be numbered as "Page 2-1, Page 2-2," and so on. To create different numbered parts of the same document, you first separate the different parts into sections by inserting section breaks. Then you can format the numbering in each section independently.

Insert a section break

In the sample document for this lesson, you will separate the first two pages from the schedule information on the remaining pages by inserting a section break between pages 2 and 3.

1 Select the paragraph mark at the very end of the second page.

2 On the Insert menu, click Break.

The Break dialog box appears. In this dialog box, you can specify the type of break to insert.

3 In the Section Breaks area, click Next Page.

This option ensures that the next section will start on the next page (rather than on the same page, an even-numbered page, or an odd-numbered page).

4 Click the OK button.

You may need to scroll upward to see the double-dotted line, labeled "End Of Section," that appears in the document. Your document looks like the following illustration.

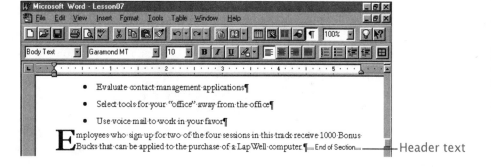

Header text

Break the link between sections

When you divide a document into sections, the header and footer information carries over from the previous section by default. To create unique headers and footers or page numbering for each section, you must break the connection between sections before you adjust the headers and footers. You break the connection between sections by clicking the Same As Previous button, which is depressed by default on the Header And Footer toolbar.

Before you adjust the page number formatting in the first section, break the link between the first and second sections. Your second section will retain the same text and paragraph formatting as the first section.

1   With the insertion point in page 3 (in the second section of the document), on the View menu, click Header And Footer.

Switch Between Header And Footer

2   On the Header And Footer toolbar, click the Switch Between Header And Footer button to move the insertion point to the footer area for this section.

In this example, the header will remain the same in both sections.

Same As Previous

3   On the Header And Footer toolbar, click the Same As Previous button.

The button is no longer depressed. This means that the current section can have a different footer from the previous section.

Restart page numbering in the second section

With the document separated into sections, and with the connection between footers no longer enabled, you can format the page numbering of each section independently. You can also create unique headers or footers in each section.

1   On the Insert menu, click Page Numbers.

2   In the Page Numbers dialog box, click the Format button.

3   In the Page Number Format dialog box, click the Start At button.

The numbering in this section is set to start at "1."

If you click OK in this dialog box (instead of clicking the Close button), Microsoft Word will insert another page number as a framed object.

4   Click the OK button to return to the Page Numbers dialog box.

5   Verify that the Show Number On First Page check box is checked.

6   Click the Close button.

Notice the page number on the first page of this section is "1," even though it is the third page of the document.

Format page numbering in the first section

Show Previous

1   On the Header And Footer toolbar, click the Show Previous button to display the footer for the previous section, Section 1.

2   On the Insert menu, click Page Numbers.

3   In the Page Numbers dialog box, click the Format button.

4   In the Page Number Format dialog box, click the arrow next to the Number Format box, and click "I, II, III."

5   Click the OK button to return the Page Numbers dialog box.

6   Verify that the Show Number On First Page check box is checked.

7   Click the Close button.

Edit the footer

1 Select the text "Page" and type a hyphen (-).

2 Press END to place the insertion point after the number, press the SPACEBAR, and then type another hyphen.

3 On the Formatting toolbar, click the Center button.

Center

Preview your footers

1 On the Standard toolbar, click the Print Preview button.

Print Preview

2 Click the Multiple Pages button, and drag horizontally across two boxes if two pages are not displayed.

Multiple Pages

3 Click near the bottom of page 2 to get a closeup view of the footer; scroll through the document to examine each of the footers on each page.

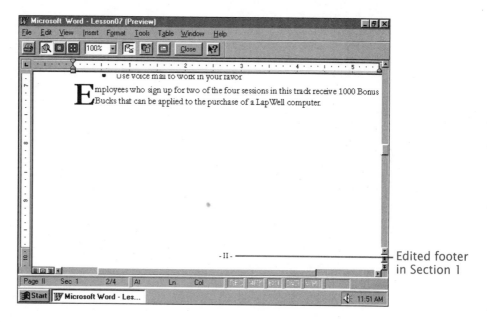

Edited footer in Section 1

4 Click the Close button to close the Print Preview window.

Creating Facing Pages

When you intend to print on both sides of paper that you plan to have bound together (for example, in a manual or book), you can create *facing pages*. For this kind of document, you want the information in the headers and footers to print differently on even-numbered and odd-numbered pages. For instance, on odd-numbered pages, you might want the page number to appear at the right margin, and on even-numbered pages, to appear at the left margin. The following illustration shows an example of a document with facing pages.

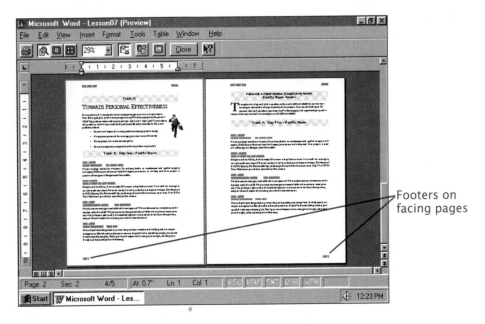

Footers on facing pages

Establish facing pages in a document

1   On the File menu, click Page Setup.

2   Click the Margins tab if it is not already displayed.

3   In the Apply To box, click the arrow, and click Whole Document.

  You also have the option to format the margins in each section or from the insertion point forward. By clicking Whole Document, the changes you make in this dialog box will affect the page setup characteristics of the entire document.

4   Click the Mirror Margins check box.

  You use this option to set up mirror margins for creating facing pages in the document. The designations for the left and right margins change to Inside and Outside.

5 In the Outside box, decrease the Outside margin to 1".

The Preview area reflects this change and shows that the inside margin is wider than the outside margin. A larger inside margin allows room for binding when the entire document is assembled and printed. You can also specify a value in the Gutter box to allow even more space for binding.

Specify different headers and footers for odd-numbered and even-numbered pages

1 Click the Layout tab.

2 In the Headers and Footers area, click the Different Odd And Even check box.

Use this option to create headers and footers that are formatted differently on odd-numbered and even-numbered pages.

3 Clear the Different First Page check box, if necessary.

Clearing this option ensures that the header and footer on the first page of a new section are the same as the headers and footers in the rest of the section.

4 Click the OK button.

Adjust a header for facing pages in section one

The headers and footers on the odd-numbered pages are already correctly formatted for facing pages, but you do need to recreate or adjust them on the even-numbered pages.

1 Press CTRL+HOME to place the insertion point in the first page of the document.

2 On the View menu, click Header And Footer.

3 Select all of the text in the odd (section 1) header.

Copy

4 On the Standard toolbar, click the Copy button.

5 On the Header And Footer toolbar, click the Show Next button to move to the even header for the first section.

Show Next

6 In the Even Header for section one, click the Paste button on the Standard toolbar.

Paste

Adjust the footer in section one

1 On the Header And Footer toolbar, click the Switch Between Header And Footer button to switch to the even footer for section one.

The Even Page Footer area for the first section contains no text, and the insertion point is already positioned at the left margin.

Switch Between Header And Footer

2 Type a hyphen (-), and press the SPACEBAR.

Page Numbers

Center

3 On the Header And Footer toolbar, click the Page Numbers button.

4 Press the SPACEBAR and type another hyphen (-).

5 On the Formatting toolbar, click the Center button.

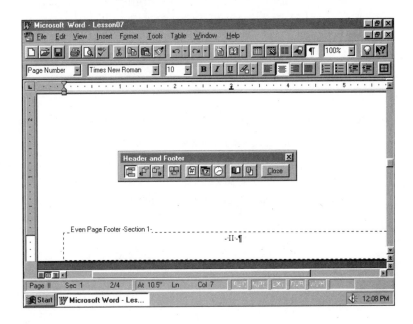

Adjust a footer for facing pages in section two

Show Next

1 On the Header And Footer toolbar, click the Show Next button twice to move to the even page footer for section two.

By default the Even Page Footer area in section two uses the same footer as the even footer in the previous section, except for differing number formats.

Same As Previous

2 On the Header And Footer toolbar, click the Same As Previous button to break the link between sections.

3 Select the first hyphen, and type **Page**

4 Press END and then press BACKSPACE twice to remove the remaining characters after the page number.

Align Left

5 On the Standard toolbar, click the Align Left button to place the footer text at the outside edge of the page.

6 On the Standard toolbar, click the Print Preview button.

Print Preview

Multiple Pages

7 Click the Multiple Pages button, and drag horizontally across one box.

8 Click near the bottom of the last page, and examine the footer. Scroll upward, and continue examining the footers on the remaining pages.

9 Click the Close button to close the Print Preview window.

One Step Further: Inserting Footnotes

In addition to footers, *footnotes* are another kind of text that can appear at the bottom of a page. When you want to make a reference to additional information in a document, you insert a footnote reference mark (for which you have the option to have Microsoft Word assign a number), and then you can enter the text. If you add or delete a footnote, Microsoft Word automatically renumbers the footnotes. Although you don't see the footnotes in normal view, you can see them in page layout view and print preview, as well as when you print them.

Insert a footnote

Normal View

In this dialog box, you can create an endnote by clicking the Endnote button. An endnote appears at the end of the document instead of at the bottom of a page.

1 Click the Normal View button to the left of the horizontal scroll bar.

2 Move the insertion point to the end of the first body paragraph on page 4.

3 On the Insert menu, click Footnote.

4 Click the OK button.

5 In the footnote area, type the following:

The Personal Effectiveness Hospitality room is available on both days of the conference.

6 Click the Close button to return to the text of the document.

7 Click the Page Layout View button, and scroll downward to see how your footnote will look when it is printed.

Page Layout View

If You Want to Continue to the Next Lesson

1 On the File menu, click Close.

2 If a message appears asking whether you want to save changes, click the Yes button.

If You Want to Quit Microsoft Word for Now

1 On the File menu, click Exit.

2 If a message appears asking whether you want to save changes, click the Yes button.

Lesson Summary

To	Do this	Button
Establish margins in a document	On the File menu, click Page Setup. Click the Margins tab. Click the scroll arrows, or enter a value, to set the desired margins.	
Create a header or footer	On the View menu, click Header And Footer. In the header or footer area, type the text, or click the buttons for the data you want to appear.	
View page numbers and headers or footers	On the View menu, click Page Layout. *or* On the File menu, click Print Preview.	
Insert a section break	On the Insert menu, click Break. In the Section Breaks area, click the type of break you want to insert. Click OK.	
Break a link between sections	On the Header And Footer toolbar, click the Same As Previous button to deselect it.	
Format page numbering	On the Insert menu, click Page Numbers. Click the Format button. Choose the desired format options, and click OK. Click Close.	
Alternate headers and footers for facing pages	On the File menu, click Page Setup. On the Layout tab, click the Different Odd and Even check box. On the Margins tab, click the Mirror Margins check box. In the Apply To box, click the desired option.	
Insert a footnote	Place the insertion point where you want the footnote reference to be. On the Insert menu, click Footnote. Select a footnote option if you want, and click OK. In the footnote area, type the text of your footnote, and click the Close button.	
Insert a date in a header or footer	On the Header And Footer toolbar, click the Date button.	
Insert a page number in a header or footer	On the Header And Footer toolbar, click the Page Number button.	

For online information about	**Use the Answer Wizard to search for**
Adjusting document margins	**margins**, and then display Changing margins
Inserting and formatting page numbers	**page numbers**, and then display Start page numbering where you want
Creating headers and footers	**headers and footers**, and then display Working with headers and footers

Preview of the Next Lesson

In the next lesson, you'll learn how to use styles to take advantage of the text formatting you've already done in a document. Styles save you time because, in a single step, you can apply a collection of format settings to characters and paragraphs.

Using Styles

In this lesson you will learn how to:

Estimated time
40 min.

- Store a combination of formats as a character style.
- Apply styles to text and paragraphs.
- Apply styles quickly using AutoFormat.
- Store a combination of formats as a paragraph style.
- Change the definition of a style.
- Apply attractive formatting to an entire document using the Style Gallery.

When creating documents, you might decide that all product names should be bold and italic or that paragraphs in a list should have a specific line spacing and right indent setting. You can save a lot of time by using *styles* to quickly apply a collection of format settings to characters and paragraphs. By applying styles, you can ensure fast and consistent formatting of text and paragraphs throughout your document. And when you modify a style, you will save time because all text formatted with that style is automatically reformatted.

In this lesson, you'll learn how to create and modify character styles to format characters, and you'll create and modify paragraph styles to format entire paragraphs. You will also learn how to use AutoFormat and the Style Gallery to apply a unified group of styles to your document.

Start the lesson

Follow the steps below to open the practice file called 08Lesson, and then save it with the new name Lesson08.

Open

To select the folder containing your practice files, refer to "Open a practice file" near the start of Lesson 2.

1   On the Standard toolbar, click the Open button.

2   In the Look In box, be sure that the Winword SBS Practice folder appears.

3   In the file list box, double-click the file named 08Lesson to open it.

4   On the File menu, click Save As.

The Save As dialog box opens. Be sure that the Winword SBS Practice folder appears in the Save In box.

5   Select and delete any text in the File Name box, and then type **Lesson08**

6   Click the Save button, or press ENTER.

If you share your computer with others who use Microsoft Word, the screen display might have changed since your last lesson. If your screen does not look similar to the illustrations as you work through this lesson, see the Appendix, "Matching the Exercises."

Formatting with Character Styles

Suppose you want to emphasize certain words, such as the name of each seminar in a conference brochure. So that the name looks different from the surrounding text, you might format the seminar names in small caps, bold, and italics. You could separately locate and select each of these settings for each seminar name, or you can create a character style and save yourself the time and effort.

By storing combinations of character formats (such as bold, italic, underline, font, and font size) as character styles, you save time and ensure consistent formatting throughout your document. The following procedure shows how to store a combination of formats so that you can later apply a set of character formats to selected text with a click of the mouse.

Apply character formatting

The easiest way to create a new style is to base the style on an example of text that already contains the formatting you want. In this exercise, you'll begin by formatting selected text to appear the way you want.

Bold

Italic

1   Select the text "Image Strategies" under the heading "Track A: Day One – Pacific Room."

2   On the Formatting toolbar, click both the Bold and the Italic buttons to change the text to bold italic.

3   On the Format menu, click Font.

The Font dialog box appears.

4   In the Effects area, click Small Caps.

5   Click OK to close the dialog box and return to the document.

Create a character style

With the selected text formatted the way you want, you can create a character style based on the formatting in your selection.

1   On the Format menu, click Style.

The Style dialog box looks like the following illustration.

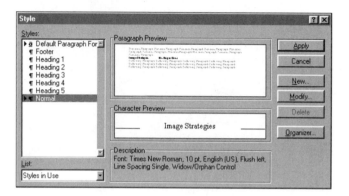

2   Click the New button to create a new style.

The New Style dialog box looks like the following illustration.

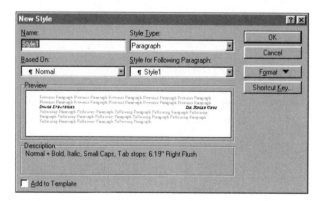

3 In the Name box, type **Seminar**

4 From the Style Type drop-down list, select Character.

This selection ensures that your style will affect only selected text, not entire paragraphs.

5 Click the OK button to return to the Style dialog box.

Your new style has been added to the list of styles in this document. The list of styles also includes the default styles provided by Microsoft Word. Character styles are identified with the letter "a" in the list.

Your Style dialog box looks like the following illustration.

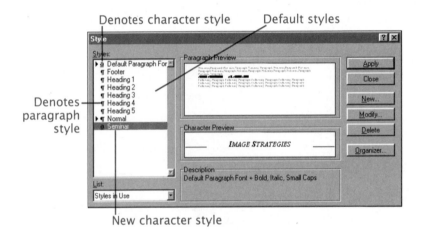

Denotes character style   Default styles

Denotes paragraph style

New character style

6 Click the Apply button to apply this new style name to the selected text and return to your document.

NOTE You can give your style a name that is up to 255 characters long, including numbers, letters, and spaces. Two styles cannot have the same name, but Microsoft Word does store uppercase and lowercase letters separately. As a result, you could have one style called "Seminar" and another called "SEMINAR."

Applying Character Styles

Once you've created a character style, you can apply it to any text you want formatted that specific way. After you apply a style, the selected text contains the same formatting as the text upon which you based the style.

Apply the Seminar character style

In this exercise, you will locate another occurrence of a seminar name in the document and apply the new character style to it.

1 Select the next seminar name in the document "Time & More."

2 At the far left of the Formatting toolbar, click the down arrow next to the Style box.

3 Click the style called Seminar.

You might need to scroll through the list to locate the style.

You can also press the repeat key F4 to repeat the last operation.

4 Locate the two remaining occurrences of a seminar name in this document, and repeat steps 1 through 3 to apply this style to each one.

When you complete applying styles, your document looks like the following illustration.

Displays a list of styles

Text formatted in Seminar character style

Formatting with Paragraph Styles

A *paragraph style* contains a collection of both paragraph and character format settings that you want to apply to an entire paragraph. This means that, in addition to specifying the appearance of text in a style, you can select the alignment, paragraph spacing, and line spacing of paragraphs. You can create paragraph styles for each kind of paragraph in a document, and then apply the different styles to ensure consistent paragraph formatting for the same kinds of paragraphs in your document. For example, you might want bold, 18-point, centered text to emphasize a heading paragraph for one of the main ideas in your document. If you create a style with these settings and name it Heading 1, you can apply all of these settings to each of the heading paragraphs for the other main ideas. All you need to do is apply the Heading 1 style.

Applying Paragraph Styles with AutoFormat

You can use the AutoFormat command to quickly review the existing text and formatting in a document and enhance the appearance of the document by applying default styles to headings, body paragraphs, and paragraphs formatted as lists. For example, the first line in a document would be formatted with a Heading 1 style. Hyphens in lists are changed to bullets. Using AutoFormat is a quick way to apply styles in a document.

 TIP   You can click the Help button on the Standard toolbar and then click the formatted text to see all the settings in effect for specific text.

Apply styles with AutoFormat

You simply click the AutoFormat button to format your document.

 NOTE   The default styles are the built-in styles provided in the default template called Normal. There are a variety of additional templates that provide collections of built-in styles for different kinds of documents. Later in this lesson, you will learn about other templates so that you can select alternate collections of styles for creating other kinds of documents.

1   Press CTRL+HOME to place the insertion point at the top of the document.

2   On the Standard toolbar, click the AutoFormat button.

Microsoft Word applies paragraph formatting using the default styles.

AutoFormat

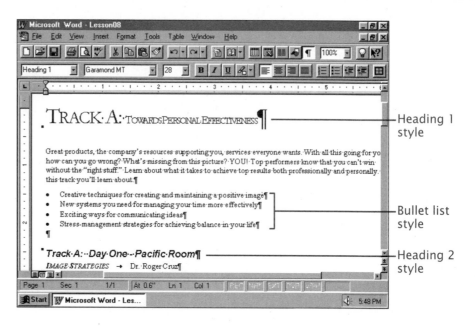

- Heading 1 style
- Bullet list style
- Heading 2 style

Show/Hide ¶

3 If paragraph marks are not currently displayed, click the Show/Hide ¶ button on the Standard toolbar.

Creating a New Paragraph Style

Creating a paragraph style is quite similar to creating a character style. You simply specify a paragraph style type in the New Style dialog box. When creating paragraph styles, you can also use a procedure that does not require you to use the Style dialog box so that you can create paragraph styles more quickly. Use this technique to create a new paragraph style for paragraphs that contain the seminar name, the speaker, and the time.

Format a paragraph

You will be formatting selected text with the settings you want. To call attention to each of the sessions, this text should be formatted with the font called Arial MT Black, and it should be centered with extra space before and after the heading.

1 Select the entire paragraph containing the seminar name "Image Strategies," as well as the next line containing the time.

2 On the Format menu, click Paragraph.

3 Press TAB until you select the Spacing Before box, and then type **3**

This setting creates 3 points of spacing before the heading.

4 Press TAB to select the Spacing After box, and then type **3**

This setting creates 3 points of spacing after the heading.

5 Click the Alignment arrow, and select Centered.

6 Click the OK button to close the dialog box and return to the document.

7 On the Formatting toolbar, click the Font box and select Arial MT Black.

Your selected formatted text should look like the following illustration.

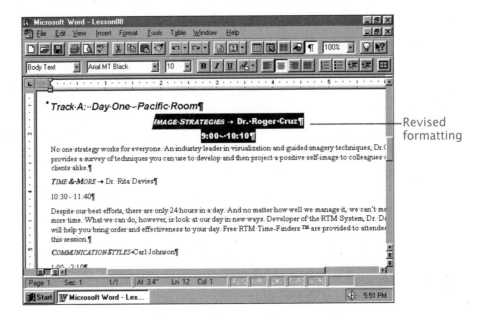

Revised formatting

Create a paragraph style for seminar headings

With the paragraph formatted the way you want, you can create a new style based on the formatting in your selection.

You can also press CTRL+SHIFT+S to move to the Style box and select the current style.

1 Click in the Style box on the Formatting toolbar.

2 In the Style box, name the style by typing **SeminarHeading**

3 Press ENTER.

You will not see a change in the document, but Microsoft Word has stored the formatting of the paragraph as the SeminarHeading style and applied the style to the selected text.

Applying Paragraph Styles

You can apply a paragraph style to any number of paragraphs in the document. Applying a paragraph style gives a paragraph the same formatting as the paragraph that served as the model for that style. Remember that paragraph styles affect entire paragraphs. If you want to add additional formatting to only a part of a paragraph, select the text, and then apply formatting with a character style or use the buttons on the Formatting toolbar.

 NOTE To create and modify character styles, use the Style command on the Format menu.

Apply the heading paragraph style

In this exercise, you will apply the SeminarHeading style to each occurrence of text containing a seminar name, speaker, and time.

1 To see more of the headings, scroll downward until the formatted heading "Time & More" is at the top of the screen.

2 Select the heading "Time & More" and the next line containing the time.

3 Click the down arrow next to the Style box to display the list of styles.

This displays the styles you've created along with some of the default styles that Microsoft Word provides (for example, the Heading 1, Heading 2, and Heading 3 styles).

4 Scroll to and select the SeminarHeading style name.

Notice that paragraph styles are identified with the symbol "¶" in the Styles list. Microsoft Word applies the formats stored in this style to the selected text. Click outside the selection for a better look at the formatting.

5 Repeat steps 3 and 4 to format the remaining paragraphs containing the seminar names, speakers, and times.

After you complete applying styles, your document looks like the following illustration.

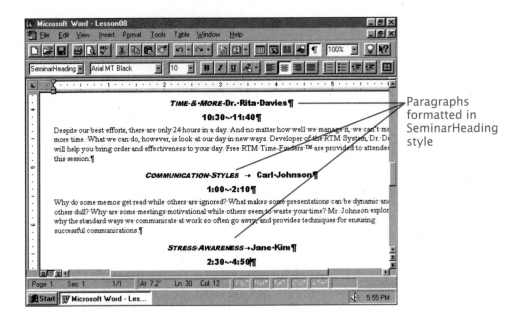

Paragraphs formatted in SeminarHeading style

Displaying styles in a document

To see all styles applied to individual paragraphs in a document, you can display the Style Area in the document window. The Style Area option is available only when you are in normal view.

Normal View

You can view the style name and all of the formatting that is applied to your text by clicking the Help button, and then clicking on the text.

1 Click the Normal View button to the left of the horizontal scroll bar.

2 On the Tools menu, click Options.

3 Click the View tab, if necessary.

4 In the Window area, in the Style Area Width box, type **1"**

This selection creates a 1-inch area in the document window in which to display style names.

5 Click the OK button.

The left side of the document window displays the name of the style applied to each paragraph. You can adjust the width of the Style Area by dragging the vertical line that separates the Style Area from the document.

6 Use the up scroll arrow to scroll line by line to the top of the document, noting the formatting and styles as you go.

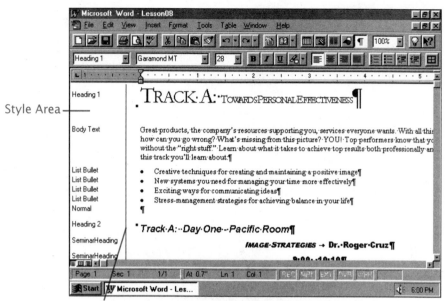

Style Area

You can drag from here to adjust the width of the Style Area.

Changing a Style

Suppose that after viewing the conference brochure, you decide to emphasize the text formatted in the Heading 2 style by increasing its size and adding a border. Instead of reformatting every heading separately, you can change the style definition. By redefining the style, you change the formatting of every paragraph formatted with that style.

Reformat a styled paragraph

In this exercise, you will make quick adjustments to the paragraph formatting before redefining the style.

1 Select the heading "Track A: Day One – Pacific Room."

2 On the Formatting toolbar, click the Font Size arrow, and select "16."

3 On the Formatting toolbar, click the Borders button.

Borders

The Borders toolbar appears. With this toolbar, you can apply lines and shading to paragraphs of text.

4 In the Line Style box on the Borders toolbar, select the 3/4 pt line style if necessary.

Top Border

5 On the Borders toolbar, click the Top Border button.

The Top Border button formats the selected paragraph so that a line appears just above the paragraph, as shown in the following illustration.

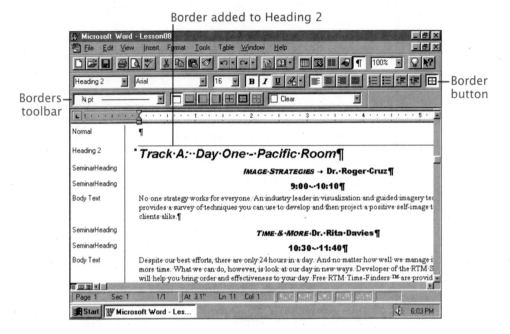

6 On the Formatting toolbar, click the Borders button to hide the toolbar.

Redefine the style

1 With the formatted paragraph still selected, select the Heading 2 text in the Style box on the Formatting toolbar, and press ENTER.

2 When you see the Reapply Style dialog box, be sure that the first option button is selected, and then click the OK button.

Every paragraph formatted with the Heading 2 style changes to reflect the new formatting.

3 Click the down scroll arrow to scroll through the document line by line to view the results of this change.

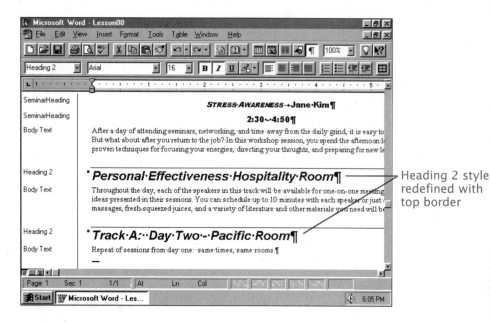

Heading 2 style redefined with top border

Save the document

Save

➤ On the Standard toolbar, click the Save button.

Microsoft Word saves the current version of the document in place of the previous version.

Hide the Style Area

You can hide the Style Area by dragging the vertical line all the way to the left of the document window.

➤ Position the pointer over the vertical line that separates the Style Area from the document text; when the pointer changes shape to a two-headed arrow, drag the line all the way to the left of the document window.

Print the document

1 Be sure that your printer connection is active.

2 On the Standard toolbar, click the Print button.

Print

Microsoft Word prints one copy of the document.

Using the Style Gallery

Once you have applied styles to your document, you can use the Style Gallery command on the Format menu to further enhance the appearance of the document. In the Style Gallery, you can choose from a list of preformatted *templates*—a master copy of standard types of documents that contain the styles that you can apply to documents of a certain type. The Style Gallery includes a Preview box in which you can see how your document will look when formatted with the styles in different templates. Using the Style Gallery, you can view different document styles and apply the styles of the template you find most appealing or appropriate to your document.

 NOTE Templates also provide boilerplate text, graphics, document settings, and other features that are standard in certain types of documents. In Lesson 9, you will learn about these other aspects of templates.

Apply styles from another template

1 Press CTRL+HOME to place the insertion point at the top of the document.

2 On the Format menu, click Style Gallery.

The Style Gallery dialog box appears.

Templates you can use to format your document

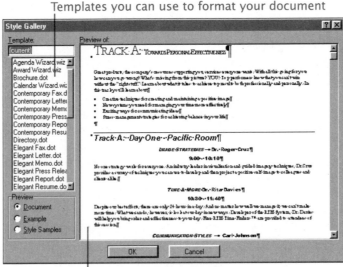

Preview of your document formatted with styles from the currently selected template

3 In the Template box, click Brochure.

A sample of the document formatted with the Brochure template styles appears in the Preview box.

4 Click the OK button.

Microsoft Word applies the styles contained in the Brochure template to the document. Among other formatting changes in the document, the text formatted in the Heading 2 style has a bottom border (instead of a top border), and the bullets in the bulleted list at the beginning of the document are square (instead of round).

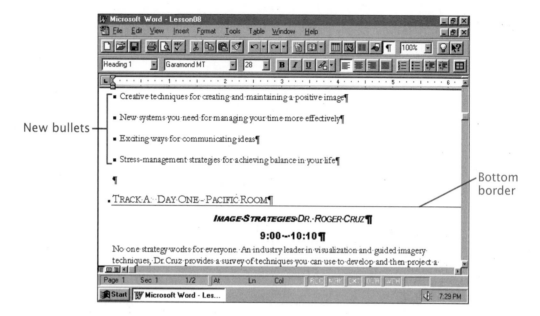

New bullets

Bottom border

Basing Styles on Other Styles

To ensure even greater formatting consistency in your documents, consider basing a new style on the formatting of an existing style. For example, if you want to create a new style that differs from an existing style in only a few settings, you can base the new style on the existing one. Then, should you modify the base style, all the other styles based on it will also be updated.

Suppose you want to create another character style that uses a different font from the Seminar character style, but in all other respects is the same. By basing your new style on the Seminar style, you can be sure that the text will always have the same characteristics as the Seminar style (except for the font), even if the Seminar style changes.

To make applying styles even easier and faster, you can also specify a keyboard shortcut as an alternative to applying a style from the Formatting toolbar.

Create a character style based on another style

1 Select the speaker name next to the first seminar heading in the document, "Dr. Roger Cruz."

   To create a character style, do not select the paragraph mark at the end of the line.

2 Apply the Seminar style.

3 From the Font drop-down list on the Formatting toolbar, change the font of the text by selecting Arial.

4 On the Format menu, click Style.

5 Click the New button to create a new style.

6 In the Name box, type **Speaker**

7 In the Style Type drop-down list, select Character.

   This selection ensures that your style will affect only selected text, and not entire paragraphs. When you select Character, the Based On box changes to display the style name of the currently selected text, "Seminar."

Create a keyboard shortcut

1 In the New Style dialog box, click the Shortcut Key button to display the Customize dialog box.

2 With the insertion point in the Press New Shortcut Key box, press CTRL+SHIFT+E.

3 Click the Assign button to assign this keyboard shortcut to the character style.

4 Click the Close button to return to the New Style dialog box.

5 Click the OK button to return to the Style dialog box.

   Your new style has been added to the list of styles in this document.

Apply the style

1 In the Style dialog box, click the Apply button to apply this style to the currently selected text and return to your document.

2 Select each occurrence of a speaker's name appearing after a seminar name and apply the Speaker style to it using the keyboard shortcut CTRL+SHIFT+E.

Test your results

Change the font size of the Seminar and Speaker styles at the same time.

1 Select any text formatted with the Seminar style.

2 Press CTRL+SHIFT+> to increase the font size by one point setting, to 14 points.

3   With the formatted text still selected, select the Seminar style in the Style box on the Formatting toolbar.

4   When you see the Reapply Style dialog box, be sure that the first option button is selected, and then click the OK button.

All the text formatted with the Seminar style changes to reflect the new formatting, as does all the text formatted in the Speaker style.

5   Click the down scroll arrow to scroll through the document line by line to view the results of this change.

6   On the File menu, click Close.

7   Click the Yes button to save your changes.

Choosing this command closes the active document; it does not exit the Microsoft Word program.

One Step Further: Using Background AutoFormatting

So far, you have learned how to format existing text quickly using Microsoft Word's AutoFormatting feature. However, when you create new text, the AutoFormat As You Type feature will do much of the formatting for you. For example, if you type a hyphen (-) followed by a space or a tab at the beginning of a line (and press ENTER at the end of the line or paragraph), the AutoFormat As You Type feature will change the hyphen to a bullet and format the paragraph with a hanging indent. Other AutoFormat As You Type features include changing "1st" to "1ST," (TM) to ™, and automatically formatting headings.

Create a new document

➤   On the Standard toolbar, click the New button.

Verify AutoFormat As You Type settings

As with many Microsoft Word background features, you can specify options for the AutoFormat As You Type feature.

1   On the Tools menu, click Options.

2   Click the AutoFormat tab.

On this tab, you can see the kinds of changes Microsoft Word makes automatically as you type.

3   Click the AutoFormat As You Type option button if it is not already clicked.

4   Click the Headings check box to enable this feature, and verify that all the other check boxes on this tab are checked (enabled).

5   Click the OK button.

Format your document as you type

1   Type **Sign Up for the 3rd Annual West Coast Sales Conference**

The "rd" becomes superscripted automatically as you type.

2   Press ENTER twice.

When you follow the first paragraph of a document with two blank lines, Microsoft Word automatically formats the paragraph with the Heading 1 style. The TipWizard also appears, explaining how to undo this change if you want.

3   Type the following text to continue entering text and formatting your document. Be sure to press the SPACEBAR after typing the first hyphen.

We are pleased to bring you four exciting tracks of seminars and workshops, including:

- Towards Personal Effectiveness

- Corporate Strategies

- Targeting Sales Excellence

- Serving Up Hot Technologies

4   After typing the last item, press ENTER twice to stop the automatic formatting of bulleted paragraphs.

5   Type a series of three hyphens, and then press ENTER to create a border that spans the width of the page.

When you press ENTER, the line of hyphens changes to a solid line border.

6   Type **Register by May 25th and get a free Date Planner(TM) portfolio in your conference packet.**

You can see the automatic formatting in the date and the trademark symbol.

Name and save the document

1   On the File menu, click Save As.

2   In the File Name box, type **One Step08**

3   Click the Save button.

Save

Reset AutoFormat as You Type settings

If you share your computer with others, you can do this exercise to return the AutoFormat settings back to the default.

1   On the Tools menu, click Options.

2   Click the AutoFormat tab.

3   Click the AutoFormat As You Type option button.

4   Clear the Headings check box to disable this feature, and verify that all the other check boxes on this tab are checked (enabled).

5   Click the OK button.

If You Want to Continue to the Next Lesson

1   On the File menu, click Close.

2   If a message appears asking whether you want to save changes, click the Yes button.

> Choosing this command closes the active document; it does not exit the Microsoft Word program.

If You Want to Quit Microsoft Word for Now

1   On the File menu, click Exit.

2   If a message appears asking whether you want to save changes, choose the Yes button.

3   If a message appears asking whether you want to save changes to the Normal template, click the No button if you share your computer with others. Your styles will be available only in this document.

> Click the Yes button, if you are the only one who uses your computer and if you want to save the styles you created in this lesson so that you can use them in other documents.

Lesson Summary

To	Do this
Create a character style	Select the formatted text and click Style on the Format menu. Click the New button, and enter a new style name in the Name box. Select the Character style type from the Style Type drop-down list. Click the OK button, and then click the Apply button.
Apply a character style	Select the text you want to format, and then select the style name in the Style drop-down list on the Formatting toolbar.

To	Do this	Button
Apply automatic formatting to a document	On the Format menu, click AutoFormat. *or* On the Standard toolbar, click the AutoFormat button.	
Create a paragraph style	Select the formatted paragraph. Then type the style name in the Style box on the Formatting toolbar, and press ENTER.	
Apply a paragraph style	Select the paragraphs you want to format. Select the style name in the Style drop-down list on the Formatting toolbar.	
Display the Style Area in normal view	On the Tools menu, click Options. Click the View tab. In the Style Area Width box, type the size of the area in which to display styles. Click the OK button.	
Hide the Style Area Width	Position the pointer over the vertical line that separates the Style Area from the document text; when the pointer changes shape to a two-headed arrow, drag the line all the way to the left of the document window.	
Redefine a paragraph style	Apply the desired formatting to one of the paragraphs containing the style you want to change. In the Style list on the Formatting toolbar, select the style name and press ENTER. Verify that the first option is selected, and click the OK button to redefine the style.	
Apply styles from a predefined template	On the Format menu, click Style Gallery. In the Template box, click the template containing the styles you want to apply. Click the OK button.	

To	Do this
Create a character style based on another style	Select the formatted text containing the style you want to change. Modify the character formatting, and click Style on the Format menu. Click the New button, and enter a new style name in the Name box. Select the Character style type from the Style Type drop-down list. Click the OK button, and then click the Apply button.

For online information about	Use the Answer Wizard to search for
Defining, naming, applying, and changing character styles	**character styles**, and then display Create a style
Defining, naming, applying, and changing paragraph styles	**paragraph styles**, and then display Fast formatting techniques

Preview of the Next Lesson

In the next lesson, you'll learn how to use templates to create and set up new documents. With templates that contain the standard formatting you apply to pages and paragraphs, you'll learn how to save time when you create specific documents, such as letters, memos, or reports. You'll also learn how to create a template and use it to start a standard letter.

Saving Time with Wizards and Templates

In this lesson you will learn how to:

- Use a wizard to create a letter.
- Create an envelope.
- Use AutoFormat to create formatting and styles for a new template.
- Create a document based on a template.
- Copy styles with the Organizer.

Estimated time
35 min.

If you use several kinds of documents in your work, each requiring its own set of formatting and styles, you can save a lot of time by using wizards and templates. This lesson has two parts. In the first part, you learn how to use a wizard to create a letter and its accompanying envelope. In the second part, you open a document that has already been formatted but does not have any styles applied to it. You create a template that can be used as a basis for other documents that require the same formatting.

Using a Wizard to Create a Letter

A *wizard* guides you through the process of creating many different kinds of documents. You answer the questions posed by the wizard regarding style and other formatting options, and the wizard creates the document you requested. All the formatting, page setup information, and even styles are already created and applied for you.

Create a letter with a wizard

You start a wizard by choosing the New command on the File menu and selecting the kind of wizard you want. In this exercise, you will use a wizard to create a letter to a West Coast Sales regional manager.

1   On the File menu, click New.

The New dialog box appears. The different tabs represent the types of wizards and templates you can use to create new documents.

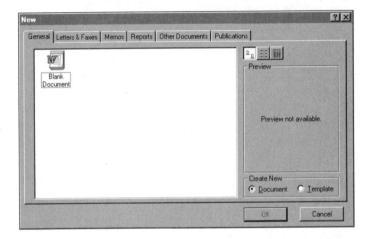

2   Click the Letters & Faxes tab.

3   In the Letters & Faxes box, click the Letter Wizard.

4   Click the OK button.

The first window of the wizard appears.

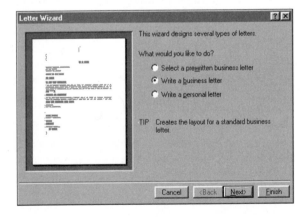

Respond to wizard questions

The wizard gives you several choices as you create your letter. There is no wrong or right answer; what you select depends on your preferences. In this exercise, you will create a classic business letter.

1   In the first wizard window, select the "Write a business letter" option.

2   Click the Next button to continue to the next window.

3   Select the Date and Enclosures check boxes, and clear any of the other check boxes that might already be selected.

   The Letter Wizard presents options for you to indicate other information to be included with your letter if you want. For example, you can specify that page numbers be automatically included in the document.

4   Click the Next button to continue to the next window.

5   Select the "Plain paper" option button.

   The Letter Wizard provides an option to allow room for a letterhead. In this case, you will not print the letter on letterhead stationery.

6   Click the Next button to continue to the next window.

7   In the Recipient box (the upper-right text box), select and delete any existing text, and then type:

   Julia Stevens
   Regional Manager
   West Coast Sales
   123 West Valley Drive
   Riverdale, MT 75661

   Be sure to press ENTER at the end of each line.

8   In the Return Address box, select and delete any existing text, and then type:

   Chris Hamilton
   West Coast Sales
   555 Plaza Avenue
   Franklin, CO 54320

9   After checking the accuracy of what you typed, click the Next button to continue to the next window.

10   Click the Professional option button.

11   Click the Next button to continue to the next window.

   The final window in the wizard looks like the following illustration.

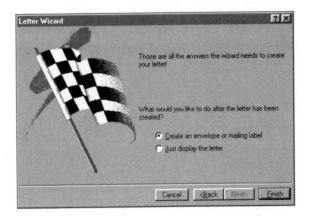

12 Be sure that the "Create an envelope or mailing label" option button is selected.

This option prepares an envelope using the name and address of the recipient you entered for your letter. You can edit the recipient's address information, as well as the return address, if necessary.

13 Click the Finish button.

The Envelopes And Labels dialog box appears.

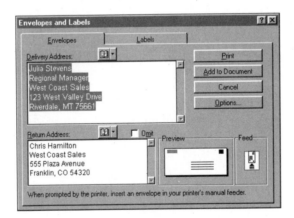

14 Make sure the Envelopes tab is active, and then click the Add To Document button.

This selection ensures that the envelope prints each time you print this letter. When you print the document, the envelope prints first. Your printer will pause until you supply an envelope, and then it will resume printing. See your printer instructions for specific procedures for using envelopes in your printer.

15 When you see the message box asking whether you want the return address information to be saved as the default return address, click the No button.

Your document looks similar to the following illustration.

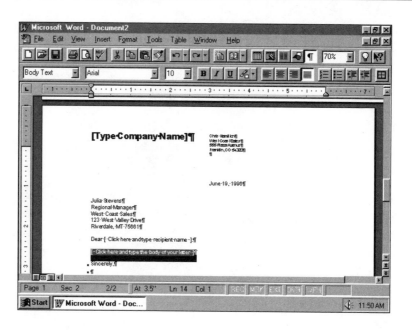

Displaying Document Views

Microsoft Word provides several views, or ways of displaying a document. Each view helps you concentrate on a different aspect of the document. For example, normal view, the view you've used most often in the preceding lessons, is best for typing and editing text. In outline view, you see the structure and organization of the document; you will learn more about working in outline view in Lesson 13.

In page layout view, you can edit the document, as well as see how it will look when printed.

Page layout view is much like print preview because it shows how your document will look when it is printed. But unlike print preview, you can see the nonprinting characters, which makes this view better for editing and formatting. When you choose page layout view, you'll see the exact arrangement of columns, graphics, and headers and footer on the page. When you use a wizard, the new document is displayed in page layout view.

View the new document

1 Scroll upward to the first page, and examine the envelope that will print when you print this document.

2 On the Standard toolbar, click Zoom Control and select 100%.

This magnification makes it easier to accomplish editing tasks.

Type your letter

When you first edit a document created by a wizard, the areas in which you enter your own text are shown inside square brackets. This makes it easy to locate where you can enter your own information. You must select and replace both the text inside the brackets and the brackets themselves with your own text for the document.

1 Scroll downward, and select both the brackets and the text "Type Company Name."

Placeholder text

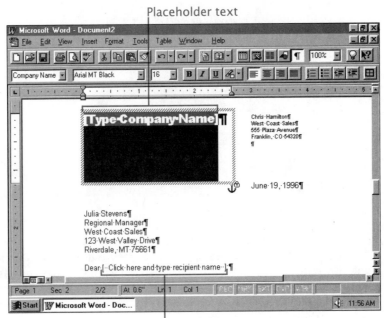

Placeholder text

2 Type **West Coast Sales**

3 Select the brackets and text after the word "Dear."

4 Type **Julia**

5 In the next line, select the next set of brackets and text, and then type the following text for the body of the letter:

I thought you would like a preview of last month's sales results. I am developing a new document type that presents the information attractively. What do you think? By the way, can you help out with a chart or some graphics?

If you see wavy lines under certain words, the automatic spell checking feature has identified these words as possibly misspelled. For more information about this feature, see "Working with Automatic Corrections" in Lesson 1.

6 Select the brackets and text after the word "Enclosures," and then type **1**

Add signature block information

The *signature block* area of a document contains the closing text "Sincerely," followed by a blank line, allowing room for your signature, your name, your title, and an enclosure notice. The small squares in the left margin next to the four lines of the signature block indicate that these lines cannot be separated by a page break.

1 Place the insertion point in front of the paragraph mark below the text "Sincerely" and press ENTER.

Notice that Microsoft Word applies the Signature Name style to the new line, inserting extra space for a handwritten signature.

2 Type **Chris Hamilton** and then press ENTER.

Microsoft Word applies the Signature Job Title style to the new line.

3 Type **CEO/West Coast Sales** and then press ENTER.

Customize the letter

The letter wizard helps you create a basic letter quickly. You can modify this letter just as you can make changes to any document you create. In this exercise, you will add visual interest to the letter by placing the date at the right margin.

Align Right

1 With the insertion point in the date paragraph near the top of the letter, click the Align Right button on the Formatting toolbar.

2 Click Zoom Control on the Standard toolbar, and then click Page Width.

Your completed document looks like the following illustration.

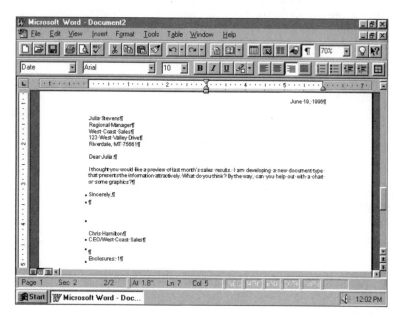

Save the document

1 On the File menu, click Save As.

2 In the File Name box, type **Lesson09**

3 Be sure that the Winword SBS Practice folder is open, and click the Save button.

4 On the File menu, click Close to close this document.

Creating a Template

As you saw in the previous section, a wizard can help you create standard kinds of business documents quickly. However, if you have document formatting requirements for which no wizards are available, you can create a document from a template. Like a wizard, a template contains all the document and paragraph formatting (in the form of styles) you need in a specific kind of document, plus boilerplate text that you can use or modify as you want. For example, if there is a standard opening or closing paragraph that your company uses in all letters, you might prefer to use a template containing this text. Unlike a wizard, a template does not ask you questions to help create a document.

Microsoft Word provides several templates for business documents, including letters, memos, and press releases. If none of these templates provide the kind of document you want, you can create your own template upon which to base future documents.

Creating a Template from an Existing Document

An easy way to create a template is to locate a document that already has many of the formatting features you want. Even if the document does not already have styles applied to the text, you can use the AutoFormat command to analyze the formatting in the document and create styles for you. Then the template you create will have the styles you need in your future documents.

Open a sample document

The document that West Coast Sales uses to create organizational reports can be adapted to create monthly sales reports. In this exercise, you'll copy and then modify this document.

Open

For information about selecting the folder containing your practice files, refer to "Open a practice file" near the start of Lesson 2.

1 On the Standard toolbar, click the Open button.

2 In the Look In box, be sure that the Winword SBS Practice folder appears.

3 In the file list box, double-click the file named 09Organization to open it.

4 On the File menu, click Save As.

Be sure that the Winword SBS Practice folder appears in the Save In box.

5 Select and delete any text in the File Name box, and then type **Organizational Report09**

6 Click the Save button, or press ENTER.

Edit the document

Before creating a template from this document, change some of the text so that it reflects sales information. You will also enter placeholder text (such as "xx"%) that represents text that must be edited each time you create a document based on the new template.

1 For fast editing, click the Normal View button if this view is not already displayed.

2 In the first heading, select the text "Organizational Overview," and replace it by typing **Monthly Sales Report**

3 For each division, add the following text to the end of each paragraph: **Growth last month was xx%. Top selling products were:**

Remember to use copying and pasting to make this step easier.

4 In place of each category listed, select the text after each hyphen, and replace it with **product**

Save your changes

Save

> On the Standard toolbar, click the Save button.

Establish styles with AutoFormat

This document has already been formatted, but it does not have styles applied to the text. You can use the AutoFormat feature to apply styles based on the formatting in the document (and add new formatting that will improve how your document looks).

The AutoFormat feature also looks for "(tm)" or "(c)" and changes them to the trademark or copyright symbols. It also changes hyphens in a list to bullets. You simply click the AutoFormat button to polish your document.

AutoFormat

> On the Standard toolbar, click the AutoFormat button.

Microsoft Word reviews your document and applies improved paragraph formatting by removing extra paragraph marks and formatting paragraphs with styles that include the proper spacing before and after each paragraph. Based on the position of text on the page and indented text, heading and body text styles are also added. Microsoft Word also adds a trademark symbol, and replaces hyphens with bullets.

NOTE   If you use the AutoFormat command on the Format menu (instead of the AutoFormat button), you can review, and then accept or reject individual changes.

153

Trademark symbol inserted

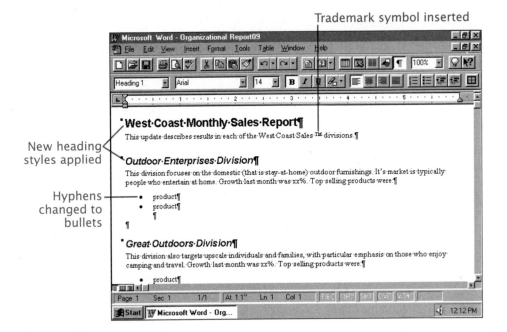

New heading styles applied

Hyphens changed to bullets

Save the document as a template and close it

Now that your document contains the standard text and formatting you need to create sales reports, you can save the document as a template. From this template, you can create standardized sales reports.

1 On the File menu, click Save As.

2 In the File Name box, type **Sales Report09**

3 In the Save As Type drop-down list, select Document Template.

   Microsoft Word adds the template extension DOT when you save the file.

4 Click the Save button to save the new template.

   Microsoft Word stores the template in a subfolder called Templates.

5 On the File menu, click Close.

Creating a New Document Based on a Template

You can get a head start on creating a sales report by using the new Sales Report09 template you created. With much of the text and formatting already in the document, you need to make only a few changes to finish the report.

Create a document from a template

1 On the File menu, click New.

2 On the General tab, find the new template, Sales Report09.

3 Double-click the template name in the list.

A new document window opens, ready for you to create a new document.

Show paragraph marks

Show/Hide ¶

➤ Click the Show/Hide ¶ button to display paragraph marks if they are not already displayed.

Working with paragraph mark displayed makes it easier to format text in your new document.

Enter text in your document

1 In the first heading, select the text "Monthly" and change it by typing **May**

NOTE The text changes you make in this document do not affect the template upon which the document was created. Your document is actually a copy of your template.

2 Select the text "xx" before each percent sign (%) in each paragraph for each division, and enter sales values as indicated here:

Outdoor Enterprises Division   **20**

Great Outdoors Division   **15**

Great Northern Division   **25**

3 Select the text "product" in each category and replace it with the products shown below.

Outdoor Enterprises Division

    Big Plaid oven mitts

    Big Plaid grill covers

Great Outdoors Division

    D-Lux 5-person tent

    Kiddie Kamper

Great Northern Division

    Cascade Down comforter covers

    Sleep Happy Featherbeds

Add text for a new division

In this exercise, you will add text announcing a new division. Later, you will apply styles to format it more attractively.

1 Place the insertion point at the end of the document, and press ENTER.

2 Type **Great Kitchens Plus Division** and press ENTER.

3 Type **Acquired last month, we are expecting great things from this new division. Hot products coming next month include:** and press ENTER.

4 Type **D-Lux Daiquiri Blender**

Apply styles to your text

1 Place the insertion point in the first new line you added, "Great Kitchens Plus Division," and then select the Heading 2 style from the Style drop-down list in the Formatting toolbar.

2 Place the insertion point in the following paragraph of text, and then select the Body Text style from the Style drop-down list.

3 Place the insertion point in the last line of text, "D-Lux Daiquiri Blender," and then select the List Bullet 2 style from the Style drop-down list.

4 With the insertion point at the end of the line, before the paragraph mark, press ENTER.

The text after this style is automatically formatted in the same style as the previous line. The insertion point appears after the bullet.

5 Type **Instant Potato Masher**

The new text in your document looks like the following illustration. As you can see in the Style box, the List Bullet 2 style has been applied.

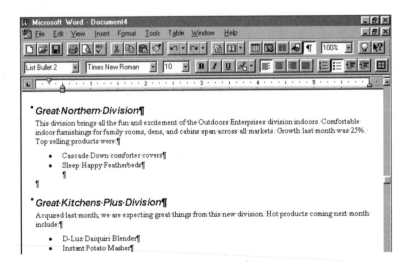

Save your new document

1 On the File menu, click Save As.

Be sure that the Winword SBS Practice folder is open.

2 In the File Name box, type **May Sales Report09**

3 Click the Save button to save the new document.

Managing Styles with the Organizer

The Organizer makes it easy to copy customized features (such as styles, AutoText entries, toolbars, and macros) from one document (or template) to another. For example, copying styles is often easier and provides more consistent formatting than attempting to apply the same formatting characteristics in two different documents. By copying styles with the Organizer, you can ensure consistent formatting across several documents.

Copy a style from one document to another

The document 09Style Sample, located in your folder, includes a style that attractively formats a report title with additional spacing before and after, plus a bottom border, and larger font. In this exercise, you will copy the style from the 09Style Sample document to your new document, using the Style Organizer.

1 On the Format menu, click Style.

2 In the Style dialog box, click the Organizer button.

The Organizer dialog box appears.

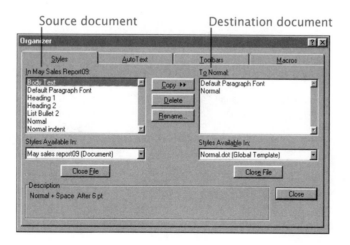

Source document   Destination document

3   On the right side of the dialog box, click the Close File button; when the label changes to Open File, click the button again.

4   In the file list, double-click 09Style Sample.

5   In the In 09Style Sample box, on the right side of the dialog box, click Title.

6   In the middle of the dialog box, click the Copy button.

7   Click the Close button.

Apply the copied style to the document

1   Press CTRL+HOME to place the insertion point at the start of the document in the "West Coast May Sales Report" line

2   In the Style drop-down list, click Title.

The report title displays the formatting characteristics copied from the Title style in the 09Style Sample document. Your document looks like the following illustration.

Style copied from another document

Save and close the document

1   On the Standard toolbar, click the Save button.

2   On the File menu, click Close.

Save

One Step Further: Creating an Agenda with the Agenda Wizard

There are many wizards included with Microsoft Word. In this exercise, you use the Agenda wizard to create an agenda that can help you prepare for an upcoming meeting.

1   On the File menu, click New.

2   Click the Other Documents tab.

3   Double-click the Agenda Wizard.

You can experiment with the different options for creating an agenda. Use your own preferences when selecting options and answering questions posed by the wizard.

If You Want to Continue to the Next Lesson

1   On the File menu, click Close.

2   If a message appears asking whether you want to save changes, click the Yes button.

3   In the Save As dialog box, type **Agenda09** and then click OK to save the new agenda document.

If You Want to Quit Microsoft Word for Now

1   On the File menu, click Exit.

2   If a message appears asking whether you want to save changes, click the Yes button.

3   In the Save As dialog box, type **Agenda09** and then click OK to save the new agenda document.

Lesson Summary

To	Do this
Create a new document using a wizard	On the File menu, click New. In the New dialog box, click the tab for the type of document you want to create. Double-click the wizard. Then, to create a document, answer the questions the wizard asks.
Edit a wizard document	Select the placeholder text and quotation marks, and replace with the text you type.

To	Do this	Button
Create a template	Open the document containing the formatting that you want. Save the document as a template by clicking Save As on the File menu and selecting Document Template from the Save As Type drop-down list.	
Apply automatic formatting to a document	On the Format menu, click AutoFormat. *or* On the Standard toolbar, click the AutoFormat button.	
Create a new document using a template	On the File menu, click New. In the New dialog box, click the tab for the type of document you want to create. Double-click the template.	

For online information about	Use the Answer Wizard to search for
Wizards and templates	**wizards and templates**, and then display Create a new document

Preview of the Next Lessons

The lessons in the next part of this book will show you how you can achieve dramatic results in your documents by formatting text in tables and columns. You will also learn how you can add charts and graphics and incorporate information from other programs. In the next lesson, you'll learn how to add visual interest to a document with tables and charts.

Review & Practice

The lessons in Part 2 helped you increase your productivity through the use of editing and proofing tools, styles, templates, and wizards. If you want to practice these skills and test your understanding before you proceed with the lessons in Part 3, you can work through the Review & Practice section following this lesson. This less structured activity allows you to increase your confidence using many of the features introduced so far.

Review & Practice

Estimated time
30 min.

You will review and practice how to:

- Save a document as a template.
- Create headers and footers.
- Add AutoText entries.
- Use AutoFormat to apply styles in a document.
- Create and apply new styles.
- Check spelling and grammar.

In this Review & Practice, you have an opportunity to fine-tune the editing and format-ting skills you learned in Part 2 of this book. You can use what you have learned about inserting repeated text, proofing, applying stored formatting, and creating documents from wizards and templates to develop a quarterly report for West Coast Sales.

Scenario

Because you create these documents four times a year in your job, and they all should contain the same formatting and much of the same text, you can save time by creating a template that has the text and formatting already stored in it. You can use AutoFor-mat to create styles based on the formatting in an existing document. To increase your productivity even more, you can add AutoCorrect and AutoText entries to the template document.

Step 1: Create a Template from a Document

1 From the Winword SBS Practice folder, open the document called P2Review.

2 Save the document as a template called TemplateP2.

Be sure to select "Document Template" in the Save As Type box.

For more information on	See
Creating a template from a document	Lesson 9

Step 2: Add AutoText Entries, Header, and Footer

1 Create AutoText entries for the following words and phrases. Do not include the paragraph mark when you select the text for the entry. Use entry names that make sense to you.

Great Outdoors Division
Outdoor Enterprises Division
Great Northern Division
Great Kitchens PLUS!

2 Create a header that says "WCS Quarterly Report" followed by the date. Create a footer that shows the page number.

For more information on	See
Using AutoText	Lesson 5
Creating headers and footers	Lesson 7

Step 3: Create Styles in the Template

Use existing styles as the basis for new styles. You will apply these new styles when you create a document based on this template.

1 Click the AutoFormat button to create styles based on the formatting in the template.

2 In the Style dialog box, create a new paragraph style based on the Heading 2 style, but change the font size so it is 2 points smaller. Call the new style Heading 2a. Do not apply the new style yet.

3 Create another new paragraph style based on the Normal indent style, but change the style so it is italic. Call the new style Indent3. Do not apply this style yet.

4 Create a character style to format text in bold and 11-point Arial. Call this style Numbers. You will use this style to format numbers in the document. Do not apply this style yet.

5 Save the template and close it.

For more information on	See
Creating Styles	Lesson 8
Using AutoFormat	Lesson 9

Step 4:   *Create a Document from a Template*

1   On the File menu, click New, and create a new document based on the template called Template P2.

2   Replace each occurrence of the placeholder text "xx" before the "%" with the values shown below. Then apply the character style called Numbers.

Great Outdoors Division	**13**
Outdoor Enterprises Division	**17**
Great Northern Division	**25**
Great Kitchens PLUS	**10**

3   Select the text "product" in each category, and replace it with the products shown below. Delete the placeholder text "product" where only one product is listed. Use the "pld" AutoCorrect entry created earlier to insert the text "Big Plaid."

Great Outdoors Division	**D-Lux DomeHome** **Big Plaid Backpacks**
Outdoor Enterprises Division	**Big Plaid Portable Refrigerator** **Big Plaid Patio Set**
Great Northern Division	**Cascade Down Curtains**
Great Kitchens PLUS!	**Big Plaid Toaster Covers**

For more information on	See
Applying styles	Lesson 8
Creating a document from a template	Lesson 9

Step 5:   *Add Text and Apply New Styles*

Add new text below the list of products for each division. You can format the new text in the new styles you created in step 3.

1   At the paragraph mark under the text "Big Plaid Backpacks," apply the Heading 2a style to the blank line. Then type **Market Focus** and press ENTER.

2   Before you type the following text, format the new paragraph in the Indent3 style. Replace "division" with the actual division name. Save time by using the AutoText entries you created in step 2 when you first modified the template.
Next quarter's new areas of concentration for the *division* include: and press ENTER.

3   Copy the text you entered in steps 1 and 2 above, and paste it in the corresponding locations under each remaining division. Edit each sentence to contain the correct division name.

4   In the new paragraph after the one formatted in the Indent3 style, type the following areas of concentration for each division. Apply the List Bullet 2 style so that each item appears with a bullet.

Great Outdoors Division	**Active seniors**
Outdoor Enterprises Division	**Affluent singles under 30** **Active seniors**
Great Northern Division	**Empty nesters** **Telecommuters**
Great Kitchens PLUS!	**Affluent singles over 30**

For more information on	**See**
Using AutoText	Lesson 5
Applying styles	Lesson 8

Step 6:   Check the Document's Spelling and Grammar

1   On the Standard toolbar, click the Spelling button.

2   Correct any words that are clearly misspelled. Add all proper names to the dictionary, and add AutoCorrect entries for words you misspell frequently.

3   On the Tools menu, click Grammar. Correct the grammar according to your style and preferences.

4   After you have finished proofing the document, save it with the name ReviewP2 in the Winword SBS Practice folder.

For more information on	**See**
Proofing a document	Lesson 6

If You Want to Continue to the Next Lesson

1   On the File menu, click Close.

2   If a message appears asking whether you want to save changes, click the Yes button.

If You Want to Quit Microsoft Word for Now

1   On the File menu, click Exit.

2   If a message appears asking whether you want to save changes, click the Yes button.

Arranging Text and Graphics

Creating Tables and Charts

In this lesson you will learn how to:

Estimated time
30 min.

- Insert a table into a document.
- Enter text in a table.
- Adjust the width of table columns.
- Insert rows and columns in a table.
- Modify borders and shading in a table using Table AutoFormat.
- Merge table cells into one.
- Create a chart from the numbers in the table.

A quick and easy way to arrange columns of numbers in a document is to create a table. You can also use tables to place paragraphs of text side by side. In this lesson, you will create a table and apply different formatting options. You'll adjust column widths and add and delete columns and rows. Then you will experiment with the Table AutoFormat command and apply your own formatting with borders. After you complete your table, you will use the built-in Microsoft Graph program to create and modify a chart based on the information in the table.

Start the lesson

Follow the steps below to open the practice file called 10Lesson, and then save it with the new name Lesson10.

Open

To select the folder containing your practice files, refer to "Open a practice file" near the start of Lesson 2.

1 On the Standard toolbar, click the Open button.

2 In the Look In box, be sure that the Winword SBS Practice folder appears.

3 In the file list box, double-click the file named 10Lesson to open it.

4 On the File menu, click Save As.

The Save As dialog box opens. Be sure that the Winword SBS Practice folder appears in the Save In box.

5 Select and delete any text in the File Name box, and then type **Lesson10**

6 Click the Save button, or press ENTER.

If you share your computer with others who use Microsoft Word, the screen display might have changed since your last lesson. If your screen does not look similar to the illustrations as you work through this lesson, see the Appendix, "Matching the Exercises."

Creating a Table

A table is a grid of rows and columns containing boxes (called *cells*) of text or graphics. Within each cell, text wraps between the borders of a cell just as it does between the margins in other parts of a document. Unlike a table that you might create using tabs, you can easily add or delete text in a table without affecting the arrangement of columns.

If you do not see the grid-lines, on the Table menu, click Gridlines to display them.

When you insert a table, Microsoft Word outlines each cell with dotted gridlines so that you can see the cells when you work in the table. Just as a paragraph mark ends every paragraph, an *end-of-cell mark* shows the end of every cell. At the end of each row, there is an *end-of-row mark* that shows the end of the row. The gridlines, end-of-cell marks, and end-of-row marks do not print.

Insert a table

Insert Table

1 Position the insertion point in front of the last paragraph mark in the document.

2 On the Standard toolbar, click the Insert Table button to display the grid.

3 Drag across the grid to select two rows and four columns.

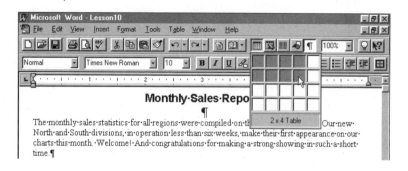

When you release the mouse button, Microsoft Word inserts an empty table that contains the number of columns and rows that you selected.

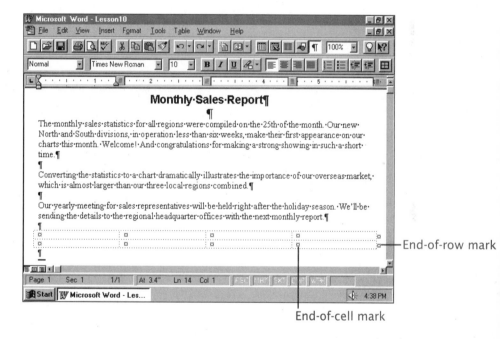

End-of-row mark

End-of-cell mark

Type the text

When you insert a table, Microsoft Word positions the insertion point in the first cell so that you are ready to type.

1 Type **North**

2 Press TAB to move to the next cell.

3 Type **Central** and press TAB.

4 Type **South** and press TAB.

5 Type **International** and press TAB.

The insertion point moves to the first cell in the next row.

6 Fill in the rest of the table as indicated below. Press TAB to move from cell to cell. A new row of blank cells appears at the bottom of the table when you press TAB in the last cell in the table.

To move to the previous cell, press SHIFT+TAB. To indent text in a table using tabs, press CTRL+TAB.

North	Central	South	International
3,209	1,091	2,343	7,809
3,429	1,908	3,485	8,988

Your table looks similar to the following illustration.

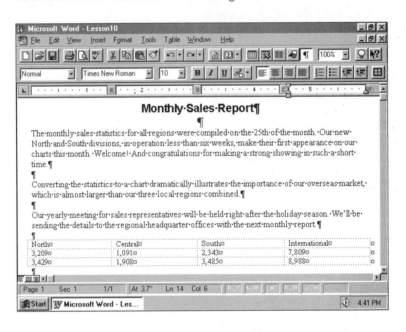

Adjust the width of the columns

To adjust the width of an entire column, not just a selected cell, be sure NOT to select any part of the table before you drag the gridlines.

You can drag the vertical gridlines in a table to adjust the width of the columns so that they better fit the text.

1 Position the pointer over the gridline between the first and second columns. When the pointer changes to a two-headed arrow, drag to the left until the column is about 0.75 inch wide.

Drag gridline to 0.75 inch.

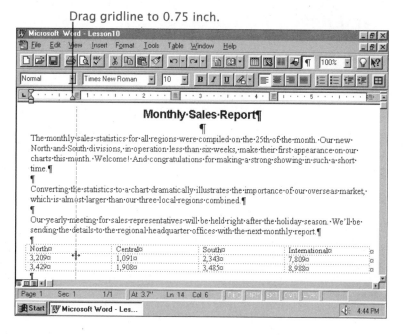

2   Drag the remaining gridlines to make the other columns narrower.

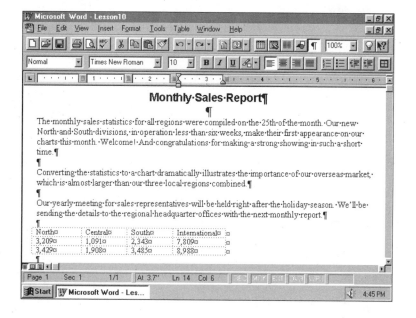

Set the "best fit" for the column width

You can have Microsoft Word determine the best fit for the width of the columns in the table. You'll need to select the entire table first.

1   On the Table menu, click Select Table.

2   On the Table menu, click Cell Height And Width, and then click the Column tab.

You can also use the right mouse button when pointing inside a table. This displays a context-sensitive menu from which you can choose the Cell Height And Width command. The dialog box looks like the following illustration.

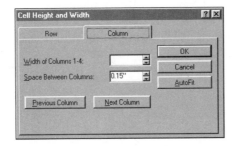

Another way to adjust column width to fit the text is to double-click a gridline.

3   Click the AutoFit button.

This option formats each column width to be only as wide as the text in the longest cell in a column.

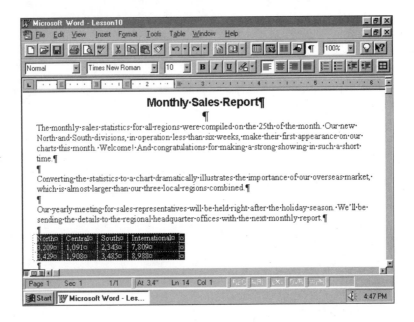

Inserting and Deleting Rows and Columns

As you work in a table you might need to add or delete a column or a row. You can use the commands on the Table menu to add rows and columns, or you can use the Insert Table button on the Standard toolbar. You can use the Cut button on the Standard toolbar to delete selected rows and columns. Or you can use the commands on the Table menu to do the same thing.

NOTE The name of the Insert Table button changes, depending on what is selected in the table. For example, if you select a row, this same button on the Standard toolbar becomes the Insert Rows button.

Insert a column

To add a column, you need to select a column to the right of where you want the new column to appear and then click the Insert Columns button on the toolbar. This button is the same as the Insert Table button, except that it inserts a column when you select a column.

1 Deselect the table by clicking outside the table, and then point near the top edge of the first column.

2 Click when the pointer changes its shape to a down arrow.

The entire column is selected.

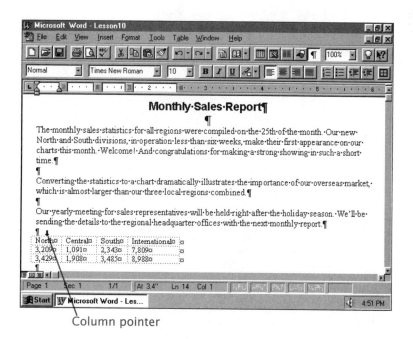

Column pointer

173

Insert Columns

3 On the Standard toolbar, click the Insert Columns button.

The remaining columns move to the right to make room for the new column.

Type text in the new column

Earlier in this lesson, you pressed TAB to move from cell to cell. You can also press arrow keys to move directly to a cell.

1 Click in the second cell of the new column, and then type **May**

2 Press the DOWN ARROW key to move down one cell, and then type **June**

Insert a column at the end of the table

Microsoft Word displays *end-of-row marks* so that you can add columns to the right side of a table. You can select these marks in the same way you select a column.

1 Point near the top and to the right of the last column, above the end-of-row marks.

2 Click when the pointer changes its shape to a down arrow.

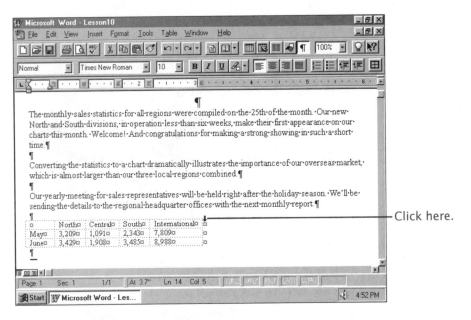

Click here.

3 On the Standard toolbar, click the Insert Columns button.

A new column appears at the end of the table.

4 Type **Totals**

The insertion point is automatically placed in the first cell of the new column when you begin typing. Leave the remaining cells in the column blank for now. Later in this lesson, you will learn to calculate totals for all the cells in each row.

Insert a row

To insert a new row, you can select the row below where you want the new row to appear and click the Insert Rows button. When you add a row, existing rows move down to make room for the new row. Microsoft Word inserts as many rows as you select.

In earlier lessons, you used an invisible selection bar to the left of paragraphs to quickly select lines and paragraphs. There is also a selection bar to the left of tables, which you can use to select entire rows.

1 Point to the left of the first row.

2 Click when the mouse pointer changes to an arrow pointing upward and to the right.

This selects the entire row. Each cell also has an invisible selection bar. Be sure that you click well to the left of the row so that you do not select the first cell by itself.

Insert Rows

To insert a new row at the end of a table, place the insertion point in the last cell of the last column, and then press TAB.

3 On the Standard toolbar, click the Insert Rows button.

This is the same button you used previously to insert columns. However, its name becomes "Insert Rows" when you have a row selected.

4 Type **Monthly Sales by Region**

The text wraps within the first cell of the new row as you type. Later in this lesson, you will learn how to center the text in a single cell that spans the width of the table.

Delete a column

Deleting a row or column is as simple as inserting one. In this exercise, you will delete the Central column.

1 Select the column labeled "Central" by positioning the mouse at the top edge of the column and clicking when the pointer changes to a down arrow.

2 On the Table menu, click Delete Columns.

You can delete rows in the same way. You select the row and then click Delete Rows on the Table menu.

Adding Borders and Shading

Although the gridlines you see on your screen make it easy to tell one cell from another, they do not print. If you want table borders to print, you can apply border formatting. You can get a head start on formatting your table by using the Table AutoFormat command. After Microsoft Word automatically formats your table, you can customize the appearance of your table even further by adding new borders.

Use Table AutoFormat to apply table borders

1   With the insertion point anywhere in the table, on the Table menu, click Table AutoFormat.

2   In the Formats box, click Classic 4.

This format applies borders to your table. An example of the formatting appears in the Preview area of the dialog box.

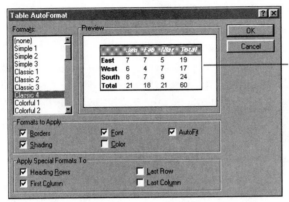

Preview the selected format.

3   Click the OK button to return to the document.

Place a border under the second row

In this exercise, you will add additional borders to a cell using the Borders toolbar.

1   Select the second row in the table.

Borders

2   On the Formatting toolbar, click the Borders button.

The Borders toolbar appears at the top of the document window above the ruler.

Bottom Border

3   Click the Bottom Border button.

TIP   You can modify the border thickness and shading percentage by selecting an option from the Line Style or Shading drop-down list on the Borders toolbar.

Formatting Text in a Table

With the borders and shading established for your table, you can format the text in individual cells in the same way you format characters and paragraphs in the rest of your document. In the next exercise, you will first merge cells to create a cell that spans all columns of the table. Then you'll center text within the table and center the table between the document margins.

Merging Cells

Sometimes you might want to combine, or *merge*, two or more selected cells within a row to create a single cell. For example, earlier in this lesson, you entered so much text in a cell that it did not fit on one line. By merging cells, you can create a cell wide enough to accommodate a heading that spans several columns.

NOTE   It's a good idea to insert and format all the columns and adjust their widths before merging cells.

Merge the cells in the top row

1   Select the first row of the table.

2   On the Table menu, click Merge Cells.

The selected cells merge into one. Your table looks like the following illustration.

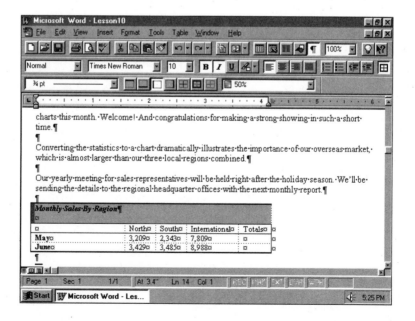

To move the insertion point to the end-of-cell mark, press the END key.

3 To delete the paragraph mark in the first cell, place the insertion point before the end-of-cell mark.

4 Press BACKSPACE to remove the extra paragraph mark.

Format the merged cell borders

The new merged cell does not have a border on the right side, because the border formatting of the first cell (which also did not have a right border) was applied to the new merged cell. This means you need to add a border to the right side of this cell.

Right Border

1 On the Borders toolbar, click the Right Border button.

2 On the Formatting toolbar, click the Borders button to hide the Borders toolbar.

Format headings

You can edit and format text in a table just as you do any other document text.

Bold

1 Select the heading "Monthly Sales by Region," and then from the Font Size drop-down list on the Formatting toolbar, select 12 points.

2 Select the headings in the second row, and then click the Bold button on the Formatting toolbar.

Adjust any column widths, if necessary, so that headings fit on one line.

Center the text in each cell

Center

1 On the Table menu, click Select Table.

2 On the Formatting toolbar, click the Center button.

Click anywhere to deselect the table and view the formatting changes. Your table looks like the following illustration.

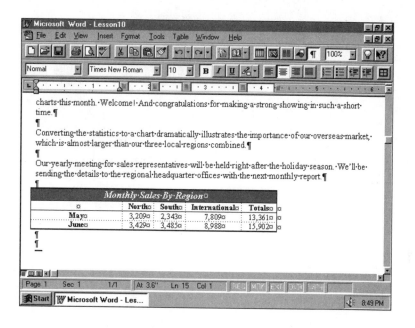

Adjust a column width

In this exercise, you will adjust the width of the first column.

➤ Drag the right vertical gridline that is between the first and second columns to approximately the 1-inch mark.

Center the table between the document margins

You can center one or more selected rows, or you can center the entire table.

1 With the insertion point anywhere in the table, on the Table menu, click Cell Height And Width.

2 Click the Row tab if it is not selected.

3 Under Alignment, click Center.

4 Click the OK button.

The table is centered between the margins of the page.

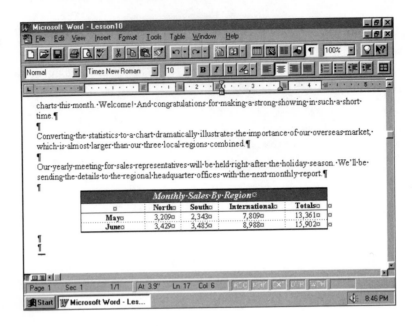

Save

Save the document

> On the Standard toolbar, click the Save button.

Creating Charts

With Microsoft Graph, a charting program that comes with Microsoft Word, you can select all or part of a table that contains numbers and then create charts similar to those in Microsoft Excel. The Setup program you use to install Microsoft Word gives you the option to install Microsoft Graph. If the program is not installed, a message will appear when you attempt to use it during the following procedure. You can run the Microsoft Word Setup program again and specify that you want to install Microsoft Graph only.

The following exercise describes the procedure for using Microsoft Graph version 5. When you start the Microsoft Graph application, Microsoft Word automatically displays the ChartWizard. This wizard guides you through the steps for creating a chart.

Create a chart of the sales figures

1   Select the bottom three rows of the table.

2   On the Insert menu, click Object.

    The Object dialog box might look different depending on the applications you have installed on your computer.

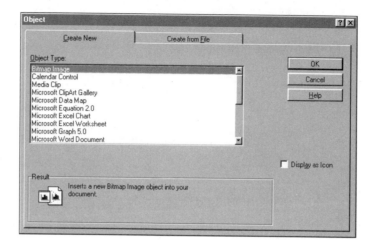

3 In the Object Type box, click Microsoft Graph 5.0, and then click OK.

The first ChartWizard window appears. In this window you can select the type of chart—bar, column, line, pie, etc.—you want to create.

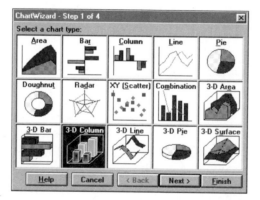

4 Be sure that the 3-D Column box is selected, and then click Next.

In the second ChartWizard window, select the format you want for the 3-D column chart.

5 Click the first option, and then click Next.

In the third ChartWizard window, specify whether the data in your table should be grouped by row or by column in the chart.

6 Click Next to accept the default settings.

In the next ChartWizard window, you can specify a title for the chart or either axis and then decide whether or not you want to include a legend.

7 Click Finish to accept the default settings, and close the ChartWizard.

8 In the Datasheet window, click the Close box.

Microsoft Word displays a column chart in the document window, as shown in the following illustration. Microsoft Graph appears with its own toolbar and menu bar. You'll use these menus to finish formatting the chart.

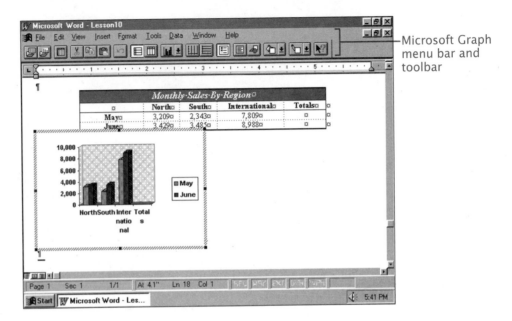

Microsoft Graph menu bar and toolbar

Resize the chart

You can resize a chart in Microsoft Graph by dragging the borders to the size you want.

1 With the chart selected, drag the lower-right corner of the chart downward and to the right until the word "International" appears on one line.

2 Select the legend to the right of the chart, and then click Selected Legend on the Format menu.

3 Click the Placement tab, click Top, and then click OK.

Your chart looks similar to the following illustration.

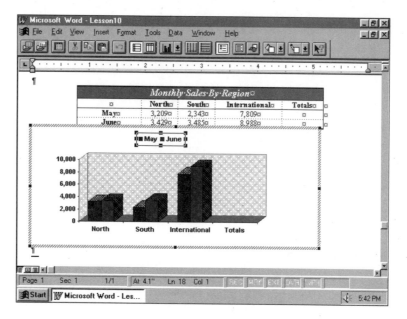

4 Click anywhere outside the graph to exit the Microsoft Graph 5 program.

 TIP You can position the chart anywhere on the page. Lesson 12, "Adding Graphics and Emphasizing Text," shows you how to position text and graphics with frames.

Save the document

Save

➤ On the Standard toolbar, click the Save button.

Microsoft Word saves this version of the document in place of the previous version.

183

One Step Further: Calculating in a Table

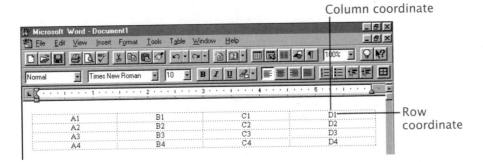

You can use Microsoft Word's Formula command to perform simple calculations in a table, including addition, subtraction, multiplication, and division, as well as basic functions, such as averages. If you are familiar with spreadsheets, such as Microsoft Excel, you already know how to refer to cells by row and column coordinates. The rows are numbered (1, 2, 3), and the columns are lettered (A, B, C). For example, the cell with the coordinates B3 is the second cell from the left in the third row. Even if you are not familiar with spreadsheets, Microsoft Word makes it easy to calculate totals in a row or column of numbers.

Calculate totals in rows

1   Click the insertion point in the first cell under the Totals label.

2   On the Table menu, click Formula.

In the dialog box, Microsoft Word suggests a formula that would sum the values in all cells to the left of the current cell. You can either accept the formula as displayed or modify it to suit your needs.

3   Click OK to accept the default formula and return to the document.

The total for the cells in this row appears in the current cell.

4   Click the insertion point in the cell below the total you calculated.

5   On the Table menu, click Formula.

This time, the formula says "SUM(ABOVE)" instead of "SUM(LEFT)." Because you want to sum the row, you must modify the formula.

6   In the formula, select "ABOVE" and type **left**, and then click OK.

TIP   If you need to edit a value in the table, you can quickly recalculate new totals by selecting the cell that contains the total and then pressing F9.

If You Want to Continue to the Next Lesson

1   On the File menu, click Close.

2   If a message appears asking whether you want to save changes, click the Yes button.

If You Want to Quit Microsoft Word for Now

1   On the File menu, click Exit.

2   If a message appears asking whether you want to save changes, click the Yes button.

Lesson Summary

To	Do this	Button
Insert a table	On the Standard toolbar, click the Insert Table button, and then drag to select the number of columns and rows you want.	
Move to the next table cell	Press the TAB key. *or* Use the arrow keys.	
Move to the previous table cell	Press SHIFT+TAB or use the arrow keys.	
Select an entire column or row	Click above the column or in the selection bar to the left of the row. Select an entire table by clicking the Select Table command on the Table menu.	
Adjust the widths of table columns	Drag the column markers on the ruler.	
Insert a new row or column	Select a row or column in the existing table, and then click the Insert Rows or Insert Columns command on the Table menu, or click the Insert Rows or Insert Columns button on the Standard toolbar.	
Delete a row or column	Select the row or column, and on the Table menu, click Delete Rows/ Columns.	
Add predefined formatting to a table		

To	Do this	Button
Add custom borders to a table	On the Table menu, click Table AutoFormat. Then select the kind of formatting you want.	
Add custom shading to a table row	On the Borders toolbar, select the borders and line width you want.	
Merge several cells into one cell	On the Borders toolbar, select the shading you want from the Shading drop-down list.	
Center text within table cells	Select the cells, and then click the Merge Cells command on the Table menu.	
	Select the table text. On the Formatting toolbar, click the Center button.	
Center a table between the page margins	Select the table. On the Table menu, click Cell Height And Width. On the Row tab under Alignment, click Center.	
Create a column chart	On the Insert menu, click Object. On the Create New tab, click Microsoft Graph 5.0 in the Object Type box. Select formatting options in the ChartWizard windows. Resize the chart if needed. Click outside the chart to return to Microsoft Word.	

For online information about	Use the Answer Wizard to search for
Tables	**tables**, and then display Tables
Sorting a table	**sorting a table**, and then display Sorting a single column in a table
Working with spreadsheet data	**spreadsheet data**, and then display Performing calculations in a table
Creating charts	**charts**, and then display Create a chart from a table

Preview of the Next Lesson

In the next lesson, you'll learn to format text into multiple columns and customize the look of the page by adding vertical lines between columns and breaking columns exactly as you want them. You'll also learn to quickly create multiple-column formatting in different parts of the same document.

Creating Columns

In this lesson you will learn how to:

Estimated time
40 min.

- Create multiple columns.
- Vary the number of columns within a document.
- Insert manual column breaks.
- Add lines between columns.
- Reduce or enlarge the display of the document on the screen.
- Vary the width of individual columns.

If the Borders toolbar is still displayed, click the Borders button on the Formatting toolbar to hide the toolbar. You will not need it in this lesson.

With Microsoft Word, you can produce "snaking" columns, in which text flows from the bottom of one column to the top of the next, as in newspaper columns. In this lesson, you'll format a document with a different number of columns for different parts (sections) of the document.

Start the lesson

Follow the steps below to open the practice file called 11Lesson, and then save it with the new name Lesson11.

Open

1 On the Standard toolbar, click the Open button.

2 In the Look In box, be sure that the Winword SBS Practice folder appears.

To select the folder containing your practice files, refer to "Open a practice file" near the start of Lesson 2.

3   In the file list box, double-click the file named 11Lesson to open it.

4   On the File menu, click Save As.

The Save As dialog box opens. Be sure that the Winword SBS Practice folder appears in the Save In box.

5   Select and delete any text in the File Name box, and then type **Lesson11**

6   Click the Save button, or press ENTER.

If you share your computer with others who use Microsoft Word, the screen display might have changed since your last lesson. If your screen does not look similar to the illustrations as you work through this lesson, see the Appendix, "Matching the Exercises."

Creating Columns

You can use a button on the Standard toolbar to create columns in a document or to change the number of columns. Microsoft Word automatically breaks each column at the bottom of the page and moves the remaining text to the top of the page to start a new column.

Create multiple columns in a document

When you use the Columns button on the Standard toolbar, Microsoft Word formats the text of the document into the number of columns you specify.

Columns button

1   On the Standard toolbar, click the Columns button.

2   Point to the left column, and drag to select two columns.

When you release the mouse button, Microsoft Word creates the number of columns that you specify. You will not see the columns in the document just yet. For now, your document looks like the following illustration.

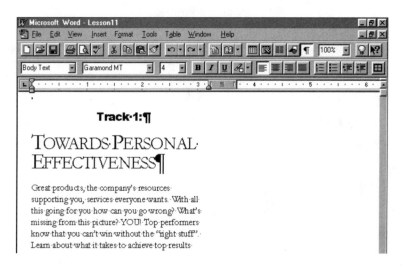

Switch to page layout view

In page layout view, you can edit the document, as well as see how it will look when printed.

When you create columns in normal view, Microsoft Word displays them in their actual width, but not side by side, as they will look when printed. To see the columns side by side, you must switch to page layout view. You can use the Page Layout View button, or you can choose the Page Layout command on the View menu.

 On the View menu, click Page Layout.

Columns now appear in your document as shown in the following illustration. Scroll through the document to view the column formatting.

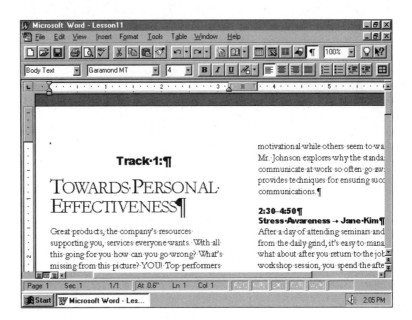

Varying Columns Within a Document

You've learned how easy it is to create columns in a document. If you need a more sophisticated page layout, you can vary how many columns appear on a page or in sections of the document. To vary the number of columns, you insert a *section break* before you create your new columns.

When you insert a section break to create differing numbers of columns in a document, indicate that you want a *continuous* break. This means that the next section immediately follows the previous section on the same page. When you insert section breaks, you divide a document into *sections,* indicated by double-dotted lines (labeled "End of Section") that do not print. You can then format each section separately. The following illustration shows a page that has been divided into three sections. The second section is formatted with two columns, while the first and third sections are formatted with one column.

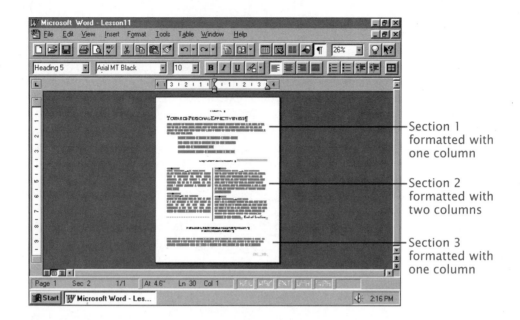

Section 1 formatted with one column

Section 2 formatted with two columns

Section 3 formatted with one column

Inserting Section Breaks

In normal view, a section break appears as a double dotted line extending the width of the page. These lines make it easy to see where section breaks occur, which is helpful when you format the sections. After you insert section breaks and create columns in each section, you can switch back to page layout view to see columns side by side.

Switch to normal view

Normal View

 On the far left of the horizontal scroll bar, click the Normal View button.

You want to be in normal view to see the section breaks you are creating in the exercise.

Insert a section break

1   Place the insertion point in front of the text "9:00–10:10."

2   On the Insert menu, click Break.

3   Under Section Breaks, select the Continuous option button so that the new section will print right after the previous section on the same page.

4   Click the OK button.

Microsoft Word inserts the section break—a double dotted line with the text "End of Section." Now the document has two sections: one above the section break and one below the section break. The status bar indicates which section contains the insertion point.

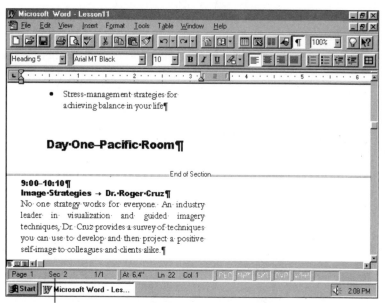

Indicates which section contains the insertion point

Insert another section break

1   Scroll down, and place the insertion point in front of the heading "Personal Effectiveness Hospitality Room."

2   On the Insert menu, click Break.

3   Under Section Breaks, click the Continuous option button.

4   Click the OK button.

Now you can format each section with the number of columns you want.

Creating Columns in Each Section

To create a different number of columns in each section, move to the section in which you want to vary the number of columns. Then use the Columns button on the Standard toolbar to create the columns. With the document divided into sections, your column formatting affects only the section containing the insertion point.

After you format your columns, you can switch to page layout view to see your columns side by side.

Format each section

Dragging the scroll box is a quick way to scroll to the beginning of the document.

1   Scroll to the top of the document.

2   Place the insertion point anywhere in the first section.

The first section should be formatted as one column.

Columns

3 On the Standard toolbar, click the Columns button, and drag to display one column.

4 Scroll down to and place the insertion point anywhere in section 3.

Be sure that the status bar displays the correct section number.

5 Use the Columns button on the Standard toolbar to create one column in the last section.

View the document in page layout

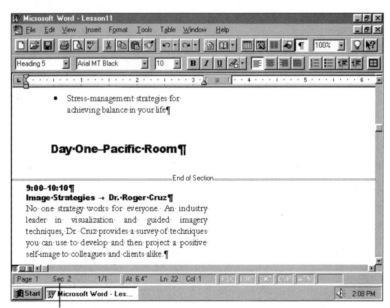

Page Layout View

▶ On the far left of the horizontal scroll bar, click the Page Layout View button.

The document looks like the following illustration.

Indicates which section contains the insertion point

Save

Save the document

▶ On the Standard toolbar, click the Save button.

Formatting Columns Within a Document

Insert a manual column break

Microsoft Word automatically breaks each column when the text reaches the bottom of the section, moving the text that follows to the top of the next column. If you want to break the columns in another location, you can insert manual column breaks.

1   Scroll to and position the insertion point in front of the text "1:00–2:10."

2   On the Insert menu, click Break.

3   Click the Column Break option.

4   Click the OK button.

The text after the column break moves to the top of the next column. Your document looks like the following illustration.

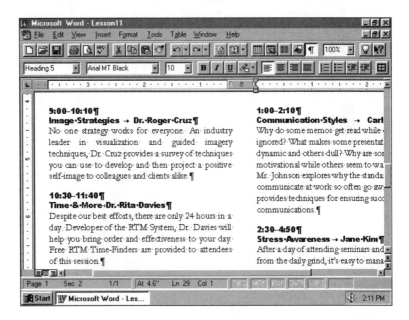

Modify formatting between columns

The Columns command includes special options for formatting columns. For example, you can use this command to place vertical lines between columns. You can also use this command to specify the space between columns or to create columns of unequal widths.

1   On the Format menu, click Columns.

Verify that the Equal Column Width check box is not checked.

2   In the Width And Spacing area, click the down arrow in the Width for Column 1 box to specify a 3-inch column width for the left column.

The width of the right column automatically increases as the left column decreases.

3   Click the down arrow under Spacing to specify a 0.3-inch space between columns.

4   Click the Line Between check box.

5   Click the OK button.

Your document looks like the following illustration.

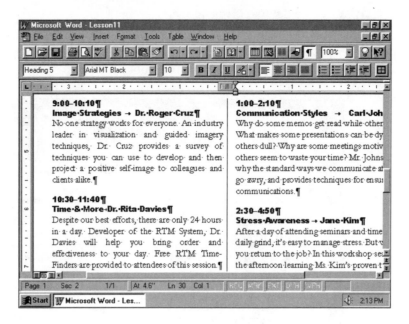

Save

Save the document

➤ On the Standard toolbar, click the Save button.

Getting an Overview of the Layout

The Zoom Control drop-down list on the Standard toolbar is useful when you are working with columns. You can use the selections in the list to change the magnification setting of the document. You can select one of the magnification settings, or you can type in an exact value.

When you change the magnification, you are changing only the way the document appears on the screen, not the size of the fonts or the length of the document.

Experiment with zooming in page layout view

1   On the Zoom Control drop-down list, select 50%.

2   In the Zoom Control list box, select the existing setting (50%). Type **40** and press ENTER.

3 In the Zoom Control drop-down list, select Whole Page.

Your document looks like the following illustration.

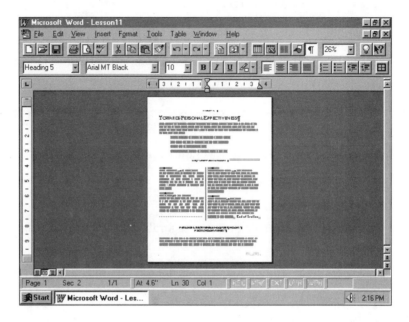

4 In the Zoom Control drop-down list, select Page Width.

One Step Further: Changing Column Width with the Ruler

For even faster formatting, you can use the column markers in the ruler to adjust the column width and spacing between columns. If the current section is formatted for columns that have the same width, dragging the column markers changes the width of the columns as well as the spacing between them. If the current section is formatted for uneven columns, dragging column markers changes only the width of the column.

Change column width using the ruler

1 Be sure that the insertion point is in the first column in section 2.

2 In the ruler, drag the left edge of the column marker to the left to the 2¾" mark.

Now you need to increase the space between the first column and the line between the paragraphs.

TIP You can increase the magnification to make finer adjustments to the column width. Also, you can hold down the ALT key when making ruler adjustments to see the column width measurements.

3 Select the paragraphs in the first column, and then drag the right indent in the ruler so that it aligns with the left edge of the column marker.

Your ruler looks like the following illustration.

Justify

4 Improve the appearance of the columns by selecting the last two paragraphs in section 2 and clicking the Justify button on the Formatting toolbar.

Print the document

Your printed document is the same regardless of which view is on the screen when you print.

Print

▶ On the Standard toolbar, click the Print button.

If You Want to Continue to the Next Lesson

1 On the File menu, click Close.

2 If a message appears asking whether you want to save changes, click the Yes button.

If You Want to Quit Microsoft Word for Now

1 On the File menu, click Exit.

2 If a message appears asking whether you want to save changes, click the Yes button.

Lesson Summary

To	Do this	Button
Create columns	On the Standard toolbar, click the Columns button, and then drag to select the number of columns you want.	
Divide a document into sections	On the Insert menu, click Break, and then select the option you want under Section Breaks.	

To	Do this	Button
Format each section in a document separately	Click in the section you want to format, and then apply formatting.	
Insert manual column breaks	On the Insert menu, click the Break command, and then select Column Break.	
View a single page of the document as it will look when printed	From Print Preview, click the One Page button. *or* In page layout view, click the Zoom Control arrow on the Standard toolbar, and then click Whole Page.	
Modify formatting between columns	On the Format menu, click Columns. To add a line between columns, select the Line Between check box. Modify spacing and column width in the Spacing and Width boxes.	
Increase or decrease the magnification of a document	On the View menu, click Zoom. In the Zoom dialog box, specify the magnification you want. *or* On the Standard toolbar, click the Zoom Control arrow, and select the magnification you want.	

For online information about	Use the Answer Wizard to search for
Columns, column breaks, and lines between columns	**columns**, and then display Newspaper columns
Working with sections	**sections**, and then display Changing the appearance of your page
Changing the view of a document	**views**, and then display Different ways to view a Microsoft Word document

Preview of the Next Lesson

In the next lesson, you will learn to emphasize important text by adding borders and shading. You'll also try your hand at turning words into art. And you'll learn how to insert and size graphics, and position them exactly where you want them on the page.

Adding Graphics and Emphasizing Text

Estimated time
40 min.

In this lesson you will learn how to:

- Insert, size, and edit a graphic.
- Create callouts to enhance a graphic.
- Insert a drop cap.
- Drag graphics and text to a new location on the page.
- Add shading, borders, and special effects to text.

You can add graphics to Microsoft Word documents to illustrate a point or to add interest to a document. In this lesson, you learn to work with the tools on the Drawing toolbar, which contains tools you can use to create and modify graphics that you can insert into your Microsoft Word documents. You also learn to use WordArt, another built-in program in which you can create special effects with text, such as curving, rotating, flipping, or stretching the text. You learn to position text and graphics on the page and to wrap text around them. In the One Step Further, you can explore inserting data or graphics from other programs, such as Microsoft Excel or Paint.

Start the lesson

Follow the steps below to open the practice file called 12Lesson, and then save it with the new name Lesson12.

Open

To select the folder containing your practice files, refer to "Open a practice file" near the start of Lesson 2.

1 On the Standard toolbar, click the Open button.

2 In the Look In box, be sure that the Winword SBS Practice folder appears.

3 In the file list box, double-click the file named 12Lesson to open it.

4 On the File menu, click Save As.

The Save As dialog box opens. Be sure that the Winword SBS Practice folder appears in the Save In box.

5 Select and delete any text in the File Name box, and then type **Lesson12**

6 Click the Save button, or press ENTER.

If you share your computer with others who use Microsoft Word, the screen display might have changed since your last lesson. If your screen does not look similar to the illustrations as you work through this lesson, see the Appendix, "Matching the Exercises."

Inserting and Sizing Graphics

If paragraph marks are not displayed, on the Standard toolbar, click the Show/Hide ¶ button to display paragraph marks for easier editing.

You can import graphics from many graphics programs into Microsoft Word. When you insert a graphic into a document and then click the graphic, eight sizing handles appear around it. You can use the sizing handles to make the graphic larger or smaller. You can also use the handles to trim, or *crop,* the graphic, hiding the portions you don't want to be displayed or printed. The sizing handles do not print.

Insert a graphic

Microsoft Word provides a collection of clip art—graphics that you can insert in documents and then edit to suit your needs. The Clipart folder contains a graphic of a speaker at a podium that you can insert into your document.

1 Position the insertion point at the beginning of the paragraph mark above the heading "Track A: Day One–Pacific Room," as shown in the following illustration.

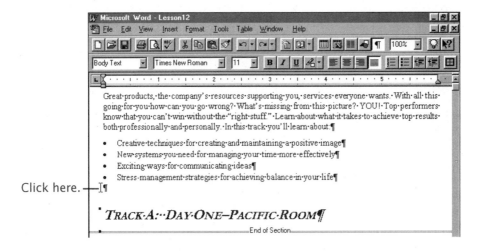

After doing step 2, if you see a message that the filter is unavailable, you need to run the Microsoft Word Setup program again, and install the Windows Metafile Filter.

2 On the Insert menu, click Picture.

Microsoft Word automatically defaults to the Clipart folder.

3 Scroll to and click the file named Speaker.wmf.

If this graphic file is not displayed in the Clipart list, you can open the Winword SBS Practice folder and select this file.

4 Click the Preview button, if it is not already selected.

5 Click the OK button.

Microsoft Word inserts the graphic in the document at the location of the insertion point.

Preview

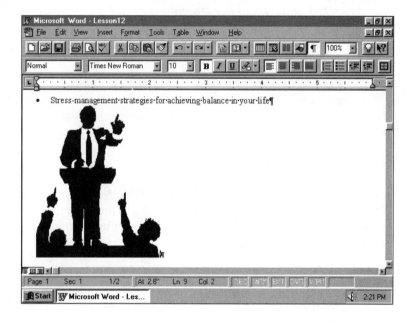

Crop the graphic

In step 1, if you accidentally double-click the graphic, click the Close Picture button on the floating toolbar to return to the document.

The graphic shows a speaker at a podium. You want to show only the top half of the graphic. You can use the cropping tool to hide the rest. When you drag a sizing handle while holding down the SHIFT key, you crop the graphic, hiding part of it. Dragging in the other direction reveals any hidden parts of the graphic. You can also eliminate any extra white space around the graphic by using the cropping tool.

1 Click the graphic once to select the graphic and display the sizing handles.

2 Hide the bottom half of the graphic by first holding down the SHIFT key and then pointing to the middle sizing handle on the bottom, as shown in the following illustration. When the pointer changes to a cropping tool, drag upward.

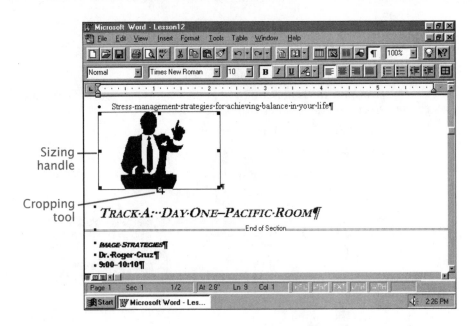

Sizing handle

Cropping tool

3 Hold down the SHIFT key, and drag the left and right sizing handles to remove as much white space as you can without hiding the graphic.

Experiment with the sizing handles

Dragging a sizing handle without holding down the SHIFT key changes the size of the graphic. You can drag any side to stretch the graphic or drag a corner to make the graphic smaller or larger proportionally.

If you want to see the vertical ruler, you can view the document in page layout view.

1 On the View menu, click Ruler if the ruler is not already displayed.

2 With the graphic selected, drag the middle handle on the bottom of the graphic downward about 1 inch to see the effect on the graphic.

3 On the Standard toolbar, click the Undo button to reverse the stretch.

4 To stretch the graphic, drag the middle handle on the right toward the right.

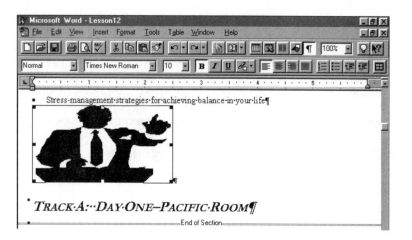

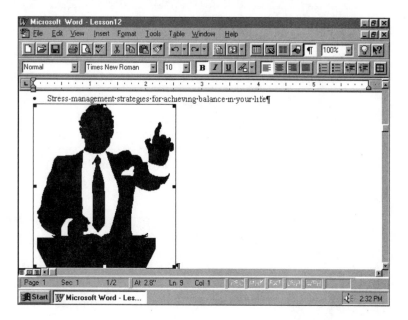

5 Click the Undo button after you've seen the effect.

Undo

6 Make the graphic larger proportionately by dragging the lower-right corner until the graphic is about 2½ inches wide. Use the ruler at the top of the screen to determine the width of the graphic.

7 Make the graphic smaller proportionately by dragging the lower-right corner until the graphic is approximately 1 inch wide.

Framing a Graphic

You can create interesting visual effects in your document, such as allowing the text to wrap around a picture by inserting a *frame* around the graphic. When you work with framed items, it's best to work in page layout view. Page layout view displays framed items in their correct location on the page. In normal view, framed items appear aligned with the left margin, marked by small, nonprinting bullets.

Insert a frame around the graphic

You must select the graphic before you can insert a frame around it. If you can see the sizing handles, the graphic is selected.

Page Layout View

1 On the horizontal scroll bar, click the Page Layout View button.

2 If you cannot see the sizing handles, click the graphic once to select it.

Drawing

3 On the Standard toolbar, click the Drawing button.

This button displays the Drawing toolbar at the bottom of the screen.

Insert Frame

4 On the right end of the Drawing toolbar, click the Insert Frame button.

You can also insert a frame by clicking the Frame command on the Insert menu.

5 On the Standard toolbar, click the Drawing button to hide the Drawing toolbar.

If you do not see the anchor, see the Appendix, "Matching the Exercises."

Framing an object allows text to flow around it. The framed object is surrounded by a shaded border that marks the frame. You also see an anchor icon next to the paragraph. The anchor indicates that the graphic is "anchored" to this paragraph. If you increase (or decrease) the amount of text before this paragraph, the framed graphic moves as well. Neither the anchor nor the shaded border around a graphic object prints.

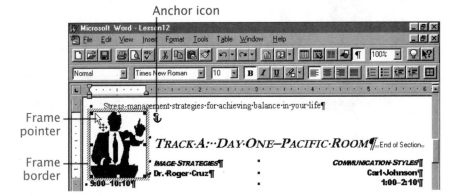

204

TIP If you don't want text to flow around a graphic, you can choose that option using the Frame command on the Format menu.

Position the graphic on the page

In addition to allowing text to flow around an object, frames allow you to drag an object anywhere on the page, using a special, four-headed pointer.

1 If the graphic is not currently selected, click it once to display the sizing handles.

2 Scroll upward, and then drag the graphic to the right of the bulleted list as shown in the following illustration. Adjust the position of the frame as necessary.

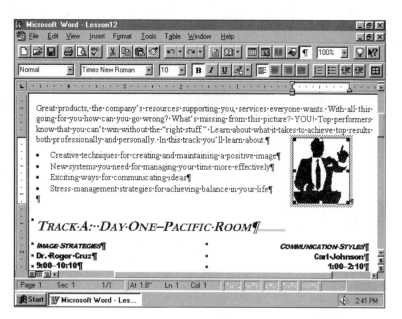

3 Click outside the graphic to hide the sizing handles and view the overall effect.

Save the document

Save

On the Standard toolbar, click the Save button.

Microsoft Word saves this version of the document in place of the previous version.

205

Making Changes to Graphics

In addition to inserting, sizing, cropping, and positioning graphics, you can edit them using the Drawing toolbar. You use this toolbar to create graphics of your own and to edit graphics that you've imported. You can also draw your own art.

Display the Drawing toolbar

With the Drawing toolbar, you can edit graphics, create special effects, and add text to graphics. This part of the lesson shows you how to edit a graphic already inserted in your document.

1   Double-click the West Coast Sales logo at the bottom of the document to display the Drawing toolbar.

2   In the Draw window, locate the small, floating toolbar window titled "Picture" and drag it to the upper-right corner of the screen if necessary.

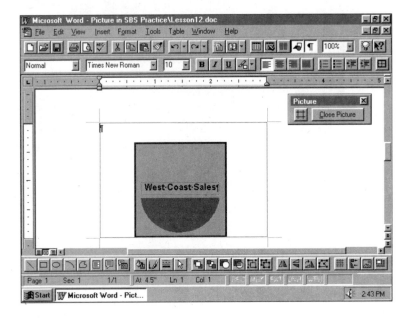

Edit the graphic

1   Select the half-circle below the text in the graphic by clicking it.

2   On the Drawing toolbar, click the Flip Vertical button.

The graphic flips over.

Flip Vertical

206

Fill Color

Select Drawing Objects

3 With the half-circle still selected, click the Fill Color button on the Drawing toolbar, and then select the color yellow from the color palette.

4 On the Drawing toolbar, click the Select Drawing Objects (pointer) button, and then drag the half-circle so that it appears above the text, as shown in the following illustration.

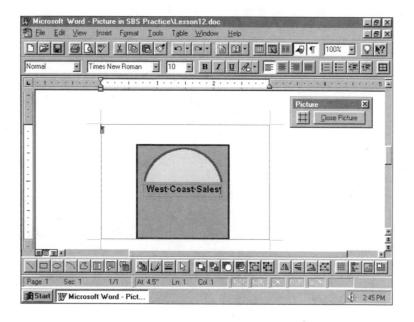

Position the graphic without Snap To Grid

If you are having trouble positioning the object exactly where you want it, you can turn off the Snap To Grid option. When the Drawing toolbar first appears, this option may be in effect to make it easy to line up objects evenly. However, if you need to make finer adjustments as you position an object, you can turn off this option to move your object freely.

Snap To Grid

1 On the Drawing toolbar, click the Snap To Grid button.

2 In the Snap To Grid dialog box, clear the Snap To Grid check box if it is selected.

3 Click the OK button to return to your drawing.

4 Position the half-circle just below the top border of the square, and center it over the text.

5 Select the square object.

6 Drag the middle sizing handle at the bottom of the square upward to just below the text in the logo.

Return to the document

➤ In the Picture window, click the Close Picture button to return to your document. The Draw window closes, and the edited graphic replaces the previous version.

Crop the graphic

1 If the sizing handles aren't displayed, click the graphic once.

2 Hold down SHIFT, and drag the bottom sizing handle upward to remove the white space.

3 Click outside the graphic to hide the sizing handles and view the overall effect.

Save the document

➤ On the Standard toolbar, click the Save button.

Save

Creating Callouts

In Microsoft Word, *callouts* are graphic objects that direct the reader's attention to a specific part of a document, graphic, or illustration, usually with a line attached to a box of text. Using the Callout button on the Drawing toolbar, you can create and position callouts in your document. Using the Format Callout button (or by double-clicking the callout), you can specify the position and orientation of the line that connects the callout to the text and whether or not you want a box around the text.

Create a callout

Because Microsoft Word retains Drawing tools settings—such as fill color, line style, and callout formatting—the initial formatting of objects you create in the following exercise will be based on any previous selections you made.

Drawing

Callout

Fill Color

1 On the Standard toolbar, click the Drawing button if the Drawing toolbar is not already displayed.

2 On the Drawing toolbar, click the Callout button.

3 Starting from the end of the last paragraph of the document, drag down and to the right about 1 inch in each direction.

A callout box appears when you release the mouse. The box may be filled with a color; however, you want the box to be transparent.

4 On the Drawing toolbar, click the Fill Color button, and select None.

Next, you want to display a line between the callout and the area to which you are drawing attention.

Line Style

Line Color

5 On the Drawing toolbar, click the Line Style button, and select the thin line that is second from the top.

Next, you want to make the lines and borders for the callout appear in black.

6 On the Drawing toolbar, click the Line Color button, and select Black.

7 With the insertion point in the callout box, type **New for WCS '96! A great way to relax...**

Format a callout

Format Callout

1 On the Drawing toolbar, click the Format Callout button.

The Format Callout dialog box appears.

2 In the Type area, select Two.

This selection formats the connecting line at an angle, but without an "elbow"-style bend.

3 From the Angle list, be sure that Any is selected.

This selection formats the connecting line with any angle.

4 From the Drop list, be sure that Center is selected.

This selection attaches the connecting line to the center of the callout box.

5 Click the Text Border check box if it is not already checked.

This selection places a border around the text in the callout. The completed dialog box should look like the following illustration.

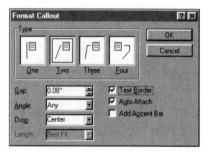

6 Click the OK button to return to the document.

7 With the callout still selected, drag the bottom-center sizing handle up until bottom border is just below the text.

8 Click outside the callout to hide the sizing handles and view the overall effect.

The callout in this part of the document should look like the following illustration.

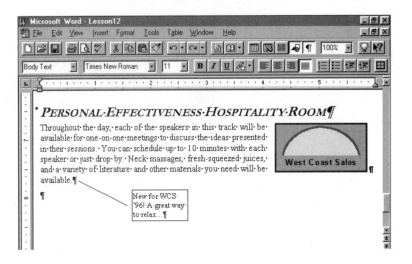

Save

Save the document

➤ On the Standard toolbar, click the Save button.

Creating Drop Caps

You can create additional effects with text using the Drop Caps command on the Format menu. This command automatically inserts a large, uppercase character as the first character of a paragraph and aligns the top edge of the character with the first line of the paragraph.

Insert a drop cap

1 Place the insertion point anywhere in the paragraph below the heading "Personal Effectiveness Hospitality Room."

2 On the Format menu, click Drop Cap.

The Drop Cap dialog box appears.

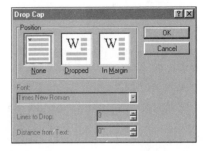

3 Under Position, click the Dropped (middle) option.

4 In the Lines to Drop box, type **2**

5 Click the OK button.

The first character in the paragraph appears enlarged in a frame, as shown in the following illustration.

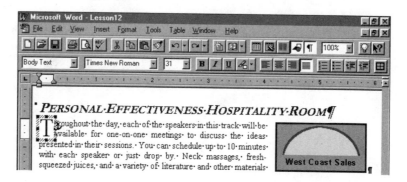

Reposition the callout

1 Position the frame pointer over the callout line.

2 Click and drag the callout to the end of the paragraph.

Working with WordArt

With WordArt, you can create graphic effects with text, such as flipping, rotating, and curving. After you insert a WordArt object in a document, you can work with it as you work with graphics. You can drag sizing handles to stretch or crop the WordArt object. You can frame a WordArt object so that text flows around it and then drag the object to other locations on the page. In the next exercises, you apply some of the WordArt effects and create a WordArt object for the sample document.

Display the WordArt dialog box

If you do not see Microsoft WordArt 2.0 in the list, WordArt might not have been installed during setup. You can run the Microsoft Word Setup program to install this feature.

1 Position the insertion point at the beginning of the paragraph mark above the heading "Track A: Day One–Pacific Room."

2 On the Insert menu, click Object.

Microsoft Word displays a dialog box that lists optional programs you can use to create objects, such as equations, graphs, charts, and drawings.

3 Scroll down, if necessary, and double-click Microsoft WordArt 2.0.

Microsoft Word displays the WordArt toolbar and the Enter Your Text Here dialog box.

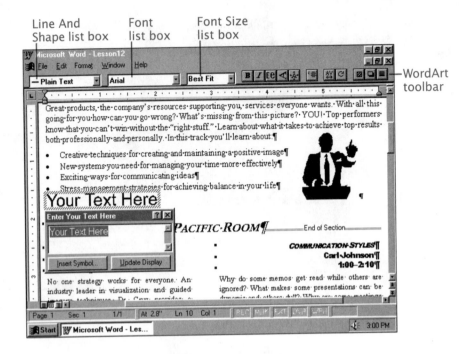

Create a WordArt object

1 In the Enter Your Text Here dialog box, select and delete any text.

2 With the insertion point in the text box, type **Track A: Personal Effectiveness**

3 Click the Update Display button.

Your text is inserted into the document.

Modify the WordArt object

1 On the WordArt toolbar, click the down arrow next to the Line And Shape list box, and then choose the sixth shape from the left in the first row.

If the Enter Your Text Here dialog box obscures your view of the WordArt object, drag the box to the lower-right corner of the screen. The text in the Line And Shape list box should read "Bottom to Top." The selected text in the document changes shape as you select different options.

2 In the Font list box, select Arial MT Black.

3 In the Font Size list box, select 30.

Shading

4   On the toolbar, click the Shading button.

The Shading dialog box appears.

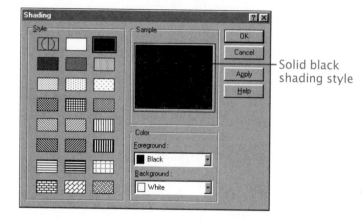

Solid black shading style

5   In the Shading dialog box, be sure that the solid black shading style is selected, and then click OK.

6   On the toolbar, click the Shadow button, and then click MORE in the lower-right corner of the options display.

Shadow

7   In the Shadow dialog box, select the third shadow from the left, and then click OK.

Return to your document

If the WordArt object appears in a black bar, click outside the bar to clear it.

▶   Click anywhere in the document to close the WordArt program.

Your screen should look similar to the following illustration.

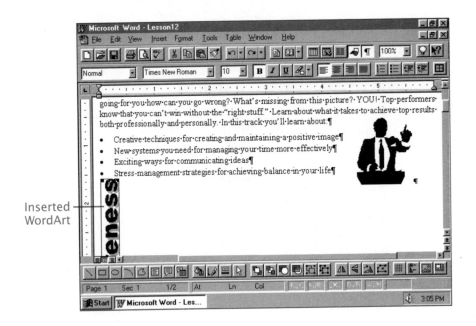

Inserted WordArt

Save the document

Save

➤ On the Standard toolbar, click the Save button.

It's a good idea to save your work often when you are making complicated changes.

Insert a frame around the WordArt graphic

You can insert a frame around the WordArt graphic so that text flows around the graphic and you can drag it to a new location.

1 Click the WordArt graphic once to select it.

2 On the Drawing toolbar, click the Insert Frame button. If a message appears asking whether you want to switch to page layout view, click the Yes button.

Insert Frame

A frame appears around the WordArt graphic.

Position the WordArt object

Framing objects gives you a great deal of flexibility in positioning an object on the page. As you see in this exercise, you can even place a framed object outside of the document margins. To make it easier to place the object, you can change the zoom magnification to see more of the page at one time.

1   On the Standard toolbar, click the Zoom Control arrow, and select 75%.

2   Drag the object upward and to the left, as shown in the following illustration.

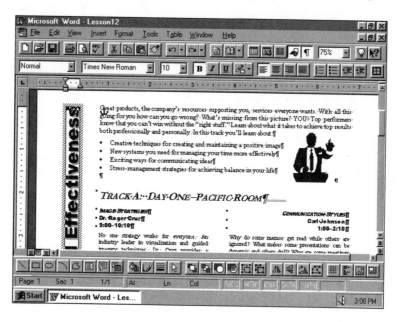

Print Preview

3   On the Standard toolbar, click the Print Preview button.

The WordArt graphic spans the length of the document outside of the left margin, as shown in the following illustration.

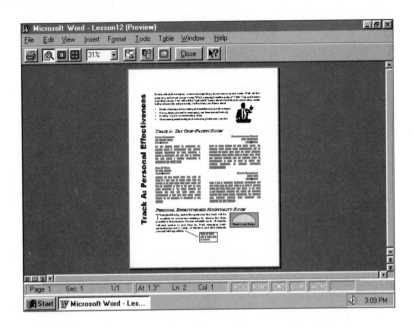

4 Click the Close button to return to the document window.

Save the document

Save

➤ On the Standard toolbar, click the Save button.

Microsoft Word saves this version of the document in place of the previous version.

Framing and Sizing Text

You can insert a frame around regular text, just as you do around a graphic. If you size the frame, the text wraps within it. Unlike when you frame a WordArt object, Microsoft Word provides a box border around framed text; the border will print. If you prefer a different style of border—perhaps a double line instead of a single line—or if you do not want a border, you can change it. You can format framed text just as you normally format text. In the following exercises, you'll create new text, put a frame around it, adjust the frame, and format the text within the frame.

Create and size a text frame

1 Position the insertion point at the beginning of the paragraph mark above the heading "Track A: Day One–Pacific Room."

216

2 Type the following text: **Last year's WCS Sales Expo played a major role in my success. I can't wait until WCS '96!**

3 Press ENTER three times and type:

Julia Ortez (press ENTER)
National Sales Leader (press ENTER)
1995

Insert Frame

4 Select all the text typed above, and then on the Drawing toolbar, click the Insert Frame button.

The text now has a border that will print and sizing handles that will not print.

5 With the two-headed arrow positioned over the right-side sizing handle, drag the right side of the frame toward the left to the 1½-inch mark, as shown in the following picture.

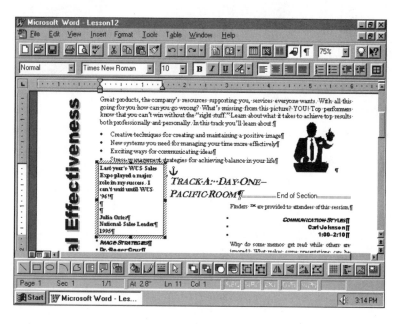

6 Click outside the frame to hide the sizing handles and view the overall effect.

Position the framed text

1 Click the framed text once to display the sizing handles.

2 Scroll downward, and then drag the graphic to the position shown in the following illustration. Adjust the position of the frame if necessary.

217

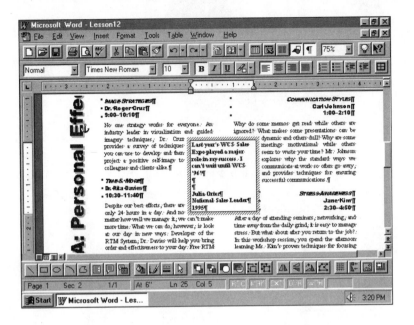

Format the framed text

You can format framed text without affecting the formatting of the surrounding text.

1   Select all of text in the first paragraph.
2   On the Format menu, click Paragraph.
3   Click the Line Spacing arrow, and select 1.5.
4   Click the OK button.
5   On the Formatting toolbar, click the Italic button.

    The surrounding text is not affected by the formatting changes.

6   Select the bottom three lines of framed text, and then click the Align Right button on the Formatting toolbar.

Italic

Align Right

Add borders and shading to the text

You can add shading to text and change the style of border around framed paragraphs. In this exercise, you will apply 20 percent shading and place a double-line border around the text.

1   Click the framed text once to display the sizing handles.
2   On the Formatting toolbar, click the Borders button.

Borders

3 On the Borders toolbar (just below the Formatting toolbar), the Shading box currently shows "Clear." Display the list of shading choices by clicking the down arrow.

4 Select 20%.

5 On the Borders toolbar, select the 1½-point double-line from the Line Style drop-down list box.

To change the line around the text, you must first select the line style and then identify what parts of the paragraph should contain the line.

Outside Border

6 On the Borders toolbar, click the Outside Border button.

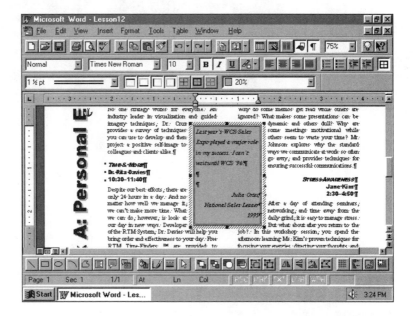

7 On the Formatting toolbar, click the Borders button to hide the Borders toolbar.

Preview the layout

Print Preview

1 On the Standard toolbar, click the Print Preview button.

2 Click the Magnifier button to deselect the Magnifier.

3 Click each framed item in turn to display the sizing handles. Then, with the four-headed arrow, drag to position each item on the page so that the document looks similar to the following illustration. Adjust the sizing and cropping, if necessary, to match the illustration.

Magnifier

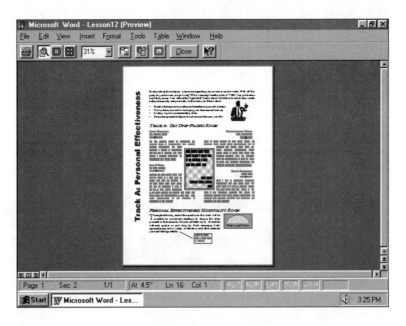

4   On the Print Preview toolbar, click the Close button to return to the document
    window.

Save and close the document

Save

1   On the Standard toolbar, click the Save button.
2   On the File menu, click Close.

One Step Further: Linking
Objects from Other Programs

As you saw earlier in this lesson, WordArt is an accessory program in which you can
create objects and insert them in your documents. However, there are many other objects
from Windows-based programs, such as Microsoft Excel worksheets or Microsoft Paint
graphics that you can insert into your documents. In addition, you can link a Microsoft
Word document to an object from other programs. Then, without ever leaving Microsoft
Word, you can double-click the object to quickly start the other program and modify the
object. The changes you make to the object are immediately reflected in the Microsoft
Word document.

Inserting and Linking Objects from Paint

The Winword SBS Practice folder contains a logo that was created using Paint (a drawing program provided with Microsoft Windows 95). You can insert this object in your document, and by linking it to Paint, you can modify the object while remaining in the Microsoft Word document.

Create a destination document

New

1   On the Standard toolbar, click the New button.

2   Type the following text, and then press ENTER three times.

    Here is the new logo for Great Kitchens Plus.

3   On the File menu, click Save As, and save the file with the name Logo Document12.

Insert a Paint object

1   On the Insert menu, click Object.

    The Object dialog box appears.

2   Click the Create From File tab.

    From this tab, you can enter the name of the file containing the object you want to insert.

3   Click the Browse button.

    Clicking the Browse button allows you to locate your file by file name and folder.

4   In the Winword SBS Practice folder, double-click the file called 12Logo.

5   When you return to the Object dialog box, click the Link to File check box.

    Selecting the Link To File option enables you to edit an object in its original program and see your changes reflected immediately in the Microsoft Word document.

6   Click the OK button to insert the object.

    The logo is inserted in the document.

Modify the Paint object

1   Double-click the logo in the document.

    The Paint program opens.

221

2 In the Paint window, on the color palette at the bottom of the window, click the light gray color.

3 On the tools palette at the left side of the window, click the Fill With Color tool.

Fill With Color

4 In the logo, click the pointer in the white cross.

The white cross changes to light gray. The color in the logo in the document also changes color. Drag the Paint window to the right side of the screen if you cannot see the logo in the Microsoft Word document window.

5 In the Paint window, click the Close button in the upper-right corner.

6 If a message appears asking if you want to save changes, click the No button.

7 On the File menu in Microsoft Word, click Close.

8 If a message appears asking if you want to save changes, click the Yes button.

Inserting and Linking Objects from Microsoft Excel

Using the Insert Object command is one way to insert and link objects from other programs into Microsoft Word; however, this method inserts the entire file. To set up an active link between only part of a file (such as a range of worksheet data), you can use a special version of the Paste command called Paste Special. With this command, you link an object (called the *source*) and the Microsoft Word document (called the *destination*). Then you can modify some of the data in the source worksheet and observe the changes in the destination document.

 TIP If you do not have Microsoft Excel installed on your computer, you can skip to the end of this lesson.

Create a destination document

New

1 On the Standard toolbar, click the New button.

2 Type the following text, and then press ENTER three times.

Below is a WCS budget summary for Q1 and Q2 of FY 1995.

3 On the File menu, click Save As, and save the file with the name Budget12.

4 Reduce the size of the Microsoft Word program window, and move it to the right half of the screen.

This will allow you to view both the source and the destination files at the same time.

Copy a source object

1   From the taskbar, start Microsoft Excel.

2   Open the file 12Worksheet in your Winword SBS Practice folder, and maximize the worksheet window within Microsoft Excel.

3   Save the file as Worksheet12.

4   Select the range A11 to E16 if it is not already selected.

This range contains the data that you want in your Microsoft Word document.

5   On the Edit menu, click Copy.

6   Reduce the Microsoft Excel window and move it to the left half of your screen. (It can partially overlap with the Microsoft Word window.)

 TIP   You can quickly set both windows side by side by using the right mouse button to click on a blank area in the taskbar, and then clicking Tile Vertically.

Link the object data from the source to the destination

1   Click in the Microsoft Word document, and be sure that the insertion point is two lines below the text.

2   On the Edit menu in Microsoft Word, click Paste Special.

The Paste Special dialog box appears.

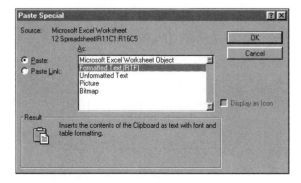

3   At the left side of the dialog box, click the Paste Link option button.

4   In the As list box, select Microsoft Excel Worksheet Object, and then click OK.

The copied portion of the worksheet appears in the Microsoft Word document, as shown in the following illustration.

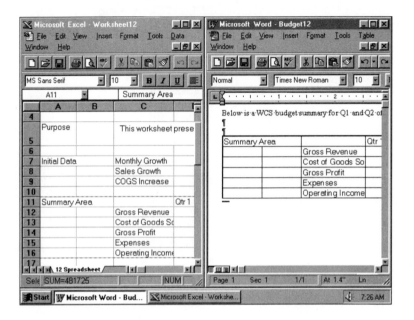

Modify the linked object

   TIP   If the source program is not running, you can usually open the program and the source document by double-clicking the destination object in the Microsoft Word document.

1   In the Microsoft Excel worksheet, select cell D12. Type **100000** and press ENTER.

2   Select cell E12. Type **150000** and press ENTER.

3   Select the Microsoft Word destination document.

The gross revenue numbers in the Microsoft Word document have been automatically updated, as shown in the following illustration.

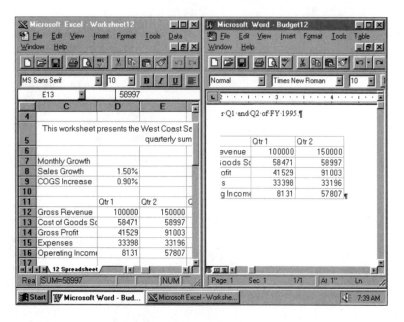

4 In Microsoft Excel, save the Worksheet12 file, and then exit the program.

If You Want to Continue to the Next Lesson

1 On the File menu in Microsoft Word, click Close.

2 If a message appears asking whether you want to save changes, click the Yes button.

If You Want to Quit Microsoft Word for Now

1 On the File menu in Microsoft Word, click Exit.

2 If a message appears asking whether you want to save changes, click the Yes button.

Lesson Summary

To	Do this
Insert a graphic	On the Insert menu, click Picture. Select the name of the graphic you want to insert.

To	Do this	Button
Size a graphic	Select the graphic. Drag the corner handles to size the graphic proportionately, or drag the middle handles to stretch the graphic.	
Display the Drawing toolbar	On the Standard toolbar, click the Drawing button.	
Frame and position a graphic	Select the object you want to position. On the Drawing toolbar, click the Insert Frame button. With the four-headed arrow, drag the item to position it on the page.	
Edit a graphic	Double-click the graphic in the document. The program in which the graphic was created opens so that you can edit the graphic. Exit the program to return to the document.	
Crop a graphic	Hold down the SHIFT key as you drag a sizing handle.	
Insert a drop cap as the first character in a paragraph	On the Format menu, click Drop Cap. In the Drop Cap dialog box, click the style of drop cap you want. Click the OK button to return to the document.	
Insert a callout	On the Drawing toolbar, click the Callout button. Drag to establish the position of the callout. Type text in the callout text box.	
Format a callout	On the Drawing toolbar, click the Format Callout button. In the dialog box, change settings for the position and orientation of the connecting line and text border.	
Start WordArt	On the Insert menu, click Object. Choose Microsoft WordArt 2.0.	
Create a WordArt object	Type the WordArt text into the dialog box. Click the Update Display button to make any changes in the text. Select the formatting options you want. Click in the document to exit WordArt.	

To	Do this	Button
Add shading to text	Select the text. On the Format menu, click Borders and Shading. Choose the Shading tab. In the Shading box, select the percent of shading that you want. You can also click the Shading box on the Borders toolbar.	
Display the Borders toolbar	On the Formatting toolbar, click the Borders button.	▦
Change the border of a framed text paragraph	Click the frame to select it. On the Format menu, click Borders And Shading. Under Line, click the type of line you want, and then click OK. *or* Click the frame to select it. On the Borders toolbar, select a line style from the Line Style drop-down list. Then click the Outside Border button.	▦
Link an object from Microsoft Excel	In the Microsoft Excel source file, copy the data you want to link. In the Microsoft Word document, position the insertion point, and then click Paste Special on the Edit menu. Select the options for Paste Link and for Microsoft Excel Worksheet Object, and then click OK.	

For online information about	Use the Answer Wizard to search for
Editing graphics	**editing graphics**, and then display Edit an embedded object
Positioning graphics and text on the page	**positioning text and graphics**, and then display Position a frame
Adding borders and shading	**borders and shading**, and then display Add borders and shading to paragraphs
Linking data between programs	**linking data**, and then display Exchanging information with other programs

Preview of the Next Lessons

The lessons in the next part of this book will show you how you can create special documents suitable for a variety of projects. For example, in the next lesson, you'll learn how to use outlining to organize large documents. In subsequent lessons, you'll learn how to locate and manage documents, create online forms, and merge form letters and labels.

Review & Practice

The lessons in Part 3 provided you with advanced skills to enhance your documents by adding tables and charts, creating multiple columns, adding graphics, and linking objects. If you want to practice these skills and test your understanding before you proceed with the lessons in Part 4, you can work through the Review & Practice section following this lesson. This less structured activity allows you to increase your confidence using many of the features introduced so far.

Review & Practice

Estimated time
35 min.

You will review and practice how to:

- Create a table and format it.
- Create a chart from a table.
- Create columns in a document.
- Use special effects with text, such as WordArt and drop caps.
- Use lines and shading to draw attention to important information in a frame.
- Modify graphics to enhance the appearance of the document.

In this Review & Practice, you have an opportunity to fine-tune the graphics and advanced layout skills you learned in Part 3 of this book. You will use what you have learned about creating and formatting tables and creating columns to develop an executive summary for West Coast Sales' quarterly report.

Scenario

After gathering information from various regions in the company, you have found two documents that contain the financial and product information you need for the executive summary. Your task is to enhance the appearance of these documents to give them greater impact.

Step 1: Create a Table and Format It

1 From your Winword SBS Practice folder, open the document called P3ReviewA.

2 Save the document as ReviewP3A.

3 With the insertion point in front of the existing paragraph mark under the heading "Financial Results," create a two-column table. Enter the following information:

Division	First Quarter
Outdoor Enterprises	22.8
Great Outdoors	17.1
Great Northern	16.3

4 Size the columns to make them narrower.

5 Add a new column in the table to report this quarter's results.

Division	Second Quarter
Outdoor Enterprises	32.4
Great Outdoors	17.9
Great Northern	18.6

6 Add a new row to the bottom of the table, and add the new division's second quarter results.

Great Kitchens PLUS	81.3

You can manually size the new column so that the text fits on one line, or you can use the AutoFit option when you use the Table AutoFormat command in the next step.

7 Add borders and shading to the table using the Table AutoFormat command from the Table menu. Select any formatting option you want. If you have not already sized the new column manually, you can select the AutoFit check box to automatically adjust the column width to fit the text in the cells.

8 Add a new row to the beginning of the table (above the current column headings), merge the cells in the new row, and give your table the title **Second Quarter Results (in Thousands)**. Add new borders as necessary to the merged row, and then center the table title.

9 Change all text in the table to 14-point Arial.

10 Adjust the column widths so that the table spans the width of the margins.

For more information on	See
Creating tables	Lesson 10
Formatting tables	Lesson 10

Step 2: Create a Chart from the Table

1 Select the data in the table, and then click the Object command on the Insert menu. Then select Microsoft Graph 5.0. Using the ChartWizard, accept the default selections. For the title of the chart, type **Second Quarter Results**.

2 Size the chart so that the labels break appropriately.

3 Crop any white space from the left side of the chart.

4 Click in the document window to close Microsoft Graph and update the chart.

For more information on	See
Creating charts	Lesson 10

Step 3: Add a Frame to the Chart and to Text

1 Using the picture at the end of these steps as a guide, frame the chart and position it above the table, as shown in the illustration.

2 Add a frame around the paragraph at the end of the document, which begins "This Executive Summary."

3 Using the Borders And Shading command from the Format menu, create a Shadow box around the text.

4 Use the Shading drop-down list on the Borders toolbar to apply a 10 percent shading pattern to the framed text.

5 Center the text in the box.

6 Size the framed text so that the frame is about 1½ inches wide and 2 inches high.

7 Position the framed text beneath the company logo, as shown in the following illustration.

West Coast Sales
Quarterly Report
Executive Summary

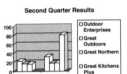

Second quarter at West Coast Sales ™ exceeded expectations of market analysts, as well as company officers. We achieved significant gains in all divisions, particularly in the Outdoor Enterprises Division. Every employee can be proud of these results.

This Executive Summary provides a financial and product overview of the information included in the Quarterly Report. Please review the enclosed Quarterly Report to get all the details.

Financial Results

Second Quarter Results (in Thousands)		
Division	First Quarter	Second Quarter
Outdoor Enterprises	22.8	32.4
Great Outdoors	17.1	17.9
Great Northern	16.3	18.6
Great Kitchens Plus		81.3

Second Quarter Results

- Outdoor Enterprises
- Great Outdoors
- Great Northern
- Great Kitchens Plus

For more information on	See
Adding a frame	Lesson 12
Shading and border	Lesson 12

Step 4: *Create Columns in a Document*

1 From your Winword SBS Practice folder, open the document called P3ReviewB, and save it as ReviewP3B.

2 Select the first line of text in the report (below the heading), and create a Shadow box as you did in Step 3 of this Review & Practice (you do not need to frame it first).

3 With the insertion point at the beginning of the heading "Exciting New Products," insert a continuous section break.

4 With the insertion point at the beginning of the heading "Outdoor Enterprises Division," insert another continuous section break.

5 With the insertion point below the section break and at the beginning of the heading "Outdoor Enterprises Division," format the text into two columns.

6 Insert a column break in front of the heading "Great Northern Division."

For more information on	See
Adding section breaks	Lesson 11
Creating columns	Lesson 11

Step 5: *Create Special Effects with Text*

1 Use WordArt to create a special effect for the heading "Exciting New Products."

Use the picture at the end of Step 6 as a guide. If the heading is not centered over the bulleted list after you exit WordArt, make sure that the WordArt object is selected, and click the Center button.

2 Add a 2-line drop cap to each of the headings in section 3.

For more information on	See
Using WordArt	Lesson 12
Inserting drop caps	Lesson 12

Step 6: *Modify Graphics*

1 Double-click the West Coast Sales logo, and then double-click the semi-circle in the logo to change the color. Return to the document.

Your final report should look similar to the following illustration.

West Coast Sales
Quarterly Report
Product Summary

West Coast Sales

This report summarizes our products by division, and our exciting new line of offerings.

Exciting New Products

- D-Lux Daiquiri Blender
- Instant Potato Masher
- Big Plaid Grill Covers
- D-Lux DomeHome

Outdoor Enterprises Division

This division focuses on the domestic (that is, stay-at-home) outdoor furnishings. Its market is typically people who entertain at home. Led by Mark Johnson, earnings increased 42% over last quarter.

- Upscale families
- Empty nesters

Great Outdoors Division

This division also targets upscale individuals and families, with particular emphasis on those who enjoy camping and travel. Products are designed for rugged use. Led by Julia Jung, earnings increased 5% over last quarter.

- Families
- Active empty nesters

Great Northern Division

This division brings all the fun and excitement of the Outdoor Enterprises division indoors. Comfortable indoor furnishings for family rooms, dens, and cabins span across all markets. Led by Angela Martinez, earnings increased 14% over last quarter.

- Professionals
- Families

Great Kitchens PLUS

This new division brings the Great Northern concept to the kitchen and dining areas. This comfortable, cozy look is enhanced with the latest labor-saving devices. Led by Henri Robert, projected earnings for next quarter are expected to be in excess of 17%.

- Professionals
- Families

2 If the Borders toolbar or Drawing toolbar still appears in your program window, select Toolbars from the View menu, and deselect the toolbar.

If You Want to Continue to the Next Lesson

1 On the File menu, click Close.

2 If a message appears asking whether you want to save changes, click the Yes button.

If You Want to Quit Microsoft Word for Now

1 On the File menu, click Exit.

2 If a message appears asking whether you want to save changes, click the Yes button.

Developing Special Project Documents

Part 4

13

Organizing a Document with Outlining

In this lesson you will learn how to:

Estimated time
35 min.

- Switch to outline view.
- Use the Outlining toolbar to promote and demote headings.
- View only selected heading levels and body text.
- Rearrange blocks of text by moving headings.
- Add numbering to an outline.

When you work with a document that is several pages long and contains many different topics or that has a hierarchical structure (with main topics and subtopics), you will find Microsoft Word's outlining feature a valuable tool. In this lesson, you will display a document in outline view to promote and demote heading levels. You will also learn how to view only specific levels of the document and reorganize your document quickly by moving headings. In addition, you will learn how to apply an outline numbering scheme to outlined text.

Start the lesson

Follow the steps below to open the practice file called 13Lesson, and then save it with the new name Lesson13.

1   On the Standard toolbar, click the Open button.

Open

2   In the Look In box, be sure that the Winword SBS Practice folder appears.

3 In the file list box, double-click the file named 13Lesson to open it.

4 On the File menu, click Save As.

To select the folder containing your practice files, refer to "Open a practice file" near the start of Lesson 2.

The Save As dialog box opens. Be sure that the Winword SBS Practice folder appears in the Save In box.

5 Select and delete any text in the File Name box, and then type **Lesson13**

6 Click the Save button, or press ENTER.

If you share your computer with others who use Microsoft Word, the screen display might have changed since your last lesson. If your screen does not look similar to the illustrations as you work through this lesson, see the Appendix, "Matching the Exercises."

Working in Outline View

To use the Microsoft Word outline feature, you need to display your document in *outline view.* The fastest way to switch between views, including outline view, is to click the view buttons just above the status bar.

Switch to outline view

Outline View

➤ Click the Outline View button located to the left of the horizontal scroll bar.

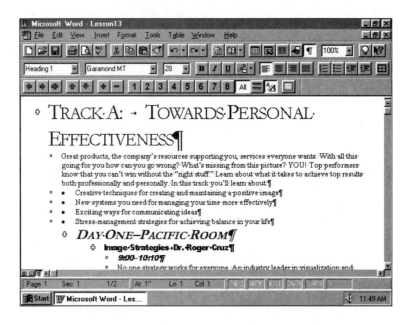

When you are in outline view, the Outlining toolbar appears below the other toolbars already displayed. Here is an overview of the buttons on the Outlining toolbar.

To	Use these buttons
Promote and demote headings	
Demote heading to body text	
Move heading and associated subheadings and text up or down one line	
Expand a heading to reveal its subordinate subheadings and associated text	
Collapse a heading to hide its subordinate subheadings and associated text	
Show all levels through the selected level	1 2 3 4 5 6 7 8 All
Show only the first line of body text in a paragraph. This button toggles to display all lines	
Show outline with or without formatting	
Display Master Document toolbar	

Display formatting

Show Formatting

➤ On the Outlining toolbar, click the Show Formatting button if it is not already selected.

Character formatting for the document is displayed. When the headings and body text are in different fonts, you can more easily distinguish headings from the rest of the document.

Understanding Outline View

When you first display your document in outline view, text that is formatted in a heading style and that also contains additional headings under it appears with an outline symbol (a plus sign) next to it. A minus sign next to a heading indicates that there are no sub-headings under it. Lower-level headings appear indented under higher-level headings. Text that is not formatted with a heading style is called body text and appears with a small square next to it. In an outline, text is associated with the preceding heading, so you can work with *blocks* of information. The following illustration identifies what you see in outline view.

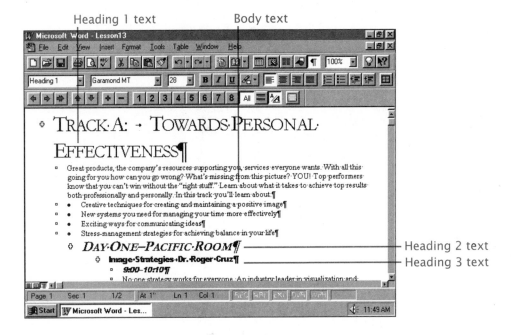

Outline view shows that the text "Track A: Towards Personal Effectiveness" is already assigned an outline heading. When you select the heading, the Style box on the Formatting toolbar indicates that this is Heading 1. The text "Day One–Pacific Room" is assigned Heading 2. The text "Image Strategies Dr. Roger Cruz" is assigned Heading 3. These headings already have heading styles applied to them, and this outline reflects that structure. The remaining text you see in the window is body text. Any text not formatted in a heading style is identified as body text in the outline and is usually indented under its heading. Text in a table, however, is not indented.

Promoting and Demoting Headings

In outline view, you can quickly change the heading levels. You can either promote a heading to a higher level or demote it to a lower level. When you promote or demote a heading, any subordinate subheadings and text are likewise affected. You can change body text to a heading level in the same way you promote or demote a heading. You can also change a heading level to body text with the Demote To Body Text button.

Promote headings

To organize this document, use the Promote and Demote buttons to establish a hierarchical structure for the remaining topics.

Promote

1 Click the heading "Track B: Serving Up Hot Technologies," and then click the Promote button on the Outlining toolbar.

This text is promoted from Heading 2 to Heading 1.

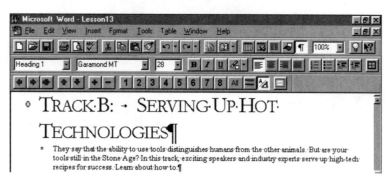

You can also drag the outline symbol to the left, to promote a heading, or to the right, to demote a heading.

2 Scroll downward, and select the text "Technology Center."

You can also place the insertion point anywhere in the line that you want to promote.

3 Click the Promote button to promote this text to Heading 2.

4 Scroll downward, and place the insertion point in the text "WCS SST System."

5 Click the Promote button twice to promote this text to Heading 3.

Your outline looks like the following illustration.

Demote headings

When you want to change an existing heading level to a lower level, use the Demote button on the Outlining toolbar. Using the Demote To Body Text button, you can change a heading to body text.

Demote

1 Click the text "Day One – Atlantic Room."

2 On the Outlining toolbar, click the Demote button to demote this text to Heading 2.

3 Click the text "Throughout the day..."

Demote To Body Text

4 On the Outlining toolbar, click the Demote To Body Text button.

This text is now body text. Your outline looks like the following illustration.

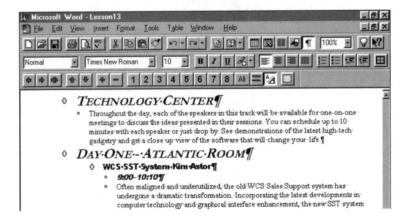

Viewing Specific Parts of the Outline

A major benefit of using outline view is that you can focus on only those parts of the document that are important to you at the moment. For example, to get the "big picture," you can display only Headings 1 and 2 and hide all the subheadings and text that are subordinate. When you are ready to focus on the details of a topic, you can view lower level headings and body text. You also have the option to see all the body text or only the first line of each paragraph.

Viewing Specified Heading Levels

When you want to focus on the higher level structure of your document or work on overview information, you might want to see only the first two or three heading levels. When you click a heading button on the Outlining toolbar, you see only those headings through the level you select. You can click any heading level button that corresponds to the level of detail you want to see. For example, if you click the Show Heading 3 button, you see heading levels 1, 2, and 3.

View first-level headings

You can click the Show Heading 1 button to get the highest level view of your document. This is useful when you want to focus on only the major elements in your document.

Show Heading 1

➤ Scroll to the beginning of the document, and click the Show Heading 1 button on the Outlining toolbar.

Your document looks like the following illustration.

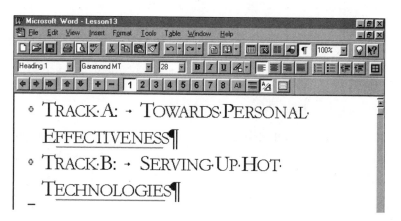

View the first three heading levels

Use lower level settings when you want to focus on specific details or individual topics in your document. Viewing only a few levels helps you see the overall structure and organization of your document without seeing more text than you need.

Show Heading 3

➤ On the Outlining toolbar, click the Show Heading 3 button.

Your document looks like the following illustration.

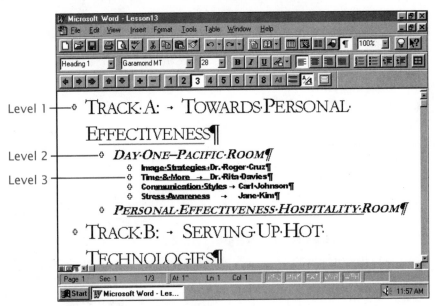

View all heading levels and body text

When you want to see all the information in your document, you can click the Show All button on the Outlining toolbar.

Show All

➤ On the Outlining toolbar, click the Show All button.

All heading levels and text in your document are displayed.

View two heading levels

Show Heading 2

➤ On the Outlining toolbar, click the Show Heading 2 button.

The first two levels in your document are displayed.

Expanding and Collapsing Headings

The heading level buttons on the Outlining toolbar affect the number of heading levels displayed for the entire outline. When you want to display more (or fewer) heading levels under a single heading, you can *collapse* or *expand* headings. The Expand and Collapse buttons on the Outlining toolbar display (or hide) subordinate headings and text of the heading containing the insertion point.

Expand a heading

You can use the Expand button to see more detail about a topic in your document. Click the button repeatedly until you see all the subordinate text.

1 Scroll downward, and place the insertion point in the heading "Day One – Atlantic Room."

Expand

2 On the Outlining toolbar, click the Expand button.

The next level of subheading under this heading is displayed.

3 Click the Expand button again so that all subordinate text and headings are displayed.

The other headings in the document remain collapsed.

TIP You can also double-click the outline symbol to expand and collapse headings. Double-clicking the outline symbol for an already expanded heading collapses the heading, while double-clicking the outline symbol for an already collapsed heading expands the heading.

Collapse a heading

Use the Collapse button to hide details for this topic in your document.

Collapse

> With the insertion point still in the heading "Day One – Atlantic Room," click the Collapse button on the Outlining toolbar.

The lowest level of subheadings and text under this heading are hidden.

Viewing Body Text

When you display body text in outline view, you can specify how much of the body text you want to see. You can choose to see all the body text, which is useful for editing. Or you can choose to see only the first line of individual paragraphs of body text, which is useful for helping you recall the content of a paragraph without displaying all of the text.

Display the first line of body text

The Show First Line Only button on the toolbar toggles to display the first line of a paragraph or to display all body text. For example, when all the body text is displayed, clicking this button hides all but the first line of text. When you click it again, all the text reappears.

Expand

Show First Line Only

1 With the insertion point still in the heading "Day One – Atlantic Room," click the Expand button.

2 On the Outlining toolbar, click the Show First Line Only button.

Only the first line of text in each paragraph appears.

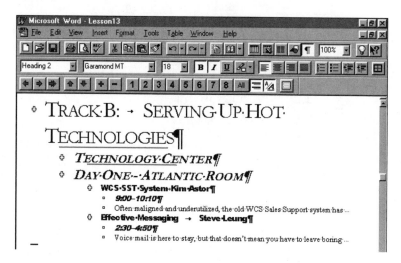

Moving Blocks of Text

Using outline view to reorganize a document ensures that all the text associated with a collapsed heading stays together as you move text around in your document. You can rearrange large blocks of text in your document without selecting all the text you want to move. You also avoid having to move your text over a long distance. In outline view, when you move a collapsed heading, all the subordinate headings and text move with the heading. If you select an expanded heading, however, only the selected text moves.

Move a block of text

To move a block of text in an outline, you collapse the heading so that all the subordinate headings are hidden. Then you use the buttons on the Outlining toolbar to move the heading up or down one line at a time. When you move the heading, the subordinate headings and body text move as well.

Show Heading 2

Move Down

Show First Line Only

Expand

You can also drag the outline symbol for the heading you want to move.

1 On the Outlining toolbar, click the Show Heading 2 button.

2 Select the heading "Technology Center."

3 On the Outlining toolbar, click the Move Down button to move the selected heading after the heading "Day One – Atlantic Room."

4 Click the Expand button, and then click the Show First Line Only button to see that all the subordinate text also moved.

Your outline looks like the following illustration.

Show Heading 3

Show All

5 On the Outlining toolbar, click the Show Heading 3 button.

6 Select the headings "Making Contact" and "Off-Site Tools."

7 On the Outlining toolbar, click the Move Down button twice.

Both headings move down together in the document.

8 On the Outlining toolbar, click the Show All button to display all of the document text.

Your completed outline looks like the following illustration.

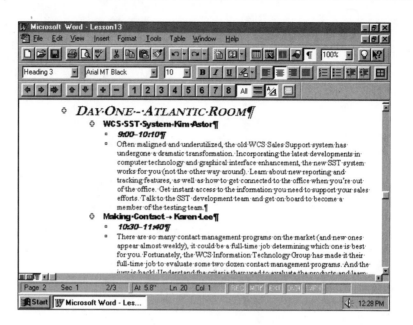

Adding Outline Numbering

Another way to reflect a hierarchical structure in your document is to apply an outline numbering scheme (I, A, 1.) to your headings, as in a report, manual, or legal document. After working in outline view to arrange text and establish your headings, you can use the Heading Numbering command to select (or modify) a numbering scheme you want to use. If you continue to rearrange headings in your outline, Microsoft Word updates the numbering sequence to reflect the new structure.

Apply outline numbering

1 On the Format menu, click Heading Numbering.

In the Heading Numbering dialog box, you can select the numbering scheme you want to use.

2 Click the first numbering option to apply the standard outline numbering scheme.

3 Click the OK button to close the dialog box and return to your document.

The headings are now formatted with the outline numbering scheme.

4 Scroll to the top of the document and, on the Outlining toolbar, click the Show Heading 3 button.

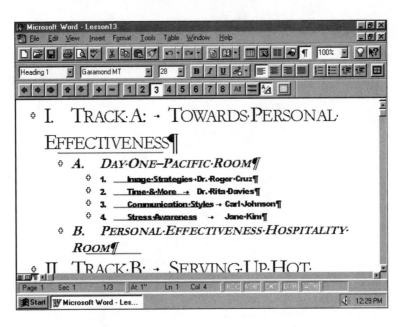

Normal View

5   Click the Normal View button next to the horizontal scroll bar and scroll through the document to view the formatting you applied in outline view.

One Step Further: Creating a Table of Contents

An added benefit of using outline view to organize your document is that assigning heading levels also applies heading styles to the text. With heading styles (such as Heading 1 and Heading 2) applied to the text, Microsoft Word makes it easy to create a table of contents for your document. When you choose the Index And Tables command on the Insert menu, you can create a table of contents that includes the range of heading levels you specify.

Create a new section for the table of contents

You will insert a table of contents at the beginning of the document. Because you want the first topic to appear on page 1, not on page 2, you can also insert a new-page section break between the table of contents and the rest of the document.

1   Make sure the insertion point is positioned before the title at the top of the document.

2   On the Insert menu, click Break.

3   Click Next Page to begin section two on the next page.

4   Click the OK button to return to the document.

5   Click in section one, and then in the Style drop-down list, click Body text.

250

Specify a starting page number for section two

1 Click in section two, and then click Page Numbers on the Insert menu.

2 Click the Format button, and then type **1** in the Start At box.

3 Click the OK button to return to the Page Numbers dialog box.

4 Click the OK button to return to your document.

With the page numbering format set for the document, you are ready to insert a table of contents in section 1.

Create a table of contents

Creating a table of contents is easy when you base the table of contents on heading styles you created in outline view.

1 Click in section one of the document.

2 On the Insert menu, click Index And Tables.

3 Click the Table Of Contents tab to display the table of contents options.

4 Click the Options button.

5 Be sure that the Styles check box is selected.

6 Click the OK button to return to the Table Of Contents tab.

7 Select the Classic style.

You can select and preview the other table of contents styles if you want.

8 Click the OK button to return to the document and generate a table of contents.

Your table of contents appears at the beginning of the document.

If You Want to Continue to the Next Lesson

1 On the File menu, click Close.

2 If a message appears asking whether you want to save changes, click the Yes button.

If You Want to Quit Microsoft Word for Now

1 On the File menu, click Exit.

2 If a message appears asking whether you want to save changes, click the Yes button.

Lesson Summary

To	Do this	Button
Display the document in outline view	Click the Outline View button next to the horizontal scroll bar.	
Promote or demote a heading	Click the Promote or Demote button.	
Demote a heading to body text	Click the Demote To Body Text button.	
Display specific headings for the entire document	Click the heading level button that corresponds to the headings you want to see.	
Hide subheadings and text for selected headings	Select the heading, and click the Collapse button.	
Display subheadings and text for selected headings	Select the heading, and click the Expand button.	
Display all headings and body text	Click the Show All button.	
Toggle the display to show the first line or all lines of body text	Expand the heading, and click the Show First Line Only button.	
Move a collapsed heading	Select the heading, and click the Move Up or Move Down button to move one line at a time.	
Set page numbers	On the Insert menu, click Page Numbers. Click the Format button, and type the starting page number in the Start At box.	
Create a table of contents	Place the insertion point where you want the table of contents to appear. On the Insert menu, click Index And Tables. Select the Table Of Contents tab. Click the Options button, and select any desired options. Click OK. Select a format for the table, and then click OK.	

For online information about	Use the Answer Wizard to search for
Outlining	**outlining**, and then display Organizing a document in outline view

Preview of the Next Lesson

In the next lesson, you'll learn efficient ways to manage your documents and work with several documents open at once. Microsoft Word provides easy ways to search for documents even if you have forgotten what you've named them. You will also learn a fast way to copy files into a new folder and to open more than one file at a time.

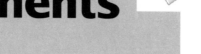
Managing Your Documents

Estimated time
25 min.

In this lesson you will learn how to:

- Search for a partial filename.
- Search for text in a document.
- Search for summary information.
- Copy documents to a folder.
- Open multiple documents at once.

After creating many documents, it can often be a challenge to locate and retrieve documents when you need them again. In this lesson, you learn to search for files three different ways. First, you will search for files when you know only a portion of the filename. Next, you'll search for a file by specifying a word that the file contains. Finally, you will search for files based on information in the Properties dialog box. You'll also learn how to copy multiple files to a folder and open two files simultaneously.

Searching for Documents

The search features in the Open dialog box give you the flexibility to locate a document even if you don't know its name or much else about it. For example, if you remember only part of the name of the document, you can search for that document by the part of the name you can remember. From the Open dialog box, you can learn a file's location, display its contents, and view other information about the file without opening it. You can also perform file-management tasks such as opening, printing, copying, and deleting one or more files.

In addition, by clicking the Advanced button in the Open dialog box, you can also locate a document by searching for almost any information you can recall—or guess—about the document. For example, you can click the Advanced button to find a document that contains a phrase, such as "annual income," or to search for documents based on information in the Properties dialog box, such as the title, subject, author, manager, as well as the date it was last saved, created, or modified.

Display the Open dialog box

➤ On the File menu, click Open.

In the Open dialog box, you see information about any previous search criteria.

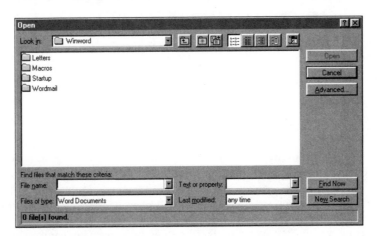

Specifying a Search Path

The *path* is the sequence of drives and folders in which Microsoft Word will search for documents. The path displayed in the Look In box of the Open and Advanced Find dialog boxes is the current search path.

Specify the search path

If you exited Microsoft Word at the end of the previous lesson, you will need to change the search path so that Microsoft Word searches for documents in the Winword SBS Practice folder. If you are continuing directly from the previous lesson, the correct search path is probably already displayed, but you can follow these steps to learn how you can change the search path when necessary.

1   In the Open dialog box, click the New Search button to remove any existing search criteria from the dialog box.

2   Click the Look In Favorites button.

3   Double-click the Winword SBS Practice folder.

    Microsoft Word will begin its search in the Winword SBS Practice folder.

Using Wildcards to Specify Part of a Filename

Now that you've identified where to search, you need to specify what you want to search for. Suppose you want to locate a document, but you cannot recall its exact filename and the filename is not immediately visible in the Open dialog box. Instead of scrolling through the list, attempting to recall the name of the file, you can enter only as much of the name as you can remember, and use a *wildcard*—or placeholder—for the rest of the name.

Search using a partial filename

You can use the asterisk (*) wildcard character to represent any character at either the start or end of a filename.

1   In the File Name box, type **Track***

    This search will locate documents whose file names start with "Track" and end with anything else, such as "Tracking," "Track Star," or "Tracked."

2   In the Files of Type box, be sure that Word Documents is selected.

    The dialog box should look similar to the following illustration. Depending on your particular configuration of drives and folders, the exact path you see might be different.

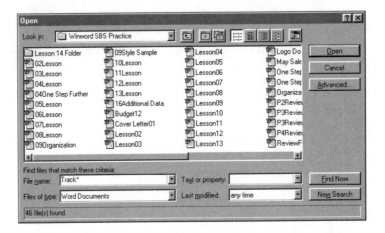

3   Click the Find Now button to begin the search.

Microsoft Word displays a list of the files that match the criterion you specified in the Open dialog box.

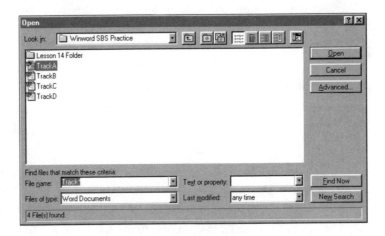

Display the search path

Preview

▶   In the Open dialog box, click the Preview button.

The contents of the first file in the list are displayed, along with the current search path.

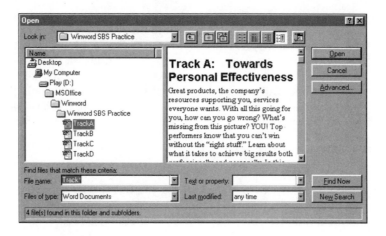

 TIP If the current path is not displayed, click the Command And Settings button, and be sure that Search Subfolders and Group Files By Folder are both selected.

Specifying Advanced Search Criteria

In the Advanced Find dialog box, you can specify additional information for which you want to search. The information you use to locate a document—filename, author, subject, and so on—is called the *search criteria*. Each time you change the search criteria, a list of the files that meet the new criteria appear in the Open dialog box. The criteria remain active until you change them.

Suppose a co-worker wants to locate any documents that refer to the "Bonus Bucks" promotion. You do not know the file names or authors, or even when the documents were written, but you guess that the materials contain the words "Bonus Bucks." That's all you need to know to search for the files.

Search based on the contents of a file

The Open dialog box still contains the information you used in your last search. In this exercise, you clear the previous search information and use instead the new search criterion—"Bonus Bucks."

TIP Unless you want to combine existing criteria with new criteria you are about to create, it is a good idea to click the New Search button in the Open dialog box. This ensures that any existing criteria are not used in your search for documents. If you do not click New Search, any additional criteria you specify will be added to the existing search; as a result, the two criteria will be combined, making the resulting search even more restrictive.

1 In the Open dialog box, click the New Search button.

2 Click the Advanced button.

In the Advanced Find dialog box, you can specify search criteria based on information in the Properties dialog box for a document or based on text in the document itself.

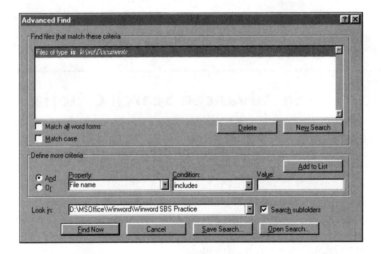

3 In the Property list box, click Contents.

4 In the Value box, type **Bonus Bucks**

5 Click the Add to List button.

6 Click the Match Case check box.

This option ensures that Microsoft Word searches for "Bonus Bucks" as a proper noun. The Advanced Find dialog box looks like the following illustration.

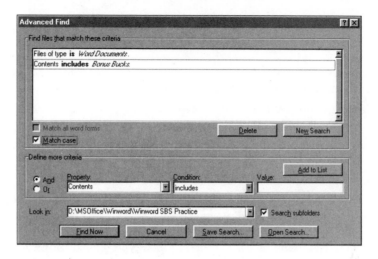

7 Click the Find Now button.

Microsoft Word closes the Advanced Find dialog box and displays the names of any files that contain the word "Bonus Bucks" in the Open dialog box. The list should include 07Lesson and 02Lesson.

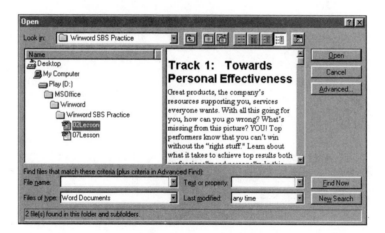

Searching for Files with Summary Information

Several types of search criteria are stored as part of each file—the filename, text, the date a file was created, the date a file was last saved, and even the author's name as it was entered when you set up Microsoft Word. But you also have the option to provide additional information about your document when you save a file.

You can provide the optional information in the Properties dialog box. If you fill in the dialog box when you save the file, later you can search for the file based on the information you provided—a title of the document, a description of the subject, or keywords that remind you of the file. You can type as many as 255 characters, including spaces and punctuation, for each category of information.

The documents you used in this lesson have several types of information stored on the Summary tab in the Properties dialog box, including:

Title   The title of the active document. Be sure to enter enough descriptive text to make it easy for you to remember.

Subject   A description of the document's contents.

Author   By default, the name assigned to your copy of the Microsoft Word program during setup. You can change the author for the active document by typing a new name. You can change the author for all future documents by choosing Options on the Tools menu, selecting the User Info tab, and then typing a new name in the Name box.

Keywords   General topics in the document or other important information, such as client names and account numbers.

Comments   Comments are notes you type to yourself or to a co-worker.

In addition to these fields, you can also enter the company name and the name of the manager for whom you are working on this document.

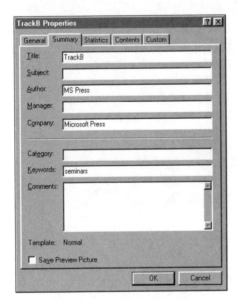

Search using a keyword

Included in the Step by Step practice files are documents that contain information about seminars for the WCS Sales Expo. When the documents were created, the word "seminars" was entered as a keyword. In this exercise, you specify a search criterion based on this keyword.

1   In the Open dialog box, click the New Search button.
2   Click the Advanced button.
3   In the Property list box, scroll down and click Keywords.
4   In the Value box, type **seminars**
5   Click the Add to List button.
6   Click the Find Now button to start the search.

Microsoft Word locates the files Track B and Track D because they have the keyword "seminars" on the Summary tab in the Properties dialog box. The first page of the first document appears in the Preview window.

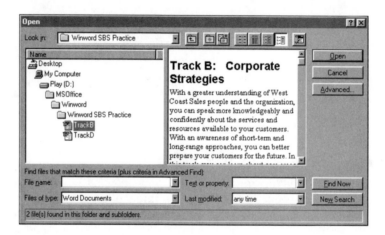

Viewing Other Information

The buttons in the Open dialog box include other kinds of information you can get about a document in the file list. In addition to the Preview button, you can click Details to see information about the file, including its name, size, type, and date the document was last saved. You can also click the Properties button to view information about the document.

View file information

You can click the Details button when knowing the size of the file or the date it was last saved will better help you identify the document. The Details button also displays the folder organization and paths of the files.

Details

> In the Open dialog box, click the Details button.
>
> If the columns are not wide enough to display the file size or the entire date, position the pointer over the column heading borders, and with the double-headed arrow, drag to adjust column widths.
>
> The dialog box should look similar to the following illustration.

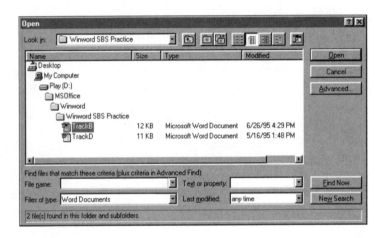

View summary information

To edit the information in the Properties dialog box, click the Commands And Settings button, and then click Properties on the drop-down menu.

You can click the Properties button to display information about the document from the Properties dialog box. You also see the number of times the document was revised, the application in which it was created, and the size of the document in terms of number of pages, words, characters, the amount of disk space, lines, and paragraphs. You can use this option when you need these details to help you identify the document.

> In the Open dialog box, click the Properties button.
>
> The Open dialog box looks like the following illustration.

Properties

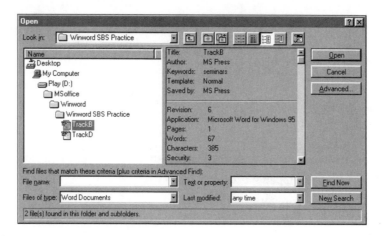

Working with Multiple Files

In this lesson, you've used only one of the many capabilities of the Open dialog box. In addition to searching for files, you can open, print, copy to another folder, or delete more than one file at a time. You can select the filenames from the list and choose the appropriate option from the Commands and Settings button. Or, from the shortcut menu, you can display by using the right mouse button.

Copy multiple files

In this exercise, you select two files to copy, paste them into a different folder, and then open both files at once.

To select a group of files listed together, select the first file. Then hold down SHIFT, and select the last file. The first and last files you clicked, and all files in between are selected.

1 In the Open dialog box, select the document Track B.

2 Hold down the CTRL key, and select the document Track D.

To select two or more filenames at once, you first select one filename, and then hold down CTRL while you select additional filenames.

3 Point to a selected file, and then press the right mouse button to display a shortcut menu.

4 Click Copy.

5 Click the Commands And Settings button, and then clear the Search Subfolders option.

6 Double-click the folder called Lesson 14 Folder, located under the Winword SBS Practice folder.

7 Point in the Name box, and use the right mouse button to click Paste.

The copied files are pasted into this folder.

265

NOTE If you see the Confirm File Replace dialog box, click Yes To All only if you are sure that it is okay to replace existing files that have the same names.

Open multiple files

1 Select the document TrackB.

2 Hold down the CTRL key, and select the document TrackD.

3 Click the Open button.

Both documents are now open.

4 Click the Window menu.

Both filenames appear in the open document list at the bottom of the Window menu, as shown in the following illustration.

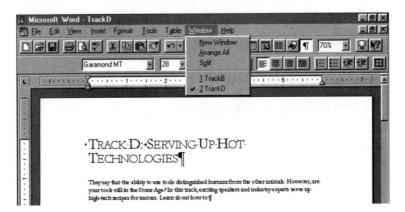

5 Click anywhere in the document window to close the menu.

6 Press CTRL+F6 to alternate displaying the two documents.

Display two documents at once

With two documents open at once, you can display them at the same time using the Arrange All command on the Window menu. Then you can scroll through both documents independently. With both documents displayed, you can use drag-and-drop techniques to copy information from one document to another.

1 On the Window menu, click Arrange All.

The document window is split into two windows. Each one contains a document. You can scroll through each window independently.

2 Scroll through the document called Track D, and select the sentence that begins "Employees who sign up."

This text is the last sentence in the document.

3 Point to the selected text. Then hold down the CTRL key, and drag the selected text to the Track B document in the other window.

4 With the insertion point at the end of the document, release the mouse.

The selected text is copied to the document.

 NOTE Be careful where you place the pointer prior to releasing the mouse button. If the tip of the arrow is near the top or bottom of the displayed portion of the document, the window will scroll too rapidly in the respective direction.

One Step Further: Creating a New Folder

You can quickly organize your documents in new folders without leaving the Microsoft Word program. For example, when saving a new document, you might realize that the document belongs in a new folder that you have not yet created. You can create a new folder from the Save As dialog box. Then, when you save the new document, it will be stored in the new folder.

Create a new folder while saving a document

1 On the File menu, click Save As.

The Save As dialog box appears.

2 Click the Create New Folder button to create a new folder.

The New Folder dialog box appears. In this dialog box, you can enter the name you want for the new folder.

3 Type **Folder 14** followed by *<your initials>*.

For example, if your initials are D J S, type **Folder 14 DJS**. Giving the folder this name ensures that you will not overwrite a folder already created by someone else working through this book.

4 Click the OK button to return to the Save As dialog box. Double-click the folder you just created, and then click the Save button to save the current document in the new folder.

If You Want to Continue to the Next Lesson

1 To close each document, on the File menu, click Close.

2 If a message appears asking whether you want to save changes, click the Yes button.

3 Repeat steps 1 and 2 to close the other document.

If You Want to Quit Microsoft Word for Now

1 On the File menu, click Exit.

2 If a message appears asking whether you want to save changes, click the Yes button.

Lesson Summary

To	Do this
Find a file	On the File menu, click Open. If the path is not what you want, select the drives and folders you want to search. Specify the filename or any portion of it along with wildcards. Click Advanced, and specify any advanced search criteria, such as keywords or author. Click the Find Now button.
Select multiple filenames	On the File menu, click Open. Search, if necessary, to display the filenames you want to use. Hold down the CTRL key, and click to select the files you want. If you accidentally select a filename that you do not want, hold down CTRL and click the filename again to remove the highlighting.
Open multiple files at once	On the File menu, click Open. Search, if necessary, to display the filenames of the files you want to open. Select the filenames, and click the Open button.
Display two files at once	On the Window menu, click Arrange All.

For online information about	Use the Answer Wizard to search for
Searching for files	**files**, and then display Finding, opening, and managing documents

Preview of the Next Lesson

In the next lesson, you'll learn to create an attractive, easy-to-complete online form. With an online form, you can supply choices of answers and easy-to-use selection options to ensure that the form is easy to complete. Plus, a form completed online is always legible—you never have to decipher someone's illegible handwriting. After you create a simple form, you will enter information in it.

Working with Forms

Estimated time
35 min.

In this lesson you will learn how to:

- Create a form template.
- Insert text fields, drop-down lists, and check boxes for easy data entry.
- Protect a form for online completion.
- Enter information in an online form.

Paper forms are often known for being difficult to complete and sometimes difficult to read after they are completed. An online form minimizes many of the disadvantages of paper forms. With Microsoft Word, you can design an online form to ensure that your forms are completed quickly and accurately.

In this lesson, you'll combine many of the features you have learned about in this book—tables, templates, frames, and borders—to create an online form, that is, a form you can fill in as a Microsoft Word document. After you create an online form, you will complete the form so that it looks similar to the following illustration.

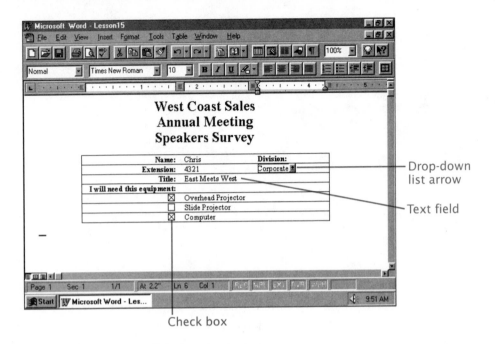

Drop-down list arrow

Text field

Check box

Understanding Online Forms

You are probably already familiar with many different kinds of paper forms: purchase order forms, expense forms, tax forms, and so on. Although there are forms too numerous to mention, they all have a few things in common:

- All forms contain both text and blank areas, or *fields*, for entering information.

- Text and fields are usually arranged in a grid, allowing space for individuals to enter information in the fields.

- Paper forms are usually known for being difficult to complete ("What am I supposed to enter here?") and, in the case of forms completed by hand, difficult to decipher ("Is this a 'one' or an 'L'?") after they are completed.

An online form minimizes many of the disadvantages of paper forms. With Microsoft Word, you can design an online form to display instructions that guide people through the process of completing the form. Your online form can also contain text fields of either a fixed length or an unlimited length. A drop-down list field provides a list of options from which the user can choose. For "yes" or "no" responses, you can create check box fields in which the user can place an "X" by clicking in the box. To make the form even easier to complete, you can also specify the "default" answer in specific fields.

Because a user completes your form online, you don't need to try to decipher someone's handwriting. In addition, if your computer is connected to a network, online forms can be completed and shared in the same way you share other documents, possibly eliminating the need for paper forms entirely.

Creating an Online Form

You create a form by first creating a template. This template contains the arrangement of text and fields you want for your form. You specify the types of fields you want and format the form. Finally, before you save the template, you protect the form elements so that when people complete the form they change only the information in the fields and not the text or format of the form.

Suppose you have been asked to help coordinate speakers for an upcoming annual company meeting. You need to create a form in which the speakers complete a short survey.

Create an online form

If you are continuing from Lesson 14, you might need to maximize the document window. Before you begin this exercise, click the Maximize button in the document window so that the document window appears full size.

1   On the File menu, click New.

2   On the General tab, verify that the Blank Document template is selected.

3   Select the Template option button.

    Your online form is a template document.

4   Click the OK button.

5   On the Standard toolbar, click the Save button.

6   In the File Name box, type **Form Template15**

    Microsoft Word automatically stores the template in the Templates folder in the Microsoft Office home folder. All templates must be stored in this folder in order for the name of the template to appear in the New dialog box.

7   Click the Save button.

Design your form

In this exercise, you enter text for the top part of the form, using the illustration at the beginning of this lesson as your guide. Later, you can format the text to make your form more attractive.

1   At the insertion point, type **West Coast Sales** and press ENTER.

2   In the next line, type **Annual Meeting** and press ENTER.

3   In the third line, type **Speakers Survey** and press ENTER twice.

    These three lines of text are the title of the form. Pressing ENTER twice creates an extra line between the title and the next part of the form.

Save

To modify the default location of your templates directory, click Options on the Tools menu. Then click the File Locations tab, and modify the location for User Templates.

Display the Forms toolbar

The Forms toolbar contains buttons that make it easy to create a form.

1   On the View menu, click Toolbars.

2   In the Toolbars dialog box, select the Forms check box.

3   Click the OK button.

The Forms toolbar appears. You might need to double-click the title bar on the Forms toolbar to move it above the workspace.

Insert a table

If you are unfamiliar with tables in Microsoft Word, see Lesson 10.

Use a table to arrange the text and fields for your form. Later, you can format your table.

➤   On the Forms toolbar, click the Insert Table button, and drag across the grid to select seven rows down by three columns across, as shown in the following illustration.

Insert Table

Drag in this grid to specify your table size.

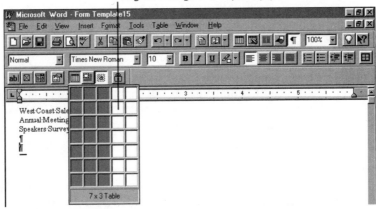

Add text to the table

To make your work easier, you can display the table gridlines by choosing Gridlines on the Table menu.

1   With the insertion point in the first cell, type **Name:**

This text is the label for the field you will create in the next step.

2   Press TAB to move to the next cell in the table.

Insert a text field

A *text field* is a field in which the user can enter text. You can allow users to enter an unlimited amount of text, or you can restrict the number of characters they are able to enter. In this exercise, you will create a text field in this cell in which users can enter a name.

Text Form Field

1 On the Forms toolbar, click the Text Form Field button.

Five small circles appear in the cell. This is a text field.

2 Double-click the text field.

Double-clicking a text field displays the Text Form Field Options dialog box. In this dialog box, you specify the options you want for the field.

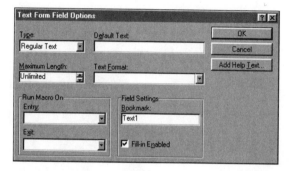

3 In the Maximum Length box, be sure that Unlimited is selected.

If it is not selected, use the arrows to select Unlimited. This selection allows the user to enter an unlimited amount of text in the field.

4 Click the OK button.

You won't see any change to the field in the table.

5 Place the insertion point in the second row of the first column.

Insert text and another text field

1 Type **Extension:**

2 Press TAB to move to the next cell in the table.

3 On the Forms toolbar, click the Text Form Field button.

4 Double-click the text field.

5 In the Maximum Length box, use the scroll up arrow to select "4."

This selection allows the user to enter only four characters in this field when filling out the form. If the user attempts to enter more characters, the program beeps.

6   Under Type, click the drop-down list, and select Number.

This selection verifies that the user has entered a number (not a letter). If the user attempts to enter a character that is not a number, a message box appears indicating that a number is required.

7   Click the OK button to return to the form.

8   Place the insertion point in the third row in the first column.

Insert text and another text field

1   Type **Title:**

2   Press TAB to move to the next cell in the table.

3   On the Forms toolbar, click the Text Form Field button.

4   Double-click the text field.

5   In the Maximum Length box, type **30**

This selection allows the user to enter up to 30 characters in this field. If the user attempts to enter more characters when completing the form online, the program beeps.

Assign help to a field

To make it easier for a user to enter the correct information in a field, you can provide information as a message that appears in the status bar or as a Help window that appears when the user presses F1. In this exercise, you will create a message in the status bar for the current field, clarifying how long the title of the speech can be.

1   In the Text Form Field Options dialog box, click the Add Help Text button.

2   In the Form Field Help Text dialog box, be sure that the Status Bar tab is selected.

3   Select the Type Your Own option button.

4   Type **Enter the exact title of your speech. You are limited to 30 characters.**

This message will appear in the status bar when the user moves to this field in the form.

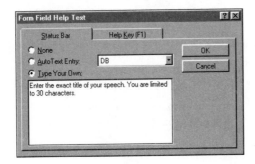

5 Click the OK button to return to the Text Form Field Options dialog box.

6 Click the OK button to return to the form.

7 Place the insertion point in the fourth row in the first column.

Add text to the form

In this exercise, you will enter a heading that describes the fields in the next part of the form.

1 Type **I will need this equipment:**

2 Press the DOWN ARROW key to place the insertion point in the cell below (the fifth row in the first column).

Insert a check box field and text

When you want the user to specify a "yes" or "no" response in a form, you can insert a check box field.

*Check Box
Form Field*

1 On the Forms toolbar, click the Check Box Form Field button.

A shaded check box appears in the cell.

2 Press TAB to move to the cell in the next column.

3 Type **Overhead Projector**

4 Place the insertion point in the first cell of the next row.

Insert two check box fields and text

1 On the Forms toolbar, click the Check Box Form Field button.

A shaded check box appears in the cell.

2 Press TAB to move to the cell in the next column, and then type **Slide Projector**

3 Place the insertion point in the first cell of the next row.

4 On the Forms toolbar, click the Check Box Form Field button.

A shaded check box appears in the cell.

5 Press TAB to move to the cell in the next column, and then type **Computer**

Save

6 On the Standard toolbar, click the Save button to save the work you have completed so far.

7 Place the insertion point in the cell at the first row of the third column.

Your screen should look like the following illustration.

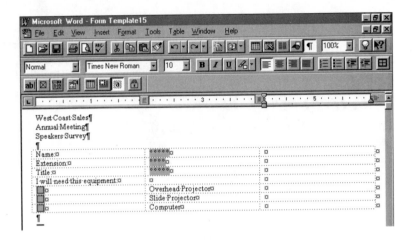

Add text to the form

In this exercise, you enter a label that describes the field you will create next.

1   Type **Division:**
2   Press the DOWN ARROW key to place the insertion point in the cell below (the second cell in the third column).

Insert a drop-down list field

To make it easy for the user to specify the division name to which he or she belongs, you can create a drop-down list of selections. The user will click this field and make a selection from the list.

*Drop-Down
Form Field*

1   On the Forms toolbar, click the Drop-Down Form Field button.
2   Double-click the drop-down list field you just created.

Double-clicking a drop-down form field displays the Drop-Down Form Field Options dialog box. In this dialog box, you can specify the options you want for the field.

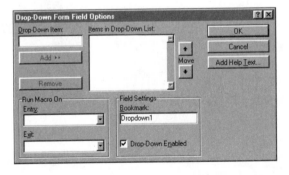

Specify selections in a drop-down list field

In this exercise, you enter the list of choices from which the user will choose when he or she completes the form.

1   In the Drop-Down Item box, type **Outdoor Enterprises**

2   Click the Add button.

The item "Outdoor Enterprises" appears in the list to the right. The first item in the list will be the default selection.

3   Type **Corporate**

4   Click the Add button.

The item "Corporate" appears in the Items in Drop-Down List box to the right.

5   Type **Great Outdoors** and then click the Add button.

6   Type **Great Northern** and then click the Add button.

7   Type **Great Kitchens PLUS** and then click the Add button.

8   Click the OK button to return to the form.

Your form looks like the following illustration.

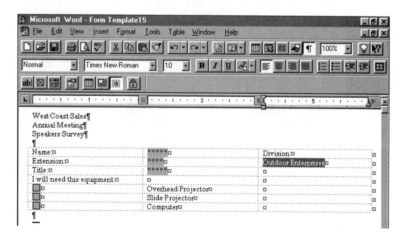

Format the table

In this exercise, you will format the table to make it more attractive and easier to read by applying borders and shading. You will also center the table between the margins.

1   On the Table menu, click Select Table.

2   On the Table menu, click Table AutoFormat.

3   From the Formats list, select the List 5 format.

4   Clear the Heading Rows check box, and then click OK.

5   On the Table menu, click Cell Height And Width.

In the Cell Height And Width dialog box, you can specify the alignment of the table.

6   Click the Row tab, if it does not appear foremost in the dialog box.

7   In the Alignment area, select the Center option button, and then click OK.

Format cells

In this exercise, you will use the Align Right button on the Formatting toolbar to align the text and fields in the first column. You will also change a cell's text style to bold and hide paragraph marks and gridlines.

1   Position the pointer near the top edge of the first column.

2   When the pointer changes shape to a down arrow, use the mouse button to select the first column.

3   On the Formatting toolbar, click the Align Right button.

Align Right

4   Select the first-row cell in the third column (the one that contains the text "Division:"), and then click the Bold button on the Formatting toolbar.

Bold

5   On the Standard toolbar, click the Show/Hide ¶ button to hide nonprinting characters.

6   On the Table menu, click Gridlines to hide the gridlines.

Show/Hide ¶

When you are making the finishing touches to your form, you might prefer to hide both the nonprinting characters and the gridlines.

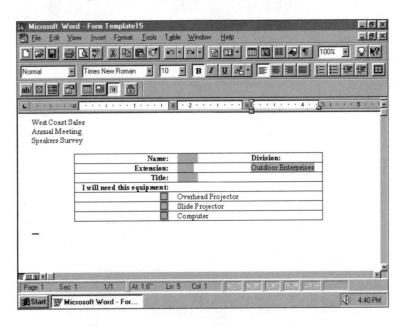

Format the title of the form

Center

1 Select the three lines of text at the top of the document (outside the table), and click the Center button on the Formatting toolbar.

2 With the text still selected, click the Bold button on the Formatting toolbar.

3 From the Font Size drop-down list on the Formatting toolbar, select "18" to create 18-point type.

Hide form shading

The default setting for the fields is shaded. You can hide the shading to improve the appearance of the form.

Form Field Shading

➤ On the Forms toolbar, click the Form Field Shading button to hide the shading.

Your form looks like the following illustration.

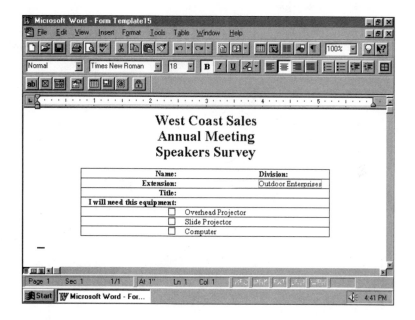

Protect the form

So that people do not inadvertently change the form when they complete it online, you can protect the form.

Protect Form

➤ On the Forms toolbar, click the Protect Form button.

281

Hide the Forms toolbar

You are finished using the Forms toolbar in this lesson.

1   On the View menu, click Toolbars.

2   In the Toolbars dialog box, select the Forms check box, and then click OK.

Save and close the form

1   On the File menu, click Close.

2   When a message appears asking whether you want to save changes, click the Yes button.

Your form is saved as a template.

Using an Online Form

Now that you have created a form, you can use Microsoft Word to complete it. To complete an online form, you create a new document based on the form's template. Each completed form is a Microsoft Word document.

Open an online form

You want to start your presentation planning on the right track. In this exercise, you will complete an online form to identify your preferences for your presentation.

1   On the File menu, click New.

2   On the General tab, select Form Template15.

3   Be sure that the Document option button is selected.

4   Click the OK button.

Complete the form on line

To move from field to field, you can press TAB. Because the form is protected, you cannot move to cells that do not contain fields.

1   In the Name field, type **Chris** and then press TAB to move to the next field.

2   In the Extension field, type **4321** and then press TAB to move to the next field.

3   Click the arrow to open the Division drop-down list.

Your screen should look like the following illustration.

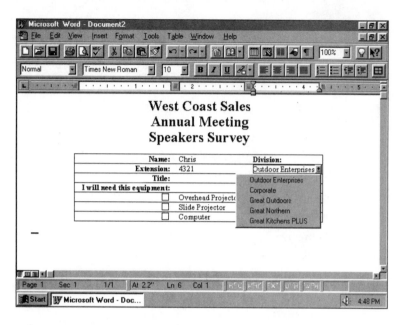

4 From the list, select Corporate.

5 Press TAB to move to the Title field, and then type **East Meets West**

6 Click both the Overhead Projector and the Computer check boxes.

Save your completed form

Save

1 On the Standard toolbar, click the Save button.

2 In the Save As dialog box, double-click the appropriate folders until Winword SBS Practice is the current folder.

The current path might have changed when you created the template document earlier in this lesson. Templates are automatically stored in the Template subfolder in the Microsoft Word home folder.

3 In the File Name box, type **Lesson15** and then click Save.

Your responses in the form are saved in this document. The original form template is unaffected.

4 On the File menu, click Close.

One Step Further: Formatting a Form's Template

You can improve the appearance of the form by increasing the row height of the rows in the table and adjusting the spacing of the text in each row.

Open another form's template

Open

1   On the Standard toolbar, click the Open button.

2   Be sure that the Winword SBS Practice folder is open. If it is not, click the Look In Favorites button, and then double-click the Winword SBS Practice folder icon.

3   Click the down arrow next to Files Of Type, and select Document Templates.

4   Double-click 15OSFTemplate.

   This practice template was copied to the Winword SBS Practice folder. To use it as a template, you need to save it in the Templates folder.

Save the template in the Templates folder with a new name

1   On the File menu, click Save As.

2   In the File Name box, type **OSF Template15**

   Be sure that the Template folder is open. If it is not, select the drive and folder for the Microsoft Word home folder, and click each subsequent folder until you locate Templates.

3   Click the Save button.

Format the table rows

1   Click in the table, and then on the Table menu, click Select Table.

2   On the Table menu, click Cell Height And Width.

3   Click the Row tab, if it does not appear foremost in the dialog box.

4   In the At box, type **30pt**

   Your row will be 30 points high.

5   Click the OK button.

Format the text

1   With the entire table still selected, click Paragraph on the Format menu.

2   In the Before box under Spacing, type **6pt**

    This will increase the spacing before the selected paragraphs by 6 points.

3   Click the OK button.

If You Want to Continue to the Next Lesson

1   On the File menu, click Close.

2   If a message appears asking whether you want to save changes, click the Yes button.

If You Want to Quit Microsoft Word for Now

1   On the File menu, click Exit.

2   If a message appears asking whether you want to save changes, click the Yes button.

Lesson Summary

To	Do this	Button
Create a form	On the File menu, click New. On the General tab, select Blank Document, and click the Template option button. Click OK, and then save the form with a new name.	
Display the Forms toolbar	On the View menu, click Toolbars, and select the Forms check box.	
Insert a text field	On the Forms toolbar, click the Text Form Field button. Double-click the text field. Specify the desired options in the dialog box, and click OK.	abl
Insert a check box	On the Forms toolbar, click the Check Box Form Field button.	⊠

To	Do this	Button
Insert a drop-down list field	On the Forms toolbar, click the Drop-Down Form Field button.	
Protect a form	On the Forms toolbar, click the Protect Form button.	
Complete an online form	On the File menu, click New. Select a form template.	

For online information about	Use the Answer Wizard to search for
Working with templates	**templates**, and then display Create a new document
Creating forms	**forms**, and then display Create a form

Preview of the Next Lesson

If you need to create many documents that are nearly identical, you can use Microsoft Word's Mail Merge feature to insert the variable information (including salutation, name, and address) where you need it. In the next lesson, you will learn how to use the Mail Merge Helper to combine documents in a way that creates personalized form letters.

Creating and Printing Merged Documents

Estimated time
35 min.

In this lesson you will learn how to:

- Create a main document with instructions for inserting variable information, such as names and addresses.
- Create a data source of names and addresses.
- Merge the data source information into the main document.
- Attach an existing data source to a main document.
- Customize documents with Microsoft Word fields.

Suppose you want to mail out several letters that are nearly identical. With Microsoft Word, you can create a *merged document*, in which customized information is combined with standard or boilerplate text, as in form letters. In this way, you can create many letters efficiently, each with a personal touch. In this lesson, you will learn how to create a main document that contains standard text. Then you will create a data source, the document that contains the individualized information. Finally, you will merge the main document and the data source to create your customized form letters. You'll also learn how to attach an existing data source (one already created for you) to a main document.

Merging Documents: Basic Techniques

Preparing any type of merged document involves two files: a *main document* and a *data source*. The main document contains the standardized text and graphics you want in each version of the merged document. The data source contains only the information that varies with each version—such as names, addresses, account numbers, and product codes. In the main document, you insert special instructions, called *merge fields*, to indicate where you want the variable information to appear. When you merge the data source and the main document, Microsoft Word inserts the appropriate information from the data source into the merge fields to create a merged document.

Whether you're printing mailing labels or personalizing a form letter, you use the same basic techniques to create the final, merged documents. The *Mail Merge Helper,* available with the Mail Merge command on the Tools menu, guides you through these steps:

Step 1   Open a new or existing document that will be the main document.

Step 2   Attach an existing data source or a create a new one.

Step 3   Insert merge field names into your main document.

Step 4   Merge the main document with the data source.

Create a main document

Suppose you want to send letters to several individuals who you met at a recent trade show, informing them of your upcoming visit to their town. You can create a main document containing boilerplate text to this effect and later merge in their names and addresses. In this exercise, you create a form letter main document. For the time being, you will not type any text in the main document until you've created the data source.

New

To set up your screen display, see the Appendix, "Matching the Exercises."

1   If you don't see a blank document, click the New button on the Standard toolbar to create a new document.

Be sure that your screen displays the Standard and Formatting toolbars, the ruler, and normal view.

2   On the Tools menu, click Mail Merge.

3   In the Main Document area of the Mail Merge Helper dialog box, click the Create button.

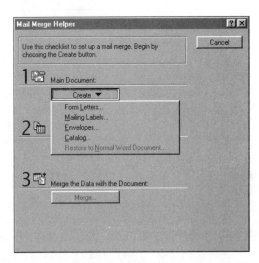

4   Click Form Letters.

A dialog box appears.

5   In the dialog box, click the Active Window button.

This selection creates a main document in the currently active document window, instead of opening a new document window.

Creating a Data Source

Now that you've created an empty main document, you're ready to create a data source. A data source contains all the text and graphics that change with each version of a merged document. Each set of related information (for a specific customer, for instance) makes up one *data record* in the data source. The different categories of information in each record—title, first name, last name, company, street address, city, state, postal code, and product—are called *fields*.

Each field name in a data source must be unique and can have as many as 32 characters. You can use letters, numbers, and underscore characters, but not spaces. The first character must be a letter.

Create and attach a data source

From the Mail Merge Helper dialog box, you can either open an existing data source or create a new one. In this exercise, you will create a new data source and select the field names to be included.

1   In the Mail Merge Helper dialog box, under Data Source, click the Get Data button.

2   Select Create Data Source.

Microsoft Word displays the Create Data Source dialog box in which you can specify the field names to include in the data source. You can start with the suggested fields already provided, remove the ones you won't use, or add your own.

3   Because you will use all but a few of the field names in the Field Name list, you can remove the ones you don't want. For each of the following field names, first select the field, and then click the Remove Field Name button to remove it from the list.

289

JobTitle
Address2
Country
HomePhone
WorkPhone

You will need to scroll downward to select field names further down in the list.

4 In the Field Name box, type **Product**

You can type over any text already selected in the Field Name box.

5 Click the Add Field Name button.

Your new field appears at the bottom of the list of field names.

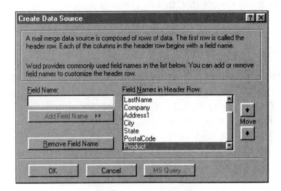

6 Click the OK button.

The Save As dialog box appears.

7 Be sure that the Winword SBS Practice folder is open. If it is not, select the drive and folder for the Microsoft Word home folder, and click each subsequent folder until you locate Winword SBS Practice.

8 In the File Name box, type **Data Source16**

9 Click the Save button.

Save

A dialog box informs you that this data source has no records in it. You can choose to add records right away, or you can return to the main document and begin adding merge fields.

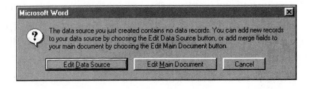

10 Click the Edit Data Source button.

The Data Form dialog box appears.

Entering Data Records

The Data Form dialog box contains the fields you specified in the data source. You enter a set of fields (data record) for each individual who you want to receive this letter. You can enter as many data records as you wish.

Complete the data source form

In this exercise, you will enter the name, address, and product information for the first person to whom you want to send a form letter.

1 Type the following information in the form. As you complete each field, press ENTER to move to the next field. Press SHIFT+TAB to move to a previous field.

Title	**Mr.**
FirstName	**Guy**
LastName	**Barton**
Company	**Victory Sports**
Address1	**1234 Central Avenue**
City	**Cascade Views**
State	**WA**
PostalCode	**98076**
Product	**camping and adventure gear**

Your completed dialog box looks like the following illustration.

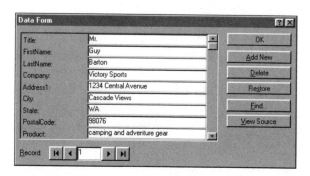

2 Click the Add New button to enter another data record.

You can also press ENTER to enter a new record.

3 Add new data records for the following individuals. For one of them, you will not enter a company name. By default, Microsoft Word will skip blank fields, so the merge is not affected if blank entries are in the data form. Remember to click the Add New button to add another data record.

Title	**Ms.**
FirstName	**Julia**
LastName	**Nelson**
Company	**Valley Sports Center**
Address1	**43908 West Old Highway 904**
City	**Riverdale**
State	**WY**
PostalCode	**87087**
Product	**camping gear**
Title	**Mr.**
FirstName	**James**
LastName	**Lee**
Company	
Address1	**Valley Heights Mall**
City	**Appleton**
State	**GA**
PostalCode	**06578**
Product	**outdoor cooking gear**

4   Click the OK button.

You return to the main document. Notice the new Mail Merge toolbar. Use the buttons on this toolbar when you are working with merged documents.

Save the main document

1   On the File menu, click Save.

2   Be sure that the Winword SBS Practice folder is open. If it is not, click the Look In Favorites button, and then double-click the Winword SBS Practice Folder.

3   Under File Name, type **Main Document16** and press ENTER.

When you save the main document at this point, you are also saving the data record information you entered. After saving, your data source is attached to the main document.

Working with Main Documents

Now that the data source is complete, you are ready to complete the main document with standard text, adding the spaces and punctuation that will print in all versions of the merged document. You also need to specify where you want variable information to appear. To do this, you insert merge fields. These fields correspond to fields in the data source. When you merge the main document with the data source, Microsoft Word replaces the merge field names with the corresponding information from each data record in the data source.

Display paragraph marks

The merge field names act as *placeholders*, that is, they reserve a place for the data source text. You must insert the same spacing and punctuation between the merge field names as you would between words. Displaying paragraph marks makes it easier to see the spaces between words and the "empty paragraphs," or blank lines, in the document.

Show/Hide ¶

> If paragraph marks are not currently displayed on the screen, click the Show/Hide ¶ button on the Standard toolbar.

Insert the date

In this exercise, you use the Date And Time command to insert the current date into the main document. If you want Microsoft Word to automatically update the information each time you print the document, you select the Automatically Update check box.

If you see "{TIME\ _}" on the screen instead of a date, you are viewing field codes that instruct Microsoft Word to insert the date into the document. To hide the codes, select Options on the Tools menu, and click Field Codes on the View tab.

1 On the Insert menu, click Date And Time.

2 Select the date format that shows the date like this: June 28, 1996.

3 Click the Automatically Update check box if it is not already selected.

4 Click the OK button.

Microsoft Word inserts a date field into the document. Each time you print the main document, Microsoft Word will update the date field with the current date.

5 Press ENTER twice to leave a blank line below the date.

Inserting Field Names in the Main Document

When you insert the merge field names into the main document, you are telling Microsoft Word where you want the variable information from the data source to appear. Microsoft Word encloses each field name in chevrons (« »).

Insert the title, first name, and last name

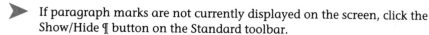

Insert Merge Field

1 On the Mail Merge toolbar, click the Insert Merge Field button.

When you click this button, a list of field names that you can insert in your main document appears. You select field names from this list.

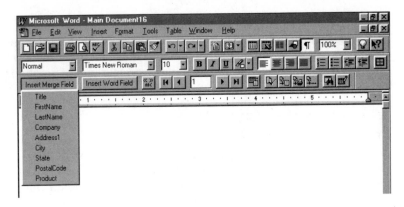

2   Click the Title merge field name to insert it into the document.

3   Press the SPACEBAR to insert a blank space between the title and the first name.

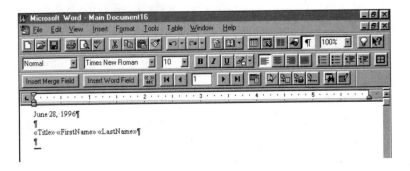

Insert Merge Field

4   Click the Insert Merge Field button to insert the next field name, and select FirstName.

5   Press the SPACEBAR to insert a blank space between the first name and the last name.

6   Click the Insert Merge Field button, and select LastName.

7   Press ENTER to move to the next line.

Insert the company name and address

1   Click the Insert Merge Field button, select Company, and press ENTER.

2   Click the Insert Merge Field button, select Address1, and press ENTER.

3   Click the Insert Merge Field button, and select City.

4   Type a comma, and press the SPACEBAR so that the punctuation will be correct between the city and state.

5   Click the Insert Merge Field button, and select State.

6   Press the SPACEBAR to insert a blank space between the state and the postal code.

7   Click the Insert Merge Field button, and select PostalCode.

8   Press ENTER twice to leave a blank line.

Type the salutation

You can use a merge field name as many times as you want in a document. In this exercise, you type the boilerplate salutation "Dear" followed by the Title and LastName merge fields, and finally a comma.

1   Type **Dear** and press the SPACEBAR. Do *not* press ENTER yet.

2   Click the Insert Merge Field button, and select Title.

3   Press the SPACEBAR to leave a space between the title and the last name.

4   Click the Insert Merge Field button, and select LastName.

5   Type a comma, and then press ENTER twice to leave a blank line.

Your document looks like the following illustration.

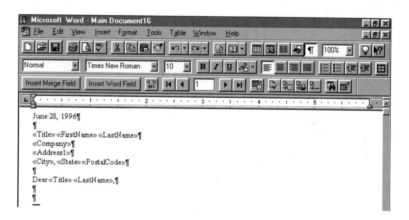

Finish typing the letter

You can use a merge field name within the body of the letter to customize the text. In this exercise, you insert the name of the city in each letter.

1   Type **Thank you for attending our trade show. We will be in**

Do *not* press ENTER yet.

2   If you have not already typed a space following "We will be in," press the SPACEBAR now.

3   Click the Insert Merge Field button, select City, and press the SPACEBAR.

4   Type **next month. We would like to show you our new** and press the SPACEBAR.

5   Click the Insert Merge Field button, and select Product.

6 Type a period. Then press ENTER twice to create a blank line between the body of the letter and the signature that you will type next.

7 Type **Sincerely**, and press ENTER three times.

8 Type **Chris Hamilton**

9 On the Standard toolbar, click the Save button.

Your completed document looks like the following illustration.

Save

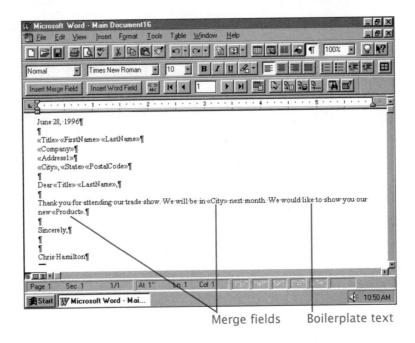

Merge fields   Boilerplate text

Merging Documents

Once you've attached a data source to a main document and inserted merge field codes into the main document, you are ready to combine the main document with the data source. You have three choices; each is available by clicking one of the following buttons on the Mail Merge toolbar.

■ Use the Check For Errors button to have Microsoft Word check the main document and the data source and alert you to errors before you merge or print.

■ Use the Merge To Printer button to merge the main document with the data source and immediately print each resulting document.

■ Use the Merge To New Document button to merge the main document and data source and store the resulting documents in a new document called Form Letters1. You can then view each version of the merged document on your screen and check formatting, spacing, and other details. This is what you will do in the following exercise. You can save this document if you want and print it later.

Merge the information into one file

Merge To New Document

▶ To merge the main document and the data source and store the results in a new file, click the Merge To New Document button on the Mail Merge toolbar.

Each form letter is separated with a double dotted line that indicates a section break. Each section is automatically formatted to begin on a new page as shown in the following illustration.

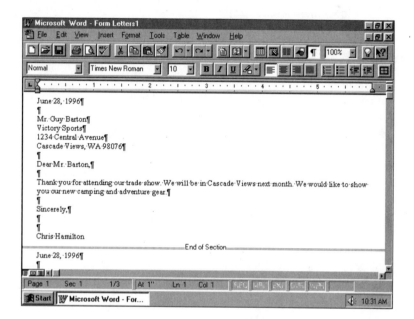

View and edit the letters

As you scroll through the letters, verify that the first two letters have a company name in the address, but that the third letter does not. Microsoft Word skips this field in the third letter because you left the company field blank in the data source. You can edit any of the text as you would edit any other document.

1 Click the down arrow on the scroll bar to examine each letter.

2 In the last letter, select the word "month" and type **week** instead. Then position the insertion point at the end of the last sentence, press the SPACEBAR, and type **Please contact Maria Mendel to set up an appointment.**

Print the merged letters

Print

▶ If you have a printer connected to your computer, be sure that the printer is turned on, and then click the Print button on the Standard toolbar.

If you don't have a printer, continue with the next exercise.

297

Close the merged document file

1   On the File menu, click Close.

2   When a message appears asking whether you want to save this document, click the No button. You do not need to save this file.

    You can quickly generate another merged document whenever you want to print these documents. The main document called Main Document16 is still open in the document window.

Attaching an Existing Data Source

You can use other existing data sources with your main documents, provided that the data source contains the same field names found in the main document. Suppose a co-worker also has a list of individuals to whom you want send your letter and has already entered the data records into a data source. You can attach your main document to that data source using the Mail Merge Helper.

NOTE The Address Book is a Windows 95 feature that you can use if you have installed Microsoft Exchange or Schedule+ on your computer. You can use the Address Book to store and then insert names, addresses, or other information into a document. To insert an individual name and address into a document, you can click the Insert Address button on the Standard toolbar. You can also use the Address Book as your data source when you merge documents.

Attach an existing data source

Included on the Step by Step practice disk is a file called 16AdditionalData. This data source contains additional data you can merge with your main document.

Mail Merge Helper

1   On the Mail Merge toolbar, click the Mail Merge Helper button.

2   In the Data Source area, click the Get Data button.

3   Select Open Data Source.

4   In the Open Data Source dialog box, double-click 16AdditionalData.

5   If you see a message box asking you to save Data Source16, click Yes.

6   When you return to the Mail Merge Helper dialog box, click the Close button.

7   Click the Merge To New Document button.

Merge To New Document

    Microsoft Word merges the main document with the data source and displays letters in a new document window called Form Letters2.

Close the merged document file

1   On the File menu, click Close.

2   Click the No button. You do not need to save this file.

Customizing Documents with Fields

Microsoft Word's fields are special instructions that direct Microsoft Word to generate or insert text (such as an index, the document name, or the date) or graphics in your document. For example, if you want to display the document name as part of a footer, you can insert the File Name field. If you revise the document name, the field is automatically updated the next time you print the document.

So that other people in your company can use your letter without making additional revisions, you can substitute a field that inserts the salesperson's name in the signature. Inserting the Author field instead of your name in the signature is another way to customize form letters efficiently.

Insert Microsoft Word's Author field

Be sure that the main document called Main Document16 is still open.

1   Select the name in the signature at the bottom of the document.

2   On the Insert menu, click Field.

3   In the Field Names box on the right, select the Author field.

4   Click the OK button.

Microsoft Word inserts the name that appears on the User Info tab of the Options dialog box. If you are working with your own copy of Microsoft Word, the Author field will supply your name.

When you share this document with someone else who works on another computer, his or her name will appear in the main document.

One Step Further: Creating Labels

As part of the preparations for an upcoming conference, you decide to print name tags for the conference attendees. Using the Mailing Labels option when you create a main document, you can select from a list of standard labels.

Create a label main document

New

1   On the Standard toolbar, click the New button to create a new document.

2   On the Tools menu, click Mail Merge.

3   In the Main Document area of the Mail Merge Helper dialog box, click the Create button.

Clicking this button reveals a list of main document options from which you can choose.

4   Click Mailing Labels.

A message window appears.

5   In the dialog box, click the Active Window button.

Attach an existing data source

1   In the Data Source area, click the Get Data button.

2   Select Open Data Source.

3   In the Open Data Source dialog box, double-click 16AdditionalData.

Set up label main document

1   Click the Set Up Main Document button to return to the main document.

2   In the Label Options dialog box, scroll through the Product Number list, and choose 5095 - Name Tag. (If your printer information specifies Dot Matrix, choose 4160 - Name Tag.)

This selection formats your labels so that they will print correctly on this kind of label.

3   Click the OK button.

4   In the Create Labels dialog box, type **Hello, my name is** and press ENTER twice to create an extra blank line.

5   Click the Insert Merge Field button, and click First Name to insert it in the label.

6   Press the SPACEBAR, then click the Insert Merge Field button, and click Last Name to insert it in the label.

7   Press ENTER twice, then click the Insert Merge Field button, and click Company to insert it in the label.

8   Click the OK button to return to the Mail Merge Helper, and then click Merge to display the Merge dialog box.

9   In the Merge dialog box, click Merge again.

Format labels

The merged label document is formatted as a table; each cell is formatted as an individual label. You can format the text as you would text in any table. To make the text easy to read on the name tags, you can change the font and the size.

1   On the Table menu, click Select Table.
2   On the Formatting toolbar, click the Font box, and choose Arial MT Black.
3   On the Formatting toolbar, click the Font Size box, and choose "16."
4   On the Formatting toolbar, click the Center button.

The merged label document looks like the following illustration.

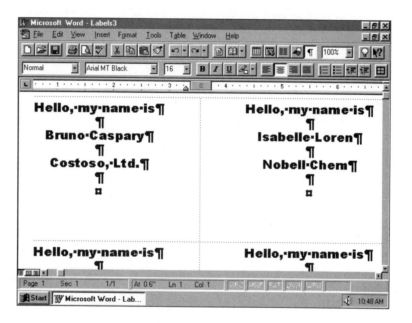

If You Want to Continue to the Review & Practice

1   On the File menu, hold down the SHIFT key and click Close All.
2   When a message appears asking whether you want to save changes, click the No button because you do not need to save the merged labels document.
3   When a message appears asking whether you want to save changes to the next open document, click the Yes button and save the main label document with the name Label Main16 in your Winword SBS Practice folder.

4 If another message appears asking whether you want to save changes to the last remaining open document, click the Yes button.

If You Want to Quit Microsoft Word for Now

1 On the File menu, click Exit.

2 When a message appears asking whether you want to save changes, click the No button because you do not need to save the merged labels document.

3 When a message appears asking whether you want to save changes to the next open document, click the Yes button and save the main label document with the name Label Main16 in your Winword SBS Practice folder.

4 If another message appears asking whether you want to save changes to last remaining open document, click the Yes button.

Lesson Summary

To	Do this	Button
Create a main document	On the Tools menu, click Mail Merge. In the dialog box, click the Create button and select a document type. Make a selection in the dialog box, and then click Close.	
Create and attach a data source	Be sure the document you want to use as the main document is open. On the Tools menu, click Mail Merge. Click the Get Data button, and select Create Data Source to open the dialog box where you add or remove field names. After you name and save the data source, click Edit Data Source to display a data form where you type the information for each record.	
Insert merge fields in a main document	With the main document open, click the Insert Merge Field button on the Mail Merge toolbar. Select the name of each field you want to insert.	Insert Merge Field
Merge a main document and a data source, and save the merged documents to a new file	With the main document open, click the Merge To New Document button on the Mail Merge toolbar to merge the information into one file that you can view and print later.	

For online information about	Use the Answer Wizard to search for
Merging documents	**merging documents**, and then display Form letters, envelopes, and mailing labels
Merging specific data records Rules	**merging specific data records**, and then display for selecting data records for mail merge

Review & Practice

The lessons in Part 4 familiarized you with some of the more sophisticated Microsoft Word features. If you want to practice these skills and test your understanding before you go on to work on special projects of your own, you can work through the Review & Practice section following this lesson. This less structured activity allows you to increase your confidence using many of the features introduced so far.

Review &
Practice

Estimated time
30 min.

You will review and practice how to:

- Search for a document.
- Use outlining techniques to reorganize a document.
- Create an online form.
- Create a main document that contains merge fields and attach it to a data source.
- Merge documents.

In this Review & Practice section, you have an opportunity to fine-tune the document management skills you learned in Part 4 of this book. Use what you have learned about outlining documents, locating files, creating forms, and merging documents to complete several special projects for West Coast Sales marketing efforts.

Scenario

To help the West Coast Sales marketing department prepare for a nationwide sales campaign, you need to modify a long document by rearranging text. Because you can't recall the document name, you need to search for the document and open it. In addition, you have been asked to prepare an on-line form to help the sales force keep track of sales calls. Finally, to help the sales representatives prepare for a series of sales meetings, you will create and modify a main document that you can merge with sales information.

Step 1: **Locate a Document**

You need to locate a document in your Winword SBS Practice folder, but you cannot remember the exact name. You do recall, however, some of the text in the Keywords field.

1   Locate the document that has the word "review04" in the Keywords field of the Properties dialog box. This document is P4Review.

2   Open the document, and save it as ReviewP4.

For more information on	See
Searching for a document	Lesson 14

Step 2: **Reorganize a Document**

Because you want to rearrange "chunks" of information in the document, use the outline feature to reorganize the document more efficiently.

1   Display the document in outline view.

2   Promote the first line of the document to Heading 1.

3   Promote all the division headings to level 2 headings.

4   Collapse the document to display only the first two heading levels.

5   Move the heading "Great Kitchens PLUS" to before the heading "Outdoor Enterprises Division," and then expand this heading to see all the subordinate text.

6   Return to normal view, and then save and close your document.

For more information on	See
Outlining a document	Lesson 13
Promoting headings	Lesson 13

Step 3: **Create an Online Form**

The sales force needs a way to summarize sales meetings. The following online form will encourage sales representatives to use the form and keep accurate records of their meetings.

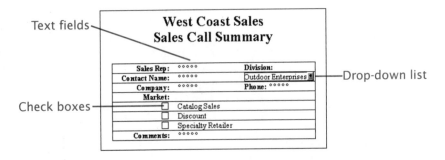

1   Create a new template based on the Blank Document template.

2   Type in the two-line table title followed by a few blank lines. Format the title similar to the preceding illustration. Display the Forms toolbar, and insert a table three columns by eight rows. In column one, enter the field names and the three check boxes. Select column one, and right align the text. In column two, insert the four text fields, and enter the check box field names. In column three, create a drop-down list for Division names and a text field for Phone.

3   Select the table. On the Table menu, click Table AutoFormat, and select a table format. On the Table menu, click Cell Height And Width, and select Center on the Row tab to center the table. Turn off the display of gridlines (on the Table menu) and form field shading (from the Forms toolbar).

4   Protect the document so that the user can modify only the form fields.

5   Save the form template in the Templates folder with the name TemplateRP4.

For more information on	See
Creating an online form	Lesson 15

Step 4:   *Complete an Online Form*

1   Create a new document based on the form template.

2   Complete the form with the following information.

Sales Rep	**Julia Martin**
Contact Name	**Darrell James**
Division	**Great Northern**
Company	**Home At Last**
Phone	**(555)888-1234**
Market	**Catalog Sales**
	Specialty Retailer
Comments	**Wants to know about discounts.**

3   Save the form document with the name Sales FormRP4 in the Winword SBS Practice folder.

For more information on	See
Completing an online form	Lesson 15

Step 5:   *Create a Main Document and Attach a Data Source*

1   Create a new copy of the form document by saving it as Main DocumentRP4.

2   Unprotect the document by clicking Unprotect Document on the Tools menu.

3   On the Tools menu, start the Mail Merge Helper.

4   Create a main form letter document based on the document in the active window.

5   Attach the data source document called RP4 Data Source from your Winword SBS Practice folder.

For more information on	See
Protecting a document	Lesson 15
Creating main documents and attaching a data source	Lesson 16

Step 6:   *Modify the Main Document and Merge Documents*

1   Select the form fields (and the check box text), and replace them with the merge fields according to the following illustration:

Sales Rep:	«SalesRep»	Division:	
Contact Name:	«ContactName»	«Division»	
Company:	«Company»	Phone: «Phone»	
Market:			
☐	«Market1»		
☐	«Market2»		
☐	«Market3»		
Comments:	«Comments»		

2   Clear any selected check boxes. (Hint: Double-click the check box. In the dialog box, clear the Check Box Enabled check box.)

3   Save your work in the main document.

4   Merge your documents to another document or directly to an attached printer. You don't need to save your merged document.

For more information on	See
Adding merge fields	Lesson 16
Merging documents	Lesson 16

If You Want to Quit Microsoft Word for Now

1   On the File menu, click Exit.

2   If a message appears asking whether you want to save changes, click the Yes button.

Appendix

Matching
the Exercises

Microsoft Word has many optional settings that can affect either the screen display or the operation of certain functions. Some exercise steps, therefore, might not produce exactly the same result on your screen as shown in the book. For example, if you could not find the Winword SBS Practice subfolder or if your screen did not look like the illustration at a certain point in a lesson, a note in the lesson might have directed you to this appendix for guidance. Or, if you did not get the outcome described in the lesson, you can use this appendix to determine whether the options you have selected are the same as the ones used in this book.

Displaying the Practice Files

You begin most of the lessons by opening one of the sample documents that came on the Step by Step Practice Files disk. The practice files should be stored on your hard disk, in a subfolder called Winword SBS Practice. The Winword SBS Practice subfolder is located in your system's Favorites folder. If you cannot locate the practice files you need to complete the lesson, follow these steps.

Open the Winword SBS Practice folder

1   On the Standard toolbar, click the Open button.

    Clicking the Open button displays the Open dialog box, where you select the name of the document to open. You must tell Microsoft Word on which drive and in which folder the document is stored.

2   In the File Open dialog box, click the Look In Favorites button.

3   Double-click the Winword SBS Practice subfolder to open it.

When you open the Winword SBS Practice subfolder, the names of the Step by Step practice files (the sample documents) appear. Click the left or right arrow in the scroll bar to see all the names.

Once you open the correct folder, you are ready to open a practice file. Return to the lesson to learn which file you need to open to complete the lesson.

Matching the Screen Display to the Illustrations

Microsoft Word makes it easy for you to set up the program window to suit your working style and preferences. If you share your computer with others, previous users might have changed the screen setup. You can easily change it back so that the screen matches the illustrations in the lessons. Use the following methods for controlling the screen display.

If you change the screen display as part of a lesson and leave Microsoft Word, the next time you open Microsoft Word, the screen looks the way you left it in the previous session.

Display or hide toolbars

If toolbars are missing at the top of the screen, previous users might have hidden them to make more room for text. You can easily display the toolbars that contain the buttons you need in the lessons.

You can also hide specialized toolbars that you no longer need so that you can see more text on the screen. However, most of the lessons require that the Standard and Formatting toolbars appear.

1   From the View menu, choose Toolbars.

2   In the Toolbars dialog box, click the check boxes for the toolbars you want to see; clear the check boxes for the toolbars you want to hide.

Most of the lessons require that the Standard and Formatting toolbars appear.

Display the ruler

If the ruler is missing from the top of the screen, previous users might have hidden it to make more room for text. Although the ruler is not required in all lessons, it is usually displayed in the illustrations. To display the ruler, do the following.

➤   From the View menu, choose Ruler.

If the vertical scroll bar does not appear

If you do not see the vertical scroll bar, a previous user might have hidden the scroll bar to make more room for text. You can easily display it again.

1   Click the Tools menu, and then choose Options.

2   Click the View tab to display the view options in the dialog box.

3 In the Window area, click the Vertical Scroll Bar check box. A check mark appears in the check box to indicate that it is selected.

If the Vertical Scroll Bar option was previously selected, click the OK button, and then see the next procedure, "If the Word for Windows program window does not fill the screen."

4 Click the OK button.

If the Word for Windows program window does not fill the screen

A previous user might have made the Microsoft Word program window smaller to allow quick access to another program. You can enlarge the document window by doing the following.

➤ Click the Maximize button in the upper-right corner of the Microsoft Word title bar.

If the right edge of the Microsoft Word window is hidden so that you cannot see the Maximize button, point to "Microsoft Word" in the title bar at the top of the screen, and then drag the title bar to the left until you see the Maximize button.

If the document does not fill the space that Microsoft Word allows

The last time Microsoft Word was used, the user might have displayed the document in a smaller size to get an overview of a document. To see your document at the normal size, use the Zoom drop-down list on the Standard toolbar.

➤ Click the down arrow next to the Zoom Control drop-down list, and select 100%.

If you see the top edge of the page on the screen

The last person to use Microsoft Word might have worked in page layout view, which displays one page of text on the screen. Return to normal view for the lesson.

Normal View

➤ Click the Normal View button to the far left of the horizontal scroll bar.
or
From the View menu, select Normal.

If spaces appear before periods when moving text

A previous user might have preferred not to use the smart-cut-and-paste feature. Because all the lessons after Lesson 1 assume that this feature is active, you can turn this feature back on.

1 From the Tools menu, choose Options.

2 Click the Edit tab to display the edit options in the dialog box.

3 Click the Use Smart Cut And Paste check box.

4 Click the OK button.

If you see words in brackets

If you see {TIME...} or {SYMBOL..} or {DATE...} in the document, you are looking at the codes that instruct Microsoft Word to insert a certain type of information. You can hide the codes and view the information that Microsoft Word inserts in place of them without changing the document in any way.

1 From the Tools menu, choose Options.

2 Click the View tab to display the view options in the dialog box.

3 Click the Field Codes check box to clear it.

4 Click the OK button.

If you see "¶" in the document

You are viewing the paragraph marks that indicate the end of paragraphs. You might also be viewing other nonprinting symbols that mark spaces or locations where the TAB key was pressed. The symbols do not appear in the document when it is printed. Many users work with the symbols on all the time. If you prefer to hide the symbols, you can do so without affecting the document in any way. Some of the instructions in the lessons require you to locate a specific paragraph mark in the document. In this case, be sure to click this button on the Standard toolbar.

Show/Hide ¶

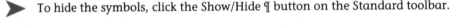 To hide the symbols, click the Show/Hide ¶ button on the Standard toolbar.

Changing Other Options

If you are not getting the results described in the lessons, follow the instructions in this section to verify that the options set in your program are the same as the ones used in this book.

Review each of the following dialog boxes to compare settings for those options that users change most often and are most likely to account for different results. You can view these dialog boxes by choosing the Options command from the Tools menu. Then you click the tab corresponding to the options you want to see.

View Options

Click the View tab to change options that affect the appearance of the document window. Here are the View settings used in this book. The first illustration displays the settings to use when a document is in normal view. The second illustration displays the settings to use when a document is in page layout view.

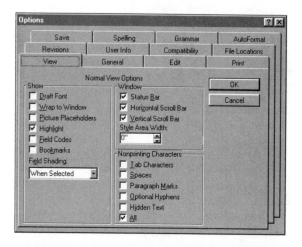

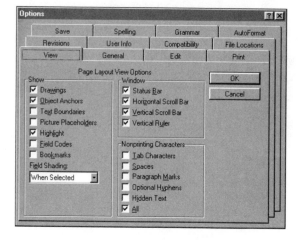

General Options

Click the General tab to change options that affect the operation of Microsoft Word in general. Here are the General settings used in this book.

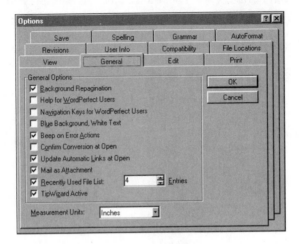

Edit Options

Click the Edit tab to change options that affect how editing operations are performed. Here are the Edit settings used in this book.

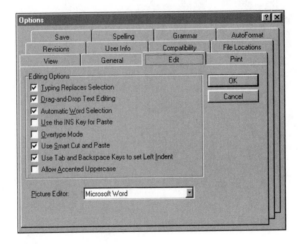

Print Options

Click the Print tab to change options that affect how printing operations are performed. Here are the Print settings used in this book.

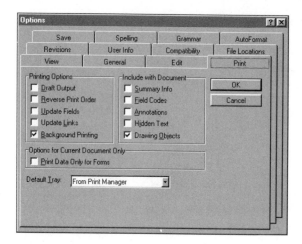

Spelling Options

Click the Spelling tab to change options that affect how the spelling check feature works. Here are the Spelling settings used in this book.

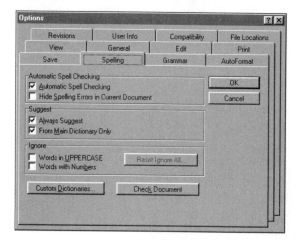

Grammar Options

Click the Grammar tab to change options that affect how the grammar check feature works. Here are the Grammar settings used in this book.

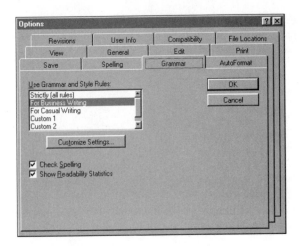

AutoFormat Options

Click the AutoFormat tab to change options that affect how the AutoFormat feature works. Here are the AutoFormat settings used in this book. The first illustration displays the settings to use when the AutoFormat option is selected. The second illustration displays the settings to use when the AutoFormat As You Type option is selected.

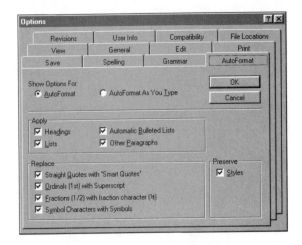

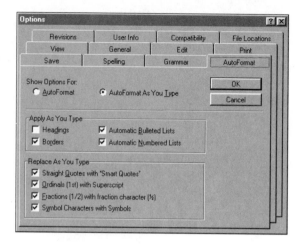

Save Options

Click the Save tab to change options that affect how your documents are saved to disk. Here are the Save settings used in this book.

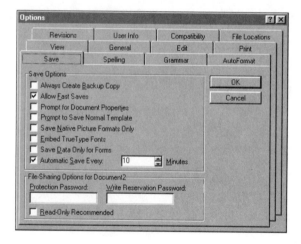

alignment   The horizontal position of text within the width of a line or between tab stops. There are three kinds of alignment in Word.

Alignment	Determines
Paragraph	Whether the lines in a paragraph are aligned with the left indent (flush left), aligned with the right indent (flush right), aligned with both indents (justified), or centered between indents (centered).
Tab	Which direction text extends from a tab position.
Section	How paragraphs are placed vertically on a page.

arrow keys   The UP ARROW, DOWN ARROW, LEFT ARROW, and RIGHT ARROW keys. Used to move the insertion point or to select from a menu or a list of options.

AutoCorrect entry   A word you misspell frequently and its corresponding correction. When you misspell a word for which you have created an AutoCorrect entry, the word is corrected as you type.

automatic save   An option that automatically saves a backup copy of your document at specified intervals. You can select or clear the Automatic Save option with the Options command on the Tools menu.

AutoText entry   An abbreviated, unique name to which you store frequently used text or graphics. To insert an AutoText entry, you type its name and then press F3 or choose AutoText from the Edit menu. Global AutoText entries are available to all documents.

border   A line that goes around text or tables. You can assign a variety of widths to a border. *See also* rule.

bullet   A mark, usually a round or square dot, often used to add emphasis or to distinguish items in a list.

cell   The basic unit of a table. In a table, the intersection of a row and a column forms one cell. You type text into cells.

click   To press and release a mouse button in one motion.

Clipboard   A temporary holding place in the computer's memory for objects that have been cut or copied (such as text or graphics). You can paste the contents of the Clipboard into any Word document or into a file of another program, such as Microsoft Excel. The Clipboard holds the information until you cut or copy another piece of text or a graphic.

Close button   The button in the upper-right corner of a Windows 95 window that you click to close the window. For example, closing the Microsoft Word program window exits the program.

column break   A place in text where you designate the end of one column and the beginning of another. In page view and print preview, and when you print your document, text after a column break appears in a new column. A column break appears as a dotted line. A break you insert is called a hard break; a break determined by the page layout is called a soft break.

crop   To trim away the parts of a graphic you don't want to display.

cut   To remove selected text or a graphic from a document so you can paste it to another place in the document or to another document. The cut information is placed in a temporary storage area called the Clipboard. The Clipboard holds the information until you cut or copy another piece of text or a graphic.

data source   A document that contains text to be merged into a main document to create form letters or other merged documents. For example, a data source for a form letter may contain names and addresses that vary for each letter. If you want to use data from another word-processing program, database, or spreadsheet, you first convert the file to Word format.

destination   A document into which an object is embedded or linked.

defaults   Predefined settings, such as page margins, tab settings, and shortcut key assignments, which are stored in the default template. The default template when you create documents is NORMAL.DOT, whose default settings include margins of 1.25 inches and no indents.

dialog box   A box that displays the available command options or list selections for you to review or change.

document Control menu   A menu with commands that control a document window. For example, you can size, position, and split a document window. To display the menu with keys, you press ALT+HYPHEN.

document window   A rectangular portion of the screen in which you view and edit a document. You can have multiple document windows open in the Word window. Each document window can be divided horizontally into two parts, called panes. When you enlarge a document window to maximum size, it shares its borders and title bar with the Word window.

drag   To hold down the mouse button while moving the mouse.

drive   The mechanism in your computer that contains a disk to retrieve and store information. Personal computers often have one hard disk drive labeled C and two drives labeled A and B that read removable floppy disks.

drop cap   A text formatting effect in which the first character of a paragraph is significantly larger than the surrounding text. The top of the character is aligned with the text at the top of paragraph, while the bottom of the character "drops" into the body of the paragraph.

edit   To add, delete, or change text and graphics.

embed   To insert an object, which is not linked to its originating (source) document, into a destination document. To edit the embedded object, you double-click it to open the source program, within the destination document.

extend selection   To lengthen a selection. When you extend a selection, it grows progressively larger each time you press F8. For example, if you select a word, you can extend the selection to a sentence by pressing F8 once. To shrink the selection, you press SHIFT+F8.

field   A set of coded instructions that inserts many types of information into your document, including the variable data inserted into form letters during printing. You can update fields to insert new information into your document automatically.

field codes   A field that appears as instructions enclosed by field characters ({}).

field result   Text or graphics inserted into a document because of the action of a field.

file   A document that has been created and saved with a unique filename. In Word, all documents are stored as files.

file format   The format in which data is stored in a file. Word usually stores a document in Word's "Normal" file format, which includes the text and all the formatting applied to the document. Word can read and save in several file formats, such as Microsoft Excel BIF, Windows WordPad, RTF, and WordPerfect.

folders   A container in which documents, program files, and other folders are stored on your disks. Using folders can help you organize your documents. For example, you can create a folder called LETTERS in which you can save all of your form letters.

font   A family of type styles, such as Geneva and Modern. Effects, such as bold or italic, are possible within one font, and various point sizes can be applied to a font.

format   The way text appears on a page. The four types of formats are character, paragraph, section, and document. Styles can be applied to any of these formats.

form letter or document   A document consisting of boilerplate text and personalized information, such as names and addresses. A form letter is created by merging the main document and the data document. The main document contains basic text that is the same in every copy of the letter. The data document contains the information that varies for each letter, such as names and addresses.

form   A special document template in which form fields allow the user to complete the form online without affecting the text and formatting of the form.

formula   A mathematical statement or expression, such as $3x = \frac{1}{2}y$. Word provides special codes to create formulas.

frame   A box you add around an area of your document—for example, a block of text, a graphic, or a chart—so that you can easily change its position on a page. Once you insert an object into a frame, you can drag it to the position you want in page layout view. Word automatically makes room for the frame at the new location.

global template   In Word, a template with the filename NORMAL.DOT that contains default menus, dialog box settings, and styles. Documents use the global template unless you specify a custom template.

hanging indent   A paragraph format in which the first line of a paragraph starts farther to the left than subsequent lines.

header and footer   A header is text or graphics that appear at the top of every page in a section. A footer appears at the bottom of every page. Headers and footers often contain page numbers, chapter titles, dates, and author names. You can edit headers and footers in the header or footer pane.

header file   In a print merge process, a document containing a header record that Word substitutes for the header record in a data document.

heading   A title for a part of a document (for example, a chapter title).

hidden text   A character format that allows you to show or hide designated text. Word indicates hidden text by underlining it with a dotted line. You can select or clear the Hidden Text option with the Options command on the Tools menu. You can omit hidden text during printing.

icon   A graphical representation of a file-level object—a disk drive, a folder, a program, a document, or other object that you can select and open.

indent   The distance between text boundaries and page margins. Positive indents make the text area narrower than the space between margins. Negative indents allow text to extend into the margins. A paragraph can have left, right, and first-line indents. Indents can also be measured relative to columns in a section, table cells, and the boundaries of positioned objects.

insertion point   The blinking vertical bar that marks the location where text is entered in a word processing document or in a dialog box. The insertion point can be moved by using the mouse to click elsewhere or by using the keyboard arrow keys.

landscape   A term used to refer to horizontal page orientation; opposite of "portrait," or vertical, orientation.

leader characters   Characters, usually dots or hyphens, that fill the space between words separated by tabs to draw the reader's eye across a line. Leader characters are often used in tables of contents. Example: Chapter 1.................Page 5

line break   A break you insert when you want to end one line and start another without starting a new paragraph. A line break is represented by the newline character, which you can display by selecting options from the Tools menu, clicking on the View tab, and then selecting the All option.

line spacing   The height of a line of text, including extra spacing. Line spacing is often measured in lines or points. The following table shows the approximate point equivalents for standard line spacing with the ruler set for 12-point type.

Spacing	Line height in points
Single	12
One-and-one-half	18
Double	24

Note: Two lines = double-spaced; 72 points = 1 inch.

link   To insert information into a destination document that is linked to its source document. When the source document is changed, the linked information (in the destination document) is updated.

list box   Part of a dialog box that contains a list of possible selections for an option. Some list boxes stay the same size; others drop down to display the list of items.

main document   In a form letter or document, the main document contains text and graphics that are the same for all the merged documents. Within the text, you insert fields that are replaced by information specific to each of the merged documents when you print.

Maximize button   The button in the upper-right corner of most windows that enlarges the window to fill the entire screen.

measurement   A measured distance. In Word, you type measurements in a dialog box with one of the following units.

Unit	Equivalent measurements
Centimeters (cm)	2.54 cm = 1 in
Inches (in or ")	1 in = 72 pt = 6 pi
Lines (li)	1 li = 1/6 in = 12 pt
Picas (pi)	1 pi = 1/6 in = 12 pt
Points (pt)	1 pt = 1/12 pi = 1/72 in

menu   A list of commands that drops down from the menu bar. The menu bar is displayed across the top of a program window and lists the menu names, such as File and Edit.

merge   To combine one or more sources of text into a single document, such as a form letter.

message   A notice on the screen that informs you of a problem or asks for more information. Messages appear in the status bar at the bottom of your screen, either in a message box or as bold text in your document. When Microsoft Word displays a message, you can press F1 for immediate help, with the following exceptions: field error messages that appear as bold text in your document, or some low-memory messages. You can get help on all messages by pressing F1 and choosing the Index button. Choose Messages under
Reference Information.

Minimize button   The button in the upper-right corner of most windows. When you click the Minimize button, the window is minimized to its button on the taskbar. The program and document remain open when the window is minimized.

normal view   The view you see when you start Word. Normal view is used for most editing and formatting tasks.

object   A table, chart, graphic, equation, or other form of information you create and edit with a program other than Word, but whose data you can import into a Word document.

OLE   A feature that allows you to import information from another source document into a destination document. The two options for importing are linking and embedding. *See also* link *and* embed.

options   The choices you have in a dialog box.

outline view   An outline shows the headings of a document indented to represent their level in the document structure. In Word, you can display the structure of your documents in outline view. Outline view makes it easy to move quickly through a document, change the importance of headings, and rearrange large amounts of text by moving headings.

overtype   An option for replacing existing characters one by one as you type. You can select overtype by pressing the INS key or by selecting the Overtype option with the Options command on the Tools menu. When you select the Overtype option, the letters "OVR" appear in the status bar at the bottom of the Word window.

page break   The point at which one page ends and another begins. In page view and print preview, and when you print your document, text after a page break appears on a new page. A break you insert, called a hard break, is created by pressing CTRL+ENTER. A break inserted automatically, as determined by the page layout, is called a soft break.

page layout view   A view that displays your document as it will appear when you print it. Items, such as headers, footnotes, and framed objects, appear in their actual positions, and you can drag them to new positions. You can edit and format text in page layout view. However, you cannot edit certain elements in this view, such as page headers and footers, and multiple columns.

Paint   The Windows 95 accessory that you can use to create, edit, and view drawings and graphic objects.

paragraph mark   In word processing, a hidden character that designates the end of a line followed by a new paragraph. You insert a paragraph mark by pressing ENTER.

paste   To insert cut or copied text into a document from the temporary storage area called the Clipboard.

path   The location of a file within a computer filing system. The path indicates the filename preceded by the disk drive, folder, and subfolders in which the file is stored. If the file is on another computer on a network, the path also includes the computer name.

point size   A measurement used for the size of text characters. There are 72 points in an inch.

portrait   A term used to refer to vertical page orientation; opposite of "landscape," or horizontal orientation.

position   The specific placement of graphics, tables, and paragraphs on a page. In Word, you can assign items to fixed positions on a page.

program   Software, such as Microsoft Word or Microsoft Excel, that helps a user create documents or perform work.

program window   A window that contains a running program. The window displays the menus and provides the workspace for any document used within the program. The program window shares its borders and title bar with document windows that are maximized.

repaginate   To calculate and insert page breaks at the correct point in your document. By default, Word repaginates whenever you make a change in your document.

rule   A straight vertical or horizontal line between columns in a section, next to paragraphs, or in a table. You can assign a variety of widths to a rule. *See also* border.

ruler   A graphical bar displayed across the top of the document window. You can use the ruler to indent paragraphs, set tab stops, adjust page margins, and change column widths in a table.

save   To store information residing in computer memory into a designated place and under a designated name on one of your computer's disks.

scale   To change the height or width of a graphic by a certain percentage. You can choose to preserve or change the relative proportions of elements within the graphic when you scale it.

scroll bar   A graphical device for moving vertically and horizontally through a document with a mouse. Scroll bars are located at the right and bottom edges of the document window. You can display or hide scroll bars with the Horizontal Scroll Bar and Vertical Scroll Bar check boxes on the View tab in the Options dialog box (Tools menu).

section   A portion of a document in which you set certain page formatting options. You create a new section when you want to change options, such as line numbering, number of columns, or headers and footers. Until you insert section breaks, Word treats your document as a single section.

section break   The point at which you end one section and begin another because you want some aspect of page formatting to change. In normal or draft view, a section break appears as two dotted lines.

selection bar   An invisible area at the left edge of a document window used to select text with the mouse. In a table, each cell has its own selection bar at the left edge of the cell.

shortcut menu   A menu that lists shortcut commands that directly relate to the action you are performing. In Microsoft Word, you can display a shortcut menu by clicking program elements (such as text, toolbars, and so on) with the right mouse button.

soft return   A line break created by pressing SHIFT+ENTER. This creates a new line without creating a new paragraph. *See also* line break.

special characters   Symbols displayed on the screen to indicate characters that do not print, such as tab characters or paragraph marks. You can control the display of special characters with the Options command on the Tools menu and the Show/Hide ¶ button on the ribbon.

status bar   A bar at the bottom of the program window that indicates the program status, for example, the page number, current mode, position of the insertion point, and so on. Your display of the status bar can be turned on and off.

style   A combination of formatting settings that you name and store. When you apply a style to selected characters and paragraphs, all the settings of that style are applied at once.

style area   An area to the left of the selection in which the names of applied styles are displayed. You can display the style area using the Options command for View options on the Tools menu.

summary information   Descriptions and statistics about a document such as title, author, comments, and revision number. You can view or change summary information with the Properties command on the File menu.

table   One or more rows of cells commonly used to display numbers and other items for quick reference and analysis. Items in a table are organized into rows and columns. You can convert text into a table with the Insert Table command on the Table menu.

tab stop   A measured position for placing and aligning text at a specific place on a line. Word has four kinds of tab stops, each with a different alignment: Left extends text to the right from the tab; Center centers text at the tab; Right extends text to the left from the tab until the tab's space is filled, and then it extends text to the right; and Decimal extends text before the decimal point to the left, and then it extends text after the decimal point to the right.

template   A special kind of document that provides basic tools and text for shaping a final document. Templates can contain the following elements: text, styles, glossary items, macros, menu and key assignments.

text box   A box within a dialog box where you type information needed to carry out a command.

title bar   The horizontal bar at the top of a window that shows the name of the document or program that appears in that window.

toolbar   A graphical bar with buttons that perform some of the most common commands in Word, such as opening, copying, and printing files. The toolbars you can display in Microsoft Word include the following: Standard, Formatting, Outline, Forms, Borders, Database, Word 2.0, and Drawing.

vertical alignment   The placement of text on a page in relation to the top, bottom, or center of the page.

view   A form of screen display that shows certain aspects of the document. Word has six views: normal, draft, outline, page layout, full screen, and print preview.

widow and orphan   A widow is the last line of a paragraph printed by itself at the top of a page. An orphan is the first line of a paragraph printed by itself at the bottom of a page. The default settings in Word prevent widows and orphans.

window   A rectangular area on your screen in which you view and work on documents. You can have up to nine different document windows open at one time.

wizard   An online coach you use to create documents. When you use a wizard to create a document, you are asked questions about your document preferences, and the wizard creates the document according to your specifications. The Answer Wizard allows you to pose questions about an operation or feature to get more information. The TipWizard monitors your actions as you work, and provides tips for improving your effectiveness with Word. The TipWizard appears above the ruler at the top of the document window.

wordwrap   Automatic placement of a word on the next line. When you type text and reach the right margin or indent, Word checks to see whether the entire word you typed fits on the current line. If not, Word automatically places the word on the next line.

Index

Index

J

jumping to specific pages, 34–35
justifying text, 57, 196

K

keyboard
    conventions, xix
    shortcut keys, xxix
key combinations. *See individual key names*

L

labels, for mail-merging, 299–301
landscape orientation, 324
Large Icons button, xxxi
layout. *See* page layout view
leaders, tab, 324
left-aligning text, 23
left indent, 51, 52
left margin, 60, 109
letters, form. *See* form letters
Letter Wizard, 145–48
line breaks, defined, 325
lines. *See* borders
line spacing, 59–60, 325
linking, defined, 325
linking data, 220–25
list boxes, xxxii, 325
lists
    bulleted, 50–51
    numbered, 49–50
    sorting of, 56
logo, 221

M

magnification, 62
mailing labels, creating, 299–301
mail merge fields. *See* merge fields
Mail Merge Helper, 288, 289, 298
Mail Merge toolbar, 292, 293, 296, 298
mail merging
    creating merged documents, 296–98
    data sources for, 287, 289–92, 298–99
    mailing labels, 299–301
    main documents for, 287, 288–89, 292–96, 299, 300, 325

mail merging, *continued*
    overview, 287–88
main documents, 287, 288–89, 292–96, 299, 300, 325
manual page breaks, 71, 72–73
margin pointer, 60
margins
    bottom, 109
    changing with Page Setup dialog box, 62, 108–9
    changing with ruler, 60–62
    for facing pages, 116–17
    vs. indents, 60
    left, 60, 109
    right, 109
    top, 60, 109
margins, default, 4
mathematical calculations, 184
Maximize button, xxviii, 313, 325
maximizing windows, xxviii, 313, 325
measurement units, 325
menu bar, xxviii
menus
    defined, 326
    using, xxix–xxxi
merged documents. *See also* mail merging
    closing files, 299
    creating, 296–98
    defined, 287
    editing, 297
    mailing labels as, 299–301
    overview, 287–89
    printing, 297
    viewing, 297
merge fields, 288, 293–96
Merge To New Document button, 297
merging. *See also* mail merging
    defined, 326
    table cells, 177–80
messages, defined, 326
Microsoft Excel, linking data to Microsoft Word documents, 222–25
Microsoft Graph, 180–83. *See also* charts
Microsoft Word
    dialog boxes, xxxi–xxxii
    menus, xxix–xxxi
    online Help, xxxiii–xxxvii, xli–xlii
    and practice files, xxii–xxiv, 24, 30–31, 311–12
    quitting, xliii, 26
    screen display, 312–14
    starting, xxxvii–xxxviii

Index

The
comprehensive
guide to
mastering Word
for Windows® 95.

ISBN 1-55615-848-3
1008 pages
$29.95 ($39.95

This book is both an
example-rich tutorial and
a great reference. Written by
a former member of the Word for
Windows development team, RUNNING
MICROSOFT® WORD FOR WINDOWS 95 contains scores of insights and power
tips not found in the documentation. The Running series has been overhauled
and enhanced and now provides even more information, plenty of screen shots,
and much easier to access information.

Written by experts in their fields, the Running Series offers both outstanding
instruction and in-depth information for novices and advanced users alike. These
easy-to-use books make use of step-by-step examples; hundreds of screen
illustrations; dozens of prominently displayed tips, notes, and warnings; extensive
cross-references; a rich and detailed index; and a comprehensive table of contents
as well as chapter-level tables of contents.

WHO KNOWS MORE
ABOUT WINDOWS® 95
THAN
MICROSOFT® PRESS?

ISBN 1-55615-816-5
224 pages
$19.95 ($26.95 Canada)

ISBN 1-55615-683-9
320 pages
$29.95 ($39.95 Canada)

These books are essential if you are a newcomer to Microsoft® Windows® or an upgrader wanting to capitalize on your knowledge of Windows 3.1. Both are written in a straightforward, no-nonsense way, with well-illustrated step-by-step examples, and both include practice files on disk. Learn to use Microsoft's newest operating system quickly and easily with MICROSOFT WINDOWS 95 STEP BY STEP and UPGRADING TO MICROSOFT WINDOWS 95 STEP BY STEP, both from Microsoft Press.

This is one book that you'll want to keep close to your computer!

ISBN 1-55615-659-6
336 pages
$24.95 ($33.95 Canada)

This colorful, interesting, fact-filled guide shows intermediate users how to use Office applications together to realize the full power and versatility they offer. With an emphasis on "document-centric" computing, it focuses on the interoperability, integration, and consistency of the applications in Microsoft® Office for Windows® 95. Users will learn how to share data through linking and embedding objects and how to choose the right tools from any application to complete a task intelligently. An updated and revised Question and Answer section, taken from Microsoft Product Support's most-asked questions, is included.

Microsoft Press

097-000-681

The
Step by Step
Practice Files Disk

The enclosed 3.5-inch disk contains timesaving, ready-to-use practice files that complement the lessons in this book. To use the practice files, you'll need the Windows 95 operating system.

Each *Step by Step* lesson uses practice files from the disk. Before you begin the *Step by Step* lessons, read the "Getting Ready" section of the book for easy instructions telling how to install the files on your computer's hard disk. As you work through each lesson, be sure to follow the instructions for renaming the practice files so that you can go through a lesson more than once if you need to.

Please take a few moments to read the License Agreement on the previous page before using the enclosed disk.

Register your Microsoft® Press book today, and let us know what you think.

At Microsoft Press, we listen to our customers. We update our books as new releases of software are issued, and we'd like you to tell us the kinds of additional information you'd find most useful in these updates. Your feedback will be considered when we prepare a future edition; plus, when you become a registered owner, you'll get Microsoft Press catalogs and exclusive offers on specially priced books.

Thanks!

I used this book as
- ○ A way to learn the software
- ○ A reference when I needed it
- ○ A way to find out about advanced features
- ○ Other_____

I consider myself
- ○ A beginner or an occasional computer user
- ○ An intermediate-level user with a pretty good grasp of the basics
- ○ An advanced user who helps and provides solutions for others
- ○ Other_____

I purchased this book from
- ○ A book store
- ○ A software store
- ○ A direct mail offer
- ○ Other_____

I will buy the next edition of the book when it's updated
- ○ Definitely
- ○ Probably
- ○ I will not buy the next edition

The next edition of this book should include the following additional information

1● _____

2● _____

3● _____

The most useful things about this book are _____

This book would be more helpful if _____

My general impressions of this book are _____

May we contact you regarding your comments?   ○ Yes   ○ No

Would you like to receive a Microsoft Press catalog regularly?   ○ Yes   ○ No

Name_____

Company (if applicable) _____

Address_____

City_____ State_____ Zip_____

Daytime phone number (optional) (_____)_____

Please mail back your feedback form—postage free! Fold this form as described on the other side of this card, or fax this sheet to:
Microsoft Press, Attn: Marketing Department, fax 206-936-7329

NO POSTAGE
NECESSARY
IF MAILED
IN THE
UNITED STATES

BUSINESS REPLY MAIL

FIRST-CLASS MAIL   PERMIT NO. 108   REDMOND, WA

POSTAGE WILL BE PAID BY ADDRESSEE

ATTN: MARKETING DEPT
MICROSOFT PRESS
ONE MICROSOFT WAY
REDMOND WA 98052-9953